Homophobia

Homophobia

HOW WE ALL PAY THE PRICE

edited by Warren J. Blumenfeld

BEACON PRESS ■ BOSTON

Beacon Press
25 Beacon Street
Boston, Massachusetts 02108-2892

Beacon Press books
are published under the auspices of
the Unitarian Universalist Association of Congregations

99 98 97 96 95 94 93   8 7 6 5 4 3

Text design by James F. Brisson

Library of Congress Cataloging-in-Publication Data

Homophobia: how we all pay the price / edited by Warren J.
Blumenfeld
    p. cm.
Includes bibliographical references.
ISBN 0-8070-7918-9. —ISBN 0-8070-7919-7 (pbk.)
    1. Homophobia—United States.   2. Sexism—United States.
I. Blumenfeld, Warren J., 1947–
HQ76.3.U5H642   1992
    305.9'0664—dc20   91-36287
                                                        CIP

For Susan,
my sister, my friend,
my ally

ACKNOWLEDGMENTS

I am thankful to a great many people who helped me make this book a reality.

To Cooper Thompson of the Campaign to End Homophobia; Joan Lester, Jamie Washington, and Carole Johnson of the Equity Institute; Kathy Obear of the Human Advantage; Ari Kane of Theseus Counseling Services; Bobbie Harro and Pat Griffin of DiversityWorks; Ann Pellegrini from the Harvard Divinity School; Susanna Stein from the John F. Kennedy School of Government at Harvard; Felice Yeskel from the University of Massachusetts—Amherst; and Walter Williams from the University of Southern California—for their advice and counsel in the formulation of the theoretical foundation for this anthology.

To Cooper Thompson, Ann Pellegrini, Arthur Lipkin, and Amanda Udis-Kessler for their valuable editorial suggestions.

To my good friends at the Gay, Lesbian, and Bisexual Speakers Bureau of Boston for their continued support and love, especially Sue Herz, Art Cohen, Will Johnston, Rheua Stakely, Robert Spencer, Paul Kowal, Leah Fygetakis, Samantha Martin, Michael Veilleux, Robyn Ochs, Linda Hirsch, and Sharon Lim-Hing. And to Michael Castellana from the Fenway Community Health Center in Boston, and Kevin Berrill, director of the Anti-Violence Project of the National Gay and Lesbian Task Force, Washington, D.C.

To my friends Berni Zisserson, David Eberly, and Alan Bob Lans who listened to my kvetching for almost three years while this book was in process.

To Deb Chasman, my editor at Beacon Press, who helped me put all the pieces of this puzzle together.

To all the wonderful, talented authors whose contributions made this anthology possible.

For his support, friendship, and unqualified belief in this project from the very beginning, to B. Jaye Miller who was taken from this world too soon by AIDS but whose legacy will live for many, many years.

And to the dedicated members of ACT UP (the AIDS Coalition to Unleash Power) who show me each day, through their energy and commitment, that individuals working together can indeed make a real difference in the world.

CONTENTS

III. Other Societal Manifestations of Homophobia

IV. Breaking Free

It is often said that, in the midst of misfortune, something unexpectedly valuable arises, and this has indeed been my experience. While traveling alone through Scandinavia one summer, I began to lose the vision in both my eyes. When I reached Denmark, I went to a hospital for an evaluation, and, after a number of tests, a physician notified me that my retinas had detached, probably because of a congenital defect. She advised immediate surgery to prevent further deterioration, and I was admitted to the Community Hospital in Copenhagen.

The next day, my sister, Susan, flew to Copenhagen to be with me for what turned out to be nearly two months.

That summer in this distant northern land, fearing the permanent loss of my vision, I lay in a narrow hospital bed longing for friends and relatives back home. But as Susan sat with me day after day, giving her love, her courage, her humor (and spectacular Danish pastries), something remarkable happened. Amid the bells of a distant church tolling away the passing hours, Susan and I genuinely got to know one another for the first time.

Although we inhabited the same house for over seventeen years, there was always some unspoken tension between us, some wall keeping us apart. Having only eighteen months separating us in age, we attended the same schools and had similar peer groups. For the first few years of our lives, we seemed to get along fine. We had a few friends in common, and we usually found time to play together most days. Our closeness, however, was soon to come to an end.

By the time I reached the age of seven or eight, I was increasingly becoming the target of harassment and attack by my peers, who perceived me as someone who was different. Names like *queer, sissy, little girl, fag*, were thrown at me like the large red ball the children hurled on the school yard in dodge ball games. During subsequent years, the situation only got worse. I tried to avoid other children and increasingly kept to myself. Susan and I grew apart. Only when we were both in our early twenties, about the time I went to Denmark, were we beginning to rediscover one another and to share the details of our lives.

While in college, I began to sort out how I had suffered as a gay male under the force of homophobia, but until my hospitalization I had very little idea how it had also affected Susan growing up as my heterosexually oriented younger sister. Smart, attractive, outgoing, she appeared to have, at least from my vantage point, plenty of friends and seemed to fit in. In Denmark, however, she confided to me that, throughout our school years, she was continually teased for having a *faggot brother.* On one occasion, she recalled some of the older boys laughing at her, asking if she were "like her brother." When she witnessed other students harassing me, peer pressure, coupled with her own fear of becoming a target, compelled her to distance herself from me by adding her voice to the chorus of insults. I felt betrayed and despised her for it.

Our time together in my hospital room permitted us the needed chance to define the basis of our past estrangement. Through the tears, the apologies, the rage at having been raised in an oppressive environment, and the regrets over losing so much precious time, we began the process of healing our relationship. As it turned out, my vision was not the only thing restored to me that summer.

This current anthology represents the growth of a seed planted in my mind back in Denmark. It centers around one primary premise: within each of the numerous forms of oppression, members of the target group (sometimes called "minority") are *oppressed,* while on some level members of the dominant group are *hurt*. Although the effects of oppression differ qualitatively for specific target and dominant groups, in the end everyone loses.

Most of us hold simultaneous membership in a number of groups based, for example, on our personal and physical characteristics, on our abilities and class backgrounds, and on our cultural, racial, or religious identifications. We may find ourselves both in groups targeted for oppression and in those dominant groups granted relatively higher degrees of power and prestige. By examining how we are disadvantaged as well as looking at the privileges we have, we can develop empathy for individuals different from ourselves and create a basis for alliances.

This book, therefore, is really about alliances: support for the maintenance and strengthening of alliances where they currently exist and assistance in forging new ones where none has existed before—specifically, alliances between and among lesbians, gay males, bisexuals, transgender people, *and* heterosexuals.

How Are Sexual Minorities Oppressed by Homophobia?

Sexual minorities—lesbians, gay males, bisexuals, and transgender people—are among the most despised groups in the United States today. Perhaps paradoxically, for many in our society, love of sameness (i.e., *homo*-sexuality) makes people different, whereas love of difference (i.e., *hetero*-sexuality) makes people the same.

Much has been written about the ways homophobia in many Western cultures targets sexual minorities, ranging from negative beliefs about these groups (which may or may not be expressed) to exclusion, denial of civil and legal protections, and, in some cases, overt acts of violence. Negative attitudes internalized by members of these groups often damage the spirit and stifle emotional growth.

Homophobia operates on four distinct but interrelated levels: the personal, the interpersonal, the institutional, and the cultural (also called the collective or societal) (Campaign to End Homophobia 1989).

Personal homophobia refers to a personal belief system (a prejudice) that sexual minorities either deserve to be pitied as unfortunate beings who are powerless to control their desires or should be hated, that they are psychologically disturbed, genetically defective, unfortunate misfits, that their existence contradicts the "laws" of nature, that they are spiritually immoral, infected pariahs, disgusting—to put it quite simply, that they are generally inferior to heterosexuals.

Interpersonal homophobia is manifested when a personal bias or prejudice affects relations among individuals, transforming prejudice into its active component—discrimination. Examples of interpersonal homophobia are name-calling or "joke" telling intended to insult or defame individuals or groups; verbal and physical harassment and intimidation as well as more extreme forms of violence; the withholding of support, rejection, abandonment by friends and other peers, coworkers, and family members; refusal of landlords to rent apartments, shop owners to provide services, insurance companies to extend coverage, and employers to hire on the basis of actual or perceived sexual identity. And the list goes on.

A study by the National Gay and Lesbian Task Force found that more than 90 percent of the respondents had experienced some form of victimization based on their sexual identity and that over 33 percent had been threatened directly with violence: "More than one in five males, and nearly one in ten females, say they were 'punched, hit, kicked, or beaten,' and approximately the same ratios suffered some form of police abuse. Assaults with weapons are reported by one in ten males and one in twenty females. Many of those who report having been harassed or assaulted further state that incidents occurred multiple times" (National Gay and Lesbian Task Force 1984, p. 4). Approximately one-third of the respondents were assaulted verbally, while more than one in fifteen were physically abused by members of their own families.

Reports of violence directed against lesbians, gay males, bisexuals, and transgender people have increased each year since the National Gay and Lesbian Task Force has been keeping records, and such incidents are only the tip of the iceberg. By no means are they isolated to certain locales; rather, they are widespread, occurring throughout the country.

Institutional homophobia refers to the ways in which governments, businesses, and educational, religious, and professional organizations systematically discriminate on the basis of sexual orientation or identity. Sometimes laws, codes, or policies actually enforce such discrimination. Few institutions have policies supportive of sexual minorities, and many actively work against not only those minorities but also heterosexuals who support them.

Consider, for example, the "Briggs" Initiative in the late 1970s: had it passed, it would have required the dismissal of California teachers who support gay, lesbian, and bisexual rights regardless of those teachers' actual sexual identification. The U.S. military has a long-standing policy excluding lesbians, gays, and bisexuals from service. In most instances, rights gained through marriage, including spousal benefits and child custody considerations, do not extend to sexual minorities. Homosexual acts are outlawed in a number of states. And although a number of municipalities and some states have extended equal protection in the areas of employment, housing, insurance, credit, and public accommodations, no such statute exists on the national level.

Although agreement concerning same-sex relationships and sexuality does not exist across the various religious communities, and while some denominations are rethinking their negative stands on homosexuality and bisexuality, others preach against such behaviors and as a matter of policy exclude people from many aspects of religious life simply on the basis of sexual identity.

Until 1973, established psychiatric associations considered homosexuality a disordered condition. People were often institutionalized against their will, made to undergo dangerous and humiliating "aversion therapy," and even, at times, lobotomized to alter their sexual desires. Same-sex lovers and friends are often still denied access to loved ones in hospital intensive-care units because of hospital policy allowing only blood relatives or a legal spouse visitation rights.

Today, although a number of practitioners within both the psychiatric and the medical professions hold genuinely enlightened attitudes regarding the realities of homosexuality and bisexuality, some, unfortunately, remain entrenched in their negative perceptions of same-sex attractions, and these perceptions often affect the manner in which they respond to their clients.

Cultural homophobia (sometimes called *collective* or *societal*) refers to the social norms or codes of behavior that, although not expressly written into law or policy, nonetheless work within a society to legitimize oppression. It results in attempts either to exclude images of lesbians, gays, bisexuals, and transgender people from the media or from history or to represent these groups in negative stereotypical terms. The theologian James S. Tinney (1983) suggests seven overlapping categories by which cultural homophobia is manifested.

1, 2. *Conspiracy to silence* and *denial of culture*. These first two categories are closely aligned. Although not expressly written into law, societies informally attempt to prevent large numbers of individuals of a particular minority (or target) group from congregating in any one place (e.g., in bars and other social centers), deny them space to hold social or political functions, deny them access to materials, attempt to restrict representation in any given educational institution or employment in any business, and inhibit frank, open, and honest discussion of topics of interest to or concerning these groups.

In societies where homophobia is present, there have been active attempts to falsify historical accounts of same-sex love—through censorship, deletion, half truths, and the altering of pronouns signifying gender—making accurate reconstruction extremely difficult. Subsequently, many members of sexual minorities grow up without significant contemporary or historical role models.

In his *Christianity, Social Tolerance, and Homosexuality*, John Boswell cites as an example of censorship a manuscript of Ovid's *The Art of Love*. The phrase that originally read "Hoc est quod pueri tanger amore minus" (A boy's love appealed to me less) was altered by a medieval moralist to read "Hoc est quod pueri tanger amore nihil" (A boy's love appealed to me not at all). An editor's note in the margin informed the reader, "Ex hoc nota quod Ovidius non frerit Sodomita" (Thus you may be sure that Ovid was not a sodomite). Boswell also provides an example of one of the first instances of a change of gender pronouns when "Michelangelo's grandnephew employed this means to render his uncle's sonnets more acceptable to the public" (Boswell 1980, 18).

3. *Denial of popular strength.* Many studies have found that a significant percentage of the population experiences same-sex desires and that these individuals often define their identity in terms of these desires. The cultural assumption exists, however, that one is heterosexual until "proven guilty." According to Tinney, "Society refuses to believe how many blacks there are in this country 'passing' for white and how many lesbians and gays (and bisexuals) there are out there passing as heterosexuals" (Tinney 1983, 5).

4. *Fear of overvisibility.* A form of homophobia is manifested each time members of a sexual minority are told that they should not define themselves in terms of their sexuality or gender identity or when they are accused of being "blatant" by expressing signs of affection in public, behaviors that heterosexual couples routinely take for granted. They are given the message that there is something inherently wrong with same-sex desire and that individuals so inclined should keep such desire well hidden and to themselves.

5. *Creation of defined public spaces.* Society tends to force disenfranchised individuals and groups into ghettos, where there is little possibility of integration into the general life of the community. Neighborhoods, business establishments, and even professions are thus set aside for sexual minorities, as they are for other target groups. Individuals enter these areas hoping to find temporary respite from the outside world's homophobia.

6. *Denial of self-labeling.* Epithets and other derogatory labels are directed at every target group. Sexual minorities have chosen terms of self-definition (e.g., *gay* and *lesbian*) to portray the positive aspects of their lives and loves more adequately. Recently, increasing numbers of lesbians, gays, bisexuals, and transgender people have reappropriated such terms as *queer, faggot,* and *dyke* in order to transform these venomous symbols of hurt and bigotry into tools of empowerment.

7. *Negative symbolism* (stereotyping). Stereotyping groups of people is used as a means of control and a further hindrance to understanding and to meaningful social change. Stereotypes about sexual minorities abound, ranging from their alleged predatory appetites, to their physical appearance, to the possible "causes" of their desires.

In addition to Tinney's categories of cultural homophobia, psychologist Dorothy Riddle (1985) suggests that the concepts of *tolerance* and *acceptance* should also be included: tolerance because it can, in actuality, be a mask for an underlying fear or even hatred (one is tolerant, e.g., of a baby crying on an airplane while simultaneously wishing it would stop or go away) and acceptance because it assumes that there is indeed something to accept.

How Homophobia Hurts Everyone

It cannot be denied that homophobia, like other forms of oppression, serves the dominant group by establishing and maintaining power and mastery over those who are marginalized or disenfranchised. Individuals maintain oppressive behaviors to gain certain rewards or to avoid punishment, to protect their self-esteem against psychological doubts or conflicts, to enhance their value systems, or to categorize others in an attempt to comprehend a complex world. By excluding entire groups of people, those in positions of power obtain economic, political, ideological, and other privileges. This book takes the position, also, that oppression ultimately limits members of the dominant group, in a number of ways.

• Homophobia locks all people into rigid gender-based roles that inhibit creativity and self-expression.

Through the process of socialization, people are expected to adhere to fairly strict social roles based on their sex. The essays in part I of this anthology develop this theme.

My own essay considers the ways in which gender-role structures hurt all males in our society. I give a personal sketch of how I was affected growing up gay and interview two heterosexual men who have challenged convention by entering "nontraditional" careers (one is a hair dresser, the other a dance instructor). I discuss how these men have overcome early socialization, how the reactions of others have affected them, and how they have dealt with their own homophobic conditioning.

Ann Pellegrini discusses the institutions of sexism and homophobia, showing the connections between women hating in general and lesbian baiting in particular and suggesting how this harms all women, regardless of their actual sexual orientation. She also discusses how the interstructuring of sexism and homophobia contributes to violence against women.

• Homophobic conditioning compromises the integrity of heterosexual people by pressuring them to treat others badly, actions contrary to their basic humanity.

Frederick Douglass, fugitive slave and abolitionist, described what he called "the dehumanizing effects" of slavery, not on slaves alone, but also on white people whose position on slavery corrupted their humanity. Within this anthology, Phillip Brian Harper discusses Douglass's perceptions and emphasizes the parallels between slavery and homophobia.

Robyn Ochs and Marcia Deihl examine the roots and manifestations of biphobia (prejudice and discrimination against bisexual people) and the limitations it places on lesbians, gay males, and heterosexuals. They also emphasize the potential benefits accruing to a society that can transcend traditional concepts of gender.

• Homophobia inhibits one's ability to form close, intimate relationships with members of one's own sex.

Young people often form close same-sex attachments during childhood. However, once they reach a certain age (usually around puberty), their elders encourage them to distance themselves from these friends, with the implication that, if they do not, their sexuality will be called into question. This means—especially for males—no more sleeping over at one another's houses, no more sharing intimate secrets, no more spending as much time together. Ultimately, this situation tends to hinder their ability, throughout their lives, to get as close to a same-sex friend as they did when they were very young.

• Homophobia generally restricts communication with a significant portion of the population and, more specifically, limits family relationships.

No matter what their constitution, families will continue to produce lesbian, gay, bisexual, and transgender offspring. The political Right argues loudly that homosexuality poses a direct threat to the stability of the "traditional" nuclear family. In actuality, however, it is homophobia that strains family relationships by restricting communication among family members, loosening the very ties that bind. Children, fearing negative reactions from parents, hold back important information about their lives. Parents, often not wanting to hear about their child's sexual or gender identity, never truly get to know their children. Even when parents and children reside in the same house, secret on secret adds up to polite estrangement and sometimes to a total break.

Members of a sexual minority often live in a psychological closet before acknowledging their sexual or gender identity to others. As they begin to "come out," family members and friends at times enter a closet of their own, owing to their own homophobic conditioning and the conditioning of others around them. They withhold the truth from friends and neighbors, remaining ever vigilant that word of their child's "deviance" stays buried. Sometimes, if the truth becomes known, they too become the target of stigmatization. In either case, the emotional toll is great.

The essays in part II examine the effects of homophobia on families and parenting. B. Jaye Miller interviews Mary Griffith, who documents the steps leading to the suicide of her son Bobby, which was due, in large measure, to the family's inability to accept his homosexuality.

Diane Raymond emphasizes that homophobia undermines the process of parenting in all families—not only that it harms those families with gay, lesbian, or bisexual children or parents, but that it also imposes great impediments to "mainstream" heterosexual families with heterosexual children.

Jean S. Gochros discusses how societal homophobia creates untenable marriages, ruins happy ones, inflicts needless pain, and stigmatizes and injures all spouses and children involved.

 • Homophobia is one cause of premature sexual involvement,

which increases the chances of teen pregnancy and the spread of sexually transmitted diseases (STDs). Young people, of all sexual identities, are often pressured to become heterosexually active to prove to themselves and others that they are "normal."

Diane Elze interviews two groups of young people—heterosexually identified and lesbian, bisexual, and gay adolescents—to discover the numerous ways that homophobia affects their lives.

• Homophobia combined with sexphobia (fear and repulsion of sex) results in the elimination of any discussion of the life-styles and sexuality of sexual minorities as part of school-based sex education, keeping vital information from all students. Such a lack of information can kill people in the age of AIDS.

Some homophobic religious and community leaders, educators, and parents actively work to prevent honest and nonjudgmental information concerning homosexuality and bisexuality—indeed, sexuality in general—from reaching young people. Students of all sexual identities need this information to make informed decisions about their sexual activity. Without it, they are placed at greater risk for unwanted pregnancy, STDs, and HIV infection.

• Homophobia can be used to stigmatize, silence, and, on occasion, target people who are perceived or defined by others as gay, lesbian, or bisexual but who are in actuality heterosexual.

For more than two millennia in the West, antihomosexual laws and decrees have been enacted by both church and state, carrying punishments ranging from the ridicule to the death of the "accused." These decrees have been used to justify the harsh treatment of those discovered or believed to have engaged in same-sex activity. But what is often forgotten or overlooked is the fact that these same laws have, on occasion, been used by individuals and governments to silence opponents, whether or not they have engaged in same-sex activity.

In our own century, Paragraph 175, the section of the German Penal Code used by the Nazi regime to incarcerate and ultimately to send great numbers of men suspected of being homosexual to their deaths, was at times employed to silence Catholic clergy, many of whom were not homosexual, as well as non-Catholic heterosexuals who opposed state authority (see Plant 1986). Sodomy laws remain on the books in many states. Although designed chiefly to harass people engaging in same-sex activity, they have also been used to prosecute heterosexuals. Recently, the Lambda Legal and Educational Defense and Educational Fund, a New York-based gay-, lesbian-, and bisexual-oriented legal organization, has defended a heterosexual man who, as a twenty-six-year-old unmarried man living in New York City with a male roommate, was perceived as gay and denied insurance.

In part III of this anthology, Carmen Vázquez documents and evaluates the ways in which heterosexuals are stigmatized and targeted for attack, profiling incidents of "queer bashing" directed against heterosexuals who were perceived as gay or lesbian. The implication is clear that all people are at risk of attack, regardless of actual sexual identity, as long as any group remains the target of hate.

Michelle M. Benecke and Kirstin S. Dodge address the problem of lesbian baiting in the military and how it is used to intimidate all military women and keep them in their place.

• Homophobia prevents heterosexuals from accepting the benefits and gifts offered by sexual minorities: theoretical insights, social and spiritual visions and options, contributions in the arts and culture, to religion, to family life, indeed to all facets of society.

David Eberly considers government-sponsored censorship of "homoerotic" art and art from other target groups and how such censorship ultimately restricts the creativity and freedom of expression of the entire artistic community.

Rabbi Margaret Holub and the Reverend Gary E. Doupe discuss not only how traditional religious teachings on homosexuality keep lesbians, gays, and bisexuals from entering religious life or from being true to themselves but also how these teachings inhibit the capacity of the entire congregation to value and celebrate human diversity and, most important, how they impede spiritual growth.

• Homophobia (along with racism, sexism, classism, sexphobia, etc.) inhibits a unified and effective governmental and societal response to AIDS.

Because of a wide-scale lack of early attention, the spread of

AIDS has reached epidemic proportions. The government and society in general have yet to make a true commitment to education, research, and treatment. Funding therefore remains insufficient. Many people have a false sense that they will not be affected and take no precautions, needlessly exposing themselves to the virus.

Jeffrey Levi examines the role of homophobia in the development (or, rather, delayed development) of AIDS public policy and how this affects the entire society.

• Homophobia inhibits appreciation of other types of diversity, making it unsafe for everyone because each person has unique traits not considered mainstream or dominant. Therefore, we are all diminished when any one of us is demeaned.

Although, as has been suggested, homophobia places limits on heterosexuals, at the same time it remains a fact that homophobia, and, indeed, all forms of oppression, is used to impose and reinforce control and mastery over others. Rewards and punishments are motivating factors for dominant group members in maintaining the status quo. Within this environment, however, members of the variety of dominant groups have become involved in antioppression work, many working to end homophobia.

Cooper Thompson discusses his personal journey as a heterosexual man involved in antihomophobia work. He focuses on his motivation and experience and on how homophobia has affected him.

• Homophobia diverts energy from more constructive endeavors.

Amanda Udis-Kessler makes the argument that, with all the problems that plague the planet and diminish the quality of life for its inhabitants, homophobia keeps us from looking at important social problems by directing attention away from the true causes of these problems and toward scapegoats.

As a counterpoint to the Western model, Walter L. Williams shows us an alternative social view by profiling nonhomophobic cultures (the native peoples of North America, Southwest Asia, and the Pacific region), pointing to the benefits that accrue to those societies in general, and families in particular, that acknowledge, support, and honor their sex- and gender-variant members.

At the conclusion of this anthology, I present a representative sample of activities for those interested in conducting antihomophobia workshops.

Why Study This Topic?

I find the questions concerning how each one of us is affected by homophobia, and more generally how any form of oppression affects us all, important and challenging. During the process of compiling this anthology, I have received encouragement from friends and acquaintances, people of all sexual identities. It must be acknowledged, however, that a few people I talked with—some lesbians, bisexuals, and gay males—have not been as receptive to the approach this book takes. Their arguments can be summarized as, "Why waste your time putting effort into discussing how homophobia hurts heterosexuals? Let them figure it out for themselves. Besides, you are trivializing our oppression by engaging in such a discussion. Also, heterosexuals who work to end homophobia do so simply because they want to be acknowledged and gain even more privilege."

These concerns are both compelling and understandable, but I believe that exploring how homophobia affects society as a whole will help us reduce, and in the long run possibly even end, oppression on many levels. How? By showing how oppression affects both target and dominant group members, we underscore the fact that, in important ways, it is indeed in everyone's *self-interest* to work to combat oppression. Such a strategy is necessary to encourage those members of dominant groups who may be hesitant to confront oppression. Moreover, it may prevent those already willing to confront oppression from either engaging in dysfunctional rescue of the target group (inappropriately attempting to "fix it") or preventing dominant group members from burning out. I therefore invite those who are struggling with the focus of this book to withhold judgment until reaching the end of the anthology.

A Note on Terminology

Within lesbian, gay, bisexual, and transgender communities, a debate is currently under way over the merits of the term *homo-*

phobia. For some, the term does not precisely convey the true and complete extent of oppression based on sexual orientation or identity. Since, in psychological terms, a *phobia* is a fear, usually irrational, some activists and theorists argue that what is conventionally called *homophobia* is far more than that. In fact, it is a prejudice often leading to acts of discrimination, sometimes abusive and violent. Besides, they continue, the prefix *homo-* (which, in Greek, means "the same") places the onus on the oppressed rather than on the agents of oppression. Proponents of this position offer alternate terms: *gay* and/or *lesbian hatred* or *hating*, *sexual orientationalism* (giving a parallel structure with *racism* and *sexism*, e.g.), and *heterosexism* (here defined as both the belief that heterosexuality is or should be the only acceptable sexual orientation and the fear and hatred of those who love and sexually desire those of the same sex). Heterosexism results in prejudice, discrimination, harassment, and acts of violence and is encouraged by fear and hatred. In this interpretation, *heterosexism* includes both the cultural precedence given to heterosexuality and also what is currently understood as *homophobia*.

While conceding many of these points, those who favor keeping the term *homophobia* point out that it is steadily gaining currency among sexual minorities, heterosexuals, and the mainstream press. Why, they argue, replace a term that adequately communicates its message?

It seems possible that we are in a transitional stage, one that could lead either to the codification of the word *homophobia*, to the creation of an altogether different word, or to agreement to employ more than one term for this complex condition.

In an attempt to allow contributors to this anthology to speak in their own voices, no attempt has been made to standardize the terminology of oppression based on sexual identity. I find myself, however, in growing sympathy with the position proposing alternative terminology, although for the purposes of this anthology I have chosen to use the term *homophobia*, however imperfect and imprecise it may be, because at this point in time it is well enough understood.

A further note. Also currently under way in the lesbian, gay, and bisexual communities is a debate concerning the effects of homophobia (and sexism) on transgender (or cross-gender) persons, that is, on those who cross the gender boundary to embrace the preferred gender role as a life-style. (Examples of transgender people are postoperative transsexuals—called *new women* and *new men; gender blenders*, who have assumed some of the attributes of both conventional gender roles and appearances; *androgynes*, who live comfortably in either gender role but are not committed to one or the other; and *gender benders*, who explode traditional notions of gender in their nonconventional combination of gender characteristics.)

Those who assert that transgender people are indeed oppressed cite the numerous areas in which they face discrimination in a homophobic culture: housing, employment, public accommodations, and other services. Those who take this position argue for a more inclusive language when listing other groups (e.g., lesbians, gays, and bisexuals) oppressed by homophobia.

On the other side of the debate are those who contend that by including transgender people one confuses gender identity with sexual orientation (or sexual identity) and that the oppression directed against transgender people, if indeed it exists, stems from a different source. Proponents of this position suggest that it is ill advised to expand the language to include transgender persons before a thorough theoretical analysis is conducted.

Transgender people are part of the culture that is rarely encouraged or even recognized. I side with those who are pushing for a more inclusive language because I believe that transgender persons, who have for so long been hidden from mainstream cultural diversity, are among those who are targeted by the institution of homophobia; I therefore include this group in my discussion here.

Conclusion: Challenging Assumptions

Over the past few years, I have appeared on a panel at the annual "Creating Change" Conference of the National Gay and Lesbian Task Force. The title of the panel for two years running was "Teaching Them about Us: Homophobia/Heterosexism Education." On the surface, this is a fairly reasonable title in that it conveys, with a certain economy of language, the intended focus of the workshop: an exchange of strategies for conducting anti-oppression education. However, on reflection, two pressing questions arise, questions that undermine the transparent assumptions of this title. Who are *they?* Who does *us* consist of?

Through its very wording, this workshop title reflects a basic opposition, a dualistic way of looking at the issue, with heterosexuals (the ones needing the education, the ones knowing very little, so the assumption goes) at one extreme and sexual minorities (those doing the educating, the ones knowing most of what they need to know) at the other.

Let us "deconstruct" this title to address some of its inherent assumptions—the major one being that heterosexuals are the ones in need of education, and that sexual minorities are doing the educating.

In truth, homophobia pervades the culture, and each of us, regardless of sexual identity, risks experiencing its harmful effects. Although homophobia did not originate with us and we are not to blame, we are all responsible for its elimination and, therefore, can all gain by a closer examination of the issues.

Lesbians, bisexuals, gay males, and transgender people have been, and continue to be, on the front lines in the fight against homophobia, and standing by our sides are supportive heterosexual allies—those women and men who have worked and continue to work through their own homophobic conditioning, who are secure with their own sexual identities, who have joined us and have not cared when others called their sexuality into question.

Although less apparent, another assumption in the workshop title is that lesbians, gay males, bisexuals, and transgender people experience homophobia in similar ways. We cannot lump all sexual minorities into one simple and unified category. Different people and groups view the world in distinct and unique ways; they appear at different points on the sexual continuum and on the path toward a definition of their identity; they regard the issue of gender identity differently; they come from disparate racial, sexual, gender, class, ethnic, religious, age, and regional backgrounds as well as physical and mental abilities. Therefore, the weight of oppression does not fall on them uniformly. Lesbians, for example, struggle against both homophobia and sexism. Lesbian, gay, bisexual, and transgender people of color must also contend with the effects of racism. Issues of class most detrimentally affect those with the least access to economic resources. Challenging standard conceptions of gender often places transgender people at risk for discrimination. Lesbians, gays, and bisexuals who can "pass" as heterosexual seem to experience less verbal harassment and acts of discrimination and violence than those who are more visible. Bisexual people, potential bridge builders between the heterosexual and the gay and lesbian communities, are often distrusted by members of all these communities.

It is, therefore, the goal of this anthology to highlight the notion that we are *all* born into a great pollution called *homophobia* (one among many forms of oppression), which falls on us like acid rain. For some people spirits are tarnished to the core, others are marred on the surface, and no one is completely protected. But neither are we to blame. We had no control over the formulation of this pollution, nor did we direct it to pour down on us. On the other hand, we all have a responsibility, indeed an opportunity, to join together to construct shelter from the corrosive effect of oppression while working to clean up the homophobic environment in which we live. Once sufficient steps are taken to reduce this pollution, we will all breathe a lot easier.

This book is dedicated to that end.

Warren J. Blumenfeld
Cambridge, Massachusetts
1992

REFERENCES

Boswell, John. *Christianity, Social Tolerance, and Homosexuality: Gay People in Western Europe from the Beginning of the Christian Era to the Fourteenth Century.* Chicago: University of Chicago Press, 1980.

Campaign to End Homophobia. "Homophobia." 1989. A pamphlet written by Cooper Thompson and Barbara Zoloth, P.O. Box 819, Cambridge, Mass. 02139.

National Gay and Lesbian Task Force. *National Anti-Gay/Lesbian Victimization Report.* New York, 1984.

Plant, Richard. *The Pink Triangle: The Nazi War against Homosexuals.* New York: Henry Holt, 1986.

Riddle, Dorothy. From *Opening Doors to Understanding and Acceptance: A Facilitiator's Guide for Presenting Workshops on Lesbian and Gay Issues,* organized by Kathy Obear and Amy Reynolds. Boston, 1985.

Tinney, James S. "Interconnections." *Interracial Books for Children Bulletin* (New York: Council on Interracial Books for Children) 14, nos. 3–4 (1983).

PART ONE

DEFINITIONS AND ORIGINS: HOMOPHOBIA AND OTHER OPPRESSIONS

1

Squeezed into Gender Envelopes

WARREN J. BLUMENFELD

[For a little girl] there are now dolls to play with and take care of, pretty clothes to try on, shiny black patent-leather shoes, and as a special reward she may help mommy with house work and stir the batter in the big white bowl. No one ever really tells her to be "domestic" or "esthetic" or "maternal" but she's learning.

A little boy, meanwhile, is learning other things. Balls and bats have miraculously appeared to play with, realistic toy pistols, and trains, blocks, and marbles. The shoes he finds in his closet are sturdy enough to take a lot of wear, and just right for running. One day there is an old tire hanging by a rope from a tree in the back yard, just right for swinging. No one ever tells him to be "active" or "aggressive" or "competitive" but somehow, he's learning. —*DEBORAH S. DAVID and ROBERT BRANNON,*
The Forty-nine Percent Majority

What is usually the first question a parent is asked by friends and family on the birth of a child? Perhaps, "How much does the baby weigh?" No, that question usually comes further down the line. What about, "Is the baby healthy?" Sometimes, but typically not first. Usually, people ask, "Is it a boy or a girl?" On the surface, this is a seemingly innocuous question. In reality, it is rife with underlying social and moral consequences.

Even before the infant's sex is inscribed on the birth certificate, assumptions have been made regarding his or her life course, assumptions based on a highly sophisticated and complex network of gender-based role expectations. The ways in which a society assigns roles to each sex reflect specific concepts of gender (social constructs in terms of "masculinity" and "femininity"). A *social role* is any pattern of behavior to which an individual is expected to conform, a *gender role* any social role linked with concepts of masculinity and feminity.

Much has been written about gender roles and how they constrain both females and males. In Western culture, concepts of masculinity and femininity promote the domination of males over females and reinforce the identification of maleness with power. Males are encouraged to be independent, competitive, goal oriented, and unemotional, to value physical courage and toughness. Females, on the other hand, are taught to be nurturing, emotional, sensitive, and expressive, to be caretakers of others while disregarding their own needs. Gender roles maintain the sexist structure of society, and heterosexism reinforces those roles—for example, by casting such epithets as *faggot, dyke,* and *homo* at people who step outside designated gender roles.

This social conditioning based on anatomical sex effectively generates great disparities between males and females, disparities evinced by the preponderance of men in upper management positions and other positions of power and prestige and by the fact that women still do not receive equal pay for equal work (Division of Labor Force Statistics 1986). There also seems to be an increased incidence of violence against women in more male-dominated societies (Mead 1935). It is evident, therefore, that females are oppressed by such a structuring of society, but what about males?

Males Hurt by Gender Roles

How are males—of any age or sexual identity—affected by rigid gender roles? How is heterosexism used to enforce gender roles? How do the family, the schools, and the media perpetuate gender-based stereotypes? While other essays in this anthology provide theoretical analyses, I concentrate primarily on the personal effect of forced gender roles, specifically on males. I profile two heterosexual men—Matt and Tom—who have chosen "non-traditional" career paths and a gay man—myself—growing up in a society with little tolerance of nonconformity. I first present a brief history of gender roles to provide a context for my discussion.

Changing Conceptualizations of Gender Roles

During the later half of the nineteenth century in England and the United States, the feminist movement emerged from the women's suffrage movement. Beyond the right to vote, women in this "first wave of American feminism" began to seek equality in politics, education, and employment and to question their traditional role within the family. Advances in birth-control technology meant that women's lives were no longer regulated by the reproductive process, and more women began to work outside the home. The availability of birth control also led to a questioning of the traditional view that the primary function of sex was procreative and that a woman's sole purpose in life was to seek fulfillment through childbearing.

With the advent of World War II, gender roles were not as strictly enforced. Most able-bodied men were drafted, their jobs—even heavy construction and factory work—often taken by women. Thousands of "Rosie the Riveters" performed extremely well under what would previously have been considered "unladylike" conditions, fulfilling what because of the national emergency suddenly became their patriotic duty. Women also enlisted in the military in large numbers.

With the victory over the Axis powers and the subsequent return of many men to civilian life, opportunities for women were again circumscribed. Government-sponsored poster and radio campaigns proclaimed it the patriotic responsibility of women who were hired during the war to relinquish their jobs to the men. Consequently, the late 1940s and the 1950s saw a return to strict gender roles.

The "second wave of feminism" in the 1960s, commonly referred to as the women's liberation movement, pushed for an end to sexism in all spheres of life, the personal as well as the political. Strategies ranged from direct confrontation to political involvement in an attempt to attain social, economic, educational, and political parity between females and males. In addition, many feminist activists and scholars challenged basic assumptions about the inevitability of sex roles and even about sexuality itself. Such questioning not only opens up greater possibilities for women to develop to their fullest potential but also relaxes some of the restrictions that inhibit men from fully expressing their individual personalities (Blumenfeld and Raymond 1988, 59–60).

The Family

The family is the primary socializing agent. It is from parents and guardians that we first learn which behaviors the culture deems appropriate to our anatomical sex—often by example.

From my earliest memories, I seemed to have questioned the ways girls and boys, women and men, were "supposed" to behave. At age five or six, I could not quite understand why my father had to be the one away at work all day while my mother stayed home and took care of my younger sister and me. With the simplicity of childhood perception, how odd I thought this arrangement was. Then and there I made a resolution that, if I ever had children, I would work only part time so that I could be at home with them.

I did not intend purposely to question the way things were; rather, I simply did not seem to fit into the arrangement. From a very young age, I had the overriding feeling that I was somehow different, that the part I was to play in this comedy (or rather drama) called life was meant for a different actor. I had been tossed onto the stage ill equipped to deliver my lines, and the audience booed me off. Consequently, I had very few friends my own age during those early years.

Helping me fill the hours was my highly developed imagination. In the isolation of my room, I performed puppet shows from within an old hollowed-out console television my parents had given me. I also enjoyed playing with my sister's dolls and sewing clothes for them out of scraps of fabric that my father brought home from the garment factory where he worked. After I turned eight, he forbade my playing with dolls. I certainly was not the son he would have chosen to have.

My father was a sports enthusiast, and baseball was particularly to his liking; he was a Giants fan long before they moved to San Francisco. He often asked me if I would like to go to the ballpark and see a big league game with him, but since the one time I remember going with him I was bored silly, I usually declined the offer.

My sister Susan, on the other hand, enjoyed athletic activities. She recalls, "I was the 'tomboy' of the family. I can remember my parents telling me that, when I got older, I should let the boys beat me in sports and games because they wouldn't like girls that could beat them. When I asked my parents why, they replied, 'It just isn't ladylike.'"

I, however, was singled out as the family member who had "a serious adjustment problem." Soon after my fifth birthday, my parents took me to a child psychotherapist for counseling. Although it strained the family budget, I attended therapy sessions twice a week for nearly eight years, until shortly before my thirteenth birthday.

There was a basic formula to each session. I walked in, took off my coat, and hung it on a hook behind the door. The therapist asked me if there was anything on my mind that I would like to talk about. I said no—since I did not understand why I was there in the first place, I surely did not trust him enough to talk to him. Then he took down a kit of a model boat or an airplane from a shelf, and we spent the remainder of the hour assembling the pieces with glue. No playing with dolls, no cooking, we simply did "boy" things. I later went on to learn that he advised my parents to encourage me to mow the lawn and take out the garbage and refrain from washing or drying the dishes, which, until that time, I was expected to do on a rotating basis with my sister.

Years later, when I asked my mother why they had sent me to "the toy doctor," as they called him, she responded, "You wouldn't have understood at the time, but we sent you because we felt you were too effeminate and we thought you would grow up to be a homosexual."

I did not understand why my parents were forcing me to

change behaviors that seemed genuine to me. I was extremely angry when they demanded that I stop crying when I was upset, or when they held my fingers still to make sure that I waved "with the whole hand and not with the fingers," or when they virtually blackmailed me into joining Little League baseball as a condition for taking up the violin. This pressure to conform continued in a curious form. When I was a teenager, my father came into my bedroom one Friday night while I was studying and put a five-dollar bill on my book, saying, "Why don't you go out and get into trouble like other boys your age." His meaning was quite clear to me; he wanted me to go out with "the guys" and cruise "the girls" on the boulevard just as he did at my age.

I have grown to understand that this drive, this near-obsessive push for me to conform, is certainly not unique to my particular family. My parents did their best to raise my sister and me in a culture that doled out rewards and punishments for adherence to and transgressions against a system firmly entrenched. My parents were simply unknowing victims attempting to fulfill their assigned parental duties. They too were squeezed into tight envelopes growing up. Later my mother told me, "We raised you and your sister the way we were raised." Serious options did not exist.

My parents' insistence that I conform to a behavioral norm stemmed, not only from their own socialization (involving hetero-sexist conditioning), but also from their desire to protect me from some of the hurt they had faced. They were concerned with my emotional and physical safety and felt powerless in the face of taunts hurled at me by my peers. For my father, this brought back harsh memories of his own youth when he, too, was labeled *different*. As one of only three Jews in his high school (the other two were his sisters), he was the target of anti-Semitic assaults. Many afternoons he returned home injured in a fight. Given the climate of the times, his own father felt obliged to Anglicize the family name in order to get a decent job.

I remember seeing my father cry only on a couple of occasions, for he tends to feel extremely uncomfortable with his own tears and those of others. On the night I "came out" to him as gay, however, his eyes welled over as he said to me, "I was hoping you wouldn't have to experience the abuse and hatred that I experienced growing up Jewish. That's one of the reasons why we took you to the therapist and why we tried to have you act like we felt you were supposed to act."

The Schools

Socializing of the child takes place mainly within the home but is reinforced in the schools. The gender oppression imposed by my schooling began the very first day I entered kindergarten at age five. As my mother dropped me off and kissed me good-bye, I felt afraid and very alone and began to cry. The teacher, in her clean yellow dress and white collar, walked up to me and said in a somewhat detached tone of voice, "Don't cry. Only sissies and little girls cry."

In retrospect, I can see that this teacher, at the time a seemingly unquestioning agent of socialization, was telling me that I must deny or, more important, learn to "control" my feelings in order to fit a preconceived notion of masculinity—a norm dictating that boys are tough and can handle any new situation, a norm asserting that a "real" boy is independent and does not depend on his mother or, for that matter, on any female. It was a norm that I did not fit and, in all likelihood, could not have fit even if I had wanted to.

Even back in those early days of kindergarten, boys and girls were channeled into gender-specific activities. Boys were encouraged to participate in sports, girls to hone such housekeeping "skills" as cooking and cleaning. This channeling seemed to grow and become more intense with each consecutive year of grade school.

During these years, I developed what has become a lifelong appreciation of music and art. When I was in the third grade, my parents rented an enormous old upright piano and allowed me to take piano lessons. (I also wanted to join my sister's ballet class, but they refused my request in no uncertain terms.) Then in the fifth grade I auditioned for the school chorus and was accepted along with only a handful of boys and about fifty girls. The reason why more boys were not included in the chorus is not because girls generally have better voices than boys at that age. The determining factor was social pressure. I and the other boys in the chorus were not well liked by our peers. In fact, several, including me, were despised and picked on by most of the other boys in our class, who viciously labeled us *the chorus girls, the fags, the sissies,* and *the fairies.* The girls, on the other hand, who "made it" into the chorus were well respected and even envied by the other girls in the school. As I was experiencing this humiliation, I repeatedly wondered why it was that kickball was considered to be more "manly" than singing. Why was it that, in order for me to be accepted by my peers, I would first have to show my physical prowess on the athletic field?

Because I did not fit into my assigned gender role, I became a prime target of verbal and physical abuse and, consequently, was involved in a great many fights. To avoid confrontation, I would arrive at school just before the opening bell sounded and leave as soon as the school day was over. Often, however, a few of the more aggressive boys would wait for me outside. I often wished I could become invisible. At night in my bed I lay weeping, wishing I were someone else, wishing I were dead.

The attitudes held by my classmates were formulated at home but reinforced at school. Teachers encouraged the girls to take advantage of the field trips to the opera each semester, and the boys to attend a local big league baseball game. The girls were allowed to help the teacher mix the paints for art period, while the boys were sometimes permitted to leave class early for recess to get the balls out of the equipment rooms. These may appear to be quite minor means of tracking a student according to sex, but they can pose enormous impediments to many school-aged children, resulting in stifled creativity and expressiveness.

The Media

Another means of socialization is the media. Although more and more men and women are depicted as equals on television and in the movies, many of the traditional, stereotyped notions of masculinity and femininity remain.

The television shows I remember from my childhood—"Father Knows Best," "The Donna Reed Show," and "Leave It to Beaver"—all reflected the popular image of the American family as white, middle class, with a nice home in the suburbs and all the characters accepting their assigned parts. Take "Father Knows Best" (the show's title in itself is telling). The Anderson family lived in the generic U.S. hometown of Springfield (we never know the state). The family profile went something like this. Betty Anderson—affectionately called "Princess" by her parents—was the eldest child, smart, pretty, fairly emotional, rarely if ever getting into trouble, always looking out for her younger brother and sister. Bud Anderson (James Jr.), possessed of "boy-next-door" good looks, was wisecracking, irresponsible, rarely emotional, independent, and frequently seen working on his car wearing a greasy T-shirt. Cathy, the youngest—affectionately called "Kitten" by her parents—was emotional, a bit of a "tomboy" in a endearing sort of way, and quite dependent on her parents and older siblings for support. Jim Anderson, the head of the household, wise, forthright, and moral, was often seen reading his newspaper over his morning orange juice and eggs before heading out to work. Margaret Anderson, emotional but steady and nurturing, was a housewife who was most often seen tidying up the living room, in the kitchen fixing breakfast for the family, or, in the late afternoon, waiting expectantly by the door to share her family's joys and deflect their trials and sorrows as they returned home from work and school.

"The Donna Reed Show" was essentially a carbon copy of "Father Knows Best," except Donna and her husband had only two lovely children, Mary and Jeff. In all other aspects, however, the Stone family was virtually interchangeable with the Andersons. And then there were the Clevers of "Leave it to Beaver," another variation on the basic theme: Wise father Ward, his caring and supportive wife June (who vacuumed in pearls), athletic older brother Wally, and "the Beaver," the freckle faced younger brother who was always getting into and out of trouble, the little scamp.

Television commercials were even worse in their depiction of

women and men in traditional roles. Women were shown ruthlessly attacking scuff marks and disheartening wax buildup on
kitchen floors, ugly, smelly toilet-bowl grime, and ring around the
collar. Behind these images of women lay the assumption that
women who failed to respond appropriately to household dirt—by
buying the advertised product—were neglecting their duty as
women. Men, on the other hand, were pictured as being in total
control. Viewers saw them seated behind the wheel of luxurious
Oldsmobiles, their adoring "better halves" by their side. Or they
were "looking smart" and "being smart" after shaving with Gillette,
with the obligatory sexy young woman feeling their smooth strong
faces. Or they were pounding one another and working up a real
sweat in the manly sport of tackle football, cooling down afterward
with a nice cold Budweiser.

These images constructed my world when I was growing up,
and many remain with us today. As a young person, I felt confused,
alienated, and extremely depressed because I believed that I was
the only one who did not fit in. Nevertheless, I do not condemn
traditional gender roles outright or unequivocally. Some people
want nothing more than to fulfill such expectations, and if, after
carefully considering their options, they choose such traditional
models, they should be free to do so. Certainly, knowing one's
proper role in a given situation can be comforting, offering a measure of stability and a framework within which to judge whether
certain forms of behavior are acceptable.

The operative word here, however, is *options*. I am angered
when any one role model or standard of behavior is held up as *the*
criterion by which all others are judged. Such a position tacks on
an added dimension to heterosexism: not only must everyone be
heterosexual, but everyone must also make sure that their behavior conforms to traditional notions of gender.

I was hurt in this system. By stepping outside my assigned
gender role, I was branded as *the faggot, the little sissie, the queer,
the homo,* whom nobody wanted to be seen with for fear of being
branded too. In many important ways, I believe I was robbed
of my childhood when my individuality, my creativity, was denied me.

> *Man for the field and woman for the hearth,*
> *Man for the sword and for the needle she,*
> *Man with the head and woman with the heart,*
> *Man to command and woman to obey,*
> *All else confusion.*
>
> ALFRED, LORD TENNYSON, *The Princess*

Opening the Envelope: Heterosexuals in "Nontraditional" Jobs

Those who violate established norms of behavior are often considered traitors to their sex and derided with heterosexist epithets, whether or not they are indeed lesbian, gay, or bisexual. There exists today a real confusion between gender-role behavior and sexual orientation. The irony is that heterosexuals, and not simply lesbians, gays, and bisexuals, are also stifled in such an environment. Although women are joining the work force in greater numbers, relatively few have yet to be promoted beyond the middle ranks in their chosen fields. In the schools, young people who are considered "different" are still commonly derided. Nevertheless, within the past few decades, cracks have appeared in the foundations underlying rigid gender roles. Females and males are now somewhat freer to participate in activities that were once strictly segregated by gender, although there is still an immensely long way to go.

Some of these changes are reflected in popular culture. Occasionally, television programs and movies depict "Mr. Mom" in his apron calling the children to dinner, power-suited women prosecuting toxic polluters, and female police officers who are the equal of any man. If you look hard enough, you can even find men crying and supported for doing so. Stereotypes, however, still remain. I took an informal survey of attitudes, asking, "What comes to your mind when I say *male hairdresser* or *female gym teacher?*" Most people's first response was "gay" or "lesbian." (A few spit out the obligatory "fag" or "dyke.")

In an attempt to understand to what extent heterosexist assumptions and stereotypes hurt heterosexual males, I interviewed two who have chosen to enter careers not traditionally considered options for men: hairdresser and dance instructor. Their names and other identifying features have been changed.

Matt grew up as one of two children in a mid-sized midwestern town in the 1960s and 1970s. He was an average student who enjoyed extracurricular activities more than academic work. He recalls that he was a pretty good football and baseball player and was fairly popular. All things considered, his high school years were some of the best of his life.

Having little desire to attend college, during his senior year he informally interviewed his friends' parents to ascertain which non-professional careers might interest him as well as pay the bills. He was particularly impressed by one friend's mother, who was a hairdresser in a trendy downtown salon. This woman told Matt that she was free to set her own schedule, enjoyed her work because she was given the opportunity to be expressive and creative, met some great people, and made a comfortable living besides. After exploring a number of options, Matt enrolled in a trade school and studied hairdressing.

At first his parents and brother and sisters had difficulty accepting his decision. His father even went so far as to tell him, "Either you forget about hair cutting, or you forget about living in this house." His elder brother, with whom he shared a room, asked him outright if he were a "fag," a question that Matt surprisingly never considered coming up over his choice of career. He had assumed that his "heterosexual credentials" were firmly intact: from his sophomore year on he hung around with the most popular young women on campus, and he dated the prom queen his senior year. These reactions from family members taught him to be selective about whom he told of his career plans.

Following graduation from trade school, he got a good job in a salon two towns away. For the first time in his life he was living away from home, alone in his own apartment. He made friends quickly at work. Among the other employees were two other men—one gay, the other—Rob—heterosexual. Rob and Matt often went to a singles bar after work to unwind. Rob counseled him never, under any circumstances, to tell new acquaintances that he was a hairdresser. Rob recounted numerous occasions when he would be hitting it off with someone, only to see a "distant, vacant stare" after mentioning where he worked. Sometimes the men would become agitated and even hostile and immediately lose interest in continuing the conversation. Within a short time, women would often offer some excuse for having to leave. Matt learned quickly to conceal his line of work from people until he became better acquainted with them, and he still does so today, after fifteen years in the trade.

Matt recounted one particularly harrowing story. One evening he met a woman at the bar, and the two "immediately clicked":

> We went home together that night and began regularly seeing one another. I told her I was a carpenter at the local construction company.
>
> Things went along smoothly for nearly a month when, as chance would have it, she came into my shop, ironically to get her hair done for our date that weekend. When she saw me holding my scissors and comb, this weird shocked expression came over her face. Needless to say, I felt like she had caught me with my pants down.
>
> She ran out of the shop, and I ran after her. She wouldn't talk to me. I kept trying to call her at work and at home, but she wouldn't return my calls. About a week later I went to see her, and she said she was really hurt. "Who and what are you anyway?" she asked. When I told her the reason why I felt like I had to lie to her, she seemed somewhat relieved. "I guess I did think you might be gay when I saw you," she said. "Now that I know you aren't, I feel angry that you didn't trust me enough to let me know the whole truth."

Matt and this young woman eventually patched up their relationship and remain together, but it seems evident, at least in Matt's case, that his choice of occupation has called his sexuality into question.

Tom seemed to have an easier time than Matt in entering a profession considered nontraditional. Growing up, Tom said he was "very shy and socially insecure" in a small Michigan town. He does not recall any strictly defined gender roles in his family. In fact, he remembers his "mother being the strong one, and father was very quiet." Both his younger brother and sister have gone on to become schoolteachers.

Tom became involved with dance quite by accident. He needed a job and saw an ad in a newspaper for extras in a small local production. He got the job and later enrolled in dance classes. Dancing for him became a way of overcoming his shyness, and it greatly improved his social skills: "I was so inhibited that it took me six months to learn to move my hips." Family and friends seemed to accept Tom's career choice easily. After his first year of teaching, he went back home. "They were all thrilled," he recalls. "They thought I was in show business." He eventually joined a small ballet troupe and today with his wife runs a dance academy outside New York city.

In the dance world, gender seems to be an overriding theme. Tom reported that 80 percent of dance instructors are women but that most choreographers are men. Asked why women are involved in dancing in significantly higher numbers than men, he responded, "Most men's masculinity is defined by a certain way of moving—very rigid and very inexpressive. Dancing betrays all that."

"There are two problems with most men dancing," Tom continued.

> One is that it makes them feel very insecure. They are afraid of looking ridiculous, awkward. Second, they are afraid that dancing will betray things that they don't know about themselves. For example, if they start dancing and begin to look "swishy," they are afraid their masculinity will start to peel away like a shell. In dancing, all traditional personas and rituals are blown to hell because you are learning to move, and as soon as you do, your body is saying things that you can't control. Although it became more acceptable for men to move their bodies during the disco craze of the 1970s, dancing still causes tremendous anxiety in men. There is still a taboo against men moving their hips and their shoulders, in fact any part of the upper body.
>
> Some of the young boys who come for dance lessons, when a male instructor moves the upper part of his body, they will say that

he is *gay*. The word *gay* is a very popular young boy term. To them it means any man who is unclassifiable to their current standards of what a man is.

Tom believes that the social movements of the 1960s and 1970s have helped relax gender roles, allowing men and women greater latitude to enter professions considered nontraditional. However, he also believes that society has a long way to go in breaking the grip of gender conformity.

Tom concluded by relating an Irish legend: "In the days of magic and emotion, people lived under a matriarchy. It was a time when people were the most important aspect of the society, when emotions and family and communicating with each other were paramount. It was only when the men began to make machines that they gained the ascendancy and took over the society from the women. Men came to power, and machines and war overrode other considerations."

Conclusion: The Burden of Masculinity

Demands that boys conform to social notions of what is manly come much earlier and are enforced with much more vigor than similar attitudes with respect to girls . . . and at an early age, when they are least able to understand either the reasons for or the nature of the demands. Moreover, these demands are frequently enforced harshly, impressing the small boy with the danger of deviating from them, while he does not quite understand what they are. (Hartley 1959, 458)

Males in our society are saddled with the heavy burden of masculinity—yes, *burden*. If we are to conform, we must be "in control." We cannot get too close to our feelings, and if we do, we certainly cannot show them. We must "keep it all together"; we cannot show vulnerability, awkwardness, doubts. We have to be "on top," in bed and out. To keep us in line, *faggot, pansy, wimp, sissy, girl,* and *homo* are thrown at us like spears to the heart.

Some psychologists believe that all people contain both a feminine and a masculine aspect and that, for individuals to be fully integrated, it is important that they recognize, appreciate, and nourish both. As they are currently constituted, however, gender roles teach males to hold in contempt anything within themselves hinting at "femininity." We thus kill a vital portion of our being.

I have come to liken gender roles to water in one regard. "The fish is the last to see the water," as the old saying goes. Likewise, many of us are unaware of an environment pervaded by traditional notions of gender. The analogy, however, is limited. While fish cannot live without water, we can all live without such strict gender roles. And unlike the fish, we don't have to be the last to see the water.

REFERENCES

Blumenfeld, Warren J., and Diane Raymond. *Looking at Gay and Lesbian Life.* Boston: Beacon, 1988.

David, Deborah S., and Robert Brannon. "The Male Sex Role: Our Culture's Blueprint of Manhood and What It's Done for Us Lately." In *The Forty-nine Percent Majority: The Male Sex Role,* ed. Deborah S. David and Robert Brannon. Reading, Mass.: Addison-Wesley, 1976.

Division of Labor Force Statistics. *Annual Report.* Washington, D.C.: Office of Current Employment Analysis, Bureau of Labor Statistics, 1986.

Hartley, R. E. "Sex-Role Pressures and the Socialization of the Male Child." *Psychology Reports* 5 (1959): 457.

Mead, Margaret. *Sex and Temperament in Three Primitive Societies.* New York: Morrow Quill, 1935.

2

S(h)ifting the Terms of Hetero/ Sexism: Gender, Power, Homophobias

ANN PELLEGRINI

Introduction

I came out and of age two years after Adrienne Rich first published her clasic "Compulsory Heterosexuality and Lesbian Existence."[1] Sometimes I think I just could not think my way through the critical challenges of surviving in a society inimical to women's wholeness and autonomy without the vocabulary and insights that Rich's demanding essay presents. Accordingly, when I was asked to write on the relation between sexism and homophobia, I was mindful of the intellectual and imaginative debt owed Adrienne Rich by women of my generation. I was also aware how much has changed in the decade since Rich first uncovered the lie of compulsory heterosexuality.

One important change has been the perceived fragmentation of the women's movement under the pressure of that much ballyhooed media darling "postfeminism." Another has been the necessary, but as yet incomplete, recognition of differences *among* women: differences negotiated along lines of race, ethnicity, class, religion, physical ability, and sexual orientation. But these political realignments have in no way severed the connections between sexism, here defined as the institution and practices of male dominance over women, and compulsory heterosexuality, the sexual economy in which women exist for men or not at all. If anything, changing times give fresh urgency to a considered reformulation of these relations.

My remarks below do not pretend to any definitive account of the relation between woman hating in general and lesbian baiting in particular. Similarly, the theoretical paradigms I propose for the reconceptualization of oppression should not be mistaken for a supertheory of oppression—with all resolved, all revealed. I cannot (or will not) aspire to such closure. Instead, I write provisionally, in the spirit of a conversation begun elsewhere and continued here in hope: the hope that, through the enunciation and elaboration of those forces that, as the poet says, hold us "rooted to an old ground," we may yet mark some slight progress in the imaginative reconstruction of the world. [2]

Unveiling the Obvious

I begin with two practical questions. How do lesbian baiting and homophobia harm *all* women? Why should heterosexual women take an interest in antihomophobia theory and activism? Both these questions might be crudely summarized as, What's in it for them? My initial response, and one that I have had to reformulate considerably, was, Is it not obvious? Obvious that heterosexism and homophobia could have no practical force, no social meaning, unless the supposedly "natural" differences between women and men had already been translated into a social, political, and economic hierarchy where women were forever subordinate to men. Obvious that the telos of female compulsory heterosexuality is not the eradication of same-sex love but the maintenance of male dominance. Obvious that proscriptions against lesbianism (when, that is, erotic, passional, and primary attachments between women have even been admitted as genuine possibilities for women) are strategies in service of a larger aim. Obvious that the real game in town (I said to myself as I plotted my appeal to heterosexual feminists) is the institution of sexism—the big *P* of Patriarchy.

All this I assumed, and more. At the very least, I expected that lesbians intuitively understood the necessity to join antihomophobia to feminist, antisexist activism. The personal observations and experience that had schooled me in this relation must also, I reasoned, have revealed the "truth" to other lesbian-feminists. It remained only to promote the alliance to heterosexual women.

Challenges

Two recent experiences have challenged these assumptions. First, in discussions with lesbian undergraduates, it has become clear to me that the costs of homophobia for heterosexual women are not uncontroversially admitted even among politically aware lesbians. Had I taken too much for granted? What sort of alliance was possible among lesbian, bisexual, and heterosexual feminists and, significantly, on whose terms? The skepticism these undergraduates expressed toward any "automatic" alliance between heterosexual and lesbian feminists has brought me to interrogate the space between *lesbian* and *feminist* in my own self-description, *lesbian-feminist*. For me, the hyphen linking *lesbian* to *feminist* points to larger political possibilities and signals strategic alliances between and among women: lesbian, bisexual, and heterosexual. But this hyphen is no straight line in either direction. Rather, political coalitions between and among women are created through a process of critical self-examination and sympathetic engagement. These alliances require work: constant, sometimes painful work together: "Two women together is a work nothing in civilization has made simple."[3]

Second, during an English seminar at Harvard on gay male representation, I was witness to an unfortunate (although scarcely inexplicable) display of homophobic anxiety and rhetoric. At the introductory meeting of the course, a heterosexual male undergraduate accused the tenured and openly gay male professor of "straight bashing." The student's homophobic accusation betrayed anxiety at his perceived exclusion from the conversation. For probably the first time in his life, the heterosexual male was not the putative subject of address. On another level, the young man's charge of "straight bashing" represents a particularly aggressive way to assert his heterosexuality. The student here usurps a place among the roster of the oppressed through and in a verbal exchange: *straight bashing*, as parasitic on the terminology that names the oppressive reality of *gay bashing,* denies by displacing the power relations that structure and enable homophobia.[4]

What I could not have predicted was the level of homophobic anxiety apparent among some of the presumably heterosexual women in the classroom. Two women joined the young man in assailing the gay address of the class. At the end of this introductory meeting, the threesome joined forces to corner the professor literally and continue their barrage. Now it seemed to me that their homophobia was not operating in the same way as their male classmates'; it had a different inflection and meaning. Because women as a group just do not have the expectation of centrality in the classroom, the homophobic anxiety of the female students could not, or so it seemed to me, represent their perceived exclusion. Put otherwise, so habituated are women to exclusion in the classroom that the experience of exclusion can of itself hold no grounds for complaint. Exclusion simply is their experience. Accordingly, I found myself unable adequately to account for the homophobia of these particular women.

Some possibilities did suggest themselves. The heterosexual women might be acting to defend male heterosexual privilege; only within the determinants of this system could they maintain what little privileges they did have as heterosexual women. On this reading, in lending their support to the young man, covering his back, the women "heterosexualized" his homophobic, homosexual panic. Or again, perhaps these women were expressing hostility to a different set of exclusions; within the field of gay male representation, they were no longer the objects of male desire. If an easy alliance between lesbian and heterosexual feminists had already proved presumptuous, relations between gay men and heterosexual women now appeared equally open to contestations. In this connection, it is interesting to consider that there is no way to refer to relationships between gay men and heterosexual women that is not pejorative. The designation *fag hag,* the most common way to denote a woman who has significant gay male friends and who spends time with them in gay male culture, is doubly burdened with negative connotations: the homophobic designation *fag* and the sexist *hag.*

Mapping the relations between homophobia and sexism was no longer so straightforward. My early claims for the "obvious" seemed to require reconceptualization and complexification; I needed to set out not just the lived realities of homophobia and sexism but also their complex and even contradictory articulations. Perhaps I was asking the wrong questions. Perhaps I had put the proverbial cart before the horse. I wanted to analyze the relations between sexism and homophobia. Did I even know how homophobia worked? What was my theory of oppression? What words would I choose to describe the presence of antigay and antilesbian attitudes and behaviors in American society? Questions of language and expression do not seem idle to me.

Discourse on Discourse: Power in Language

Language is not immaterial to the experience of oppression. Far from it. Language too has its violence. Anyone who has ever been called a *faggot* or a *dyke* knows this. In language lie the assumptions of a culture, its rules of conduct, what it will acknowledge as possible and permissible. No mirror of nature, language rather constitutes a prism through which human knowers organize, interpret, and give meaning to their experiences. Language marks out the limits of the possible. It tells us what to think because it is impossible to think outside language.

One way to illustrate this is to consider the nonrepresentation of lesbian existence in language. Lesbians are subsumed under the supposedly gender-neutral terms *homosexual* and *gay*. Yet both these terms also refer specifically to homosexual/gay men. This pattern, where the male-specific term is also the universal term, repeats the linguistic invisibility of women evident in usages of *man, mankind,* or *he* as universal subject. This invisibility in language affects the lived realities of lesbian existence. All too often there is no vocabulary to express passional love between women positively. In the absence of words naming their experiences, giving their lives shape and history, how many women, for example, have thought that they were the only ones ever to make their lives with other women? In heterosexist culture, this love that dares not speak its name suffers under an enforced silence. And silence, we should all know by now, equals death.

Even among persons particularly sensitive to the potential abuses of and in language, certain terms of expression and analysis may obfuscate the very problems they are meant to clarify by presenting paradigms that have unintended secondary meanings or that exclude in advance alternative explanations. *The feminization of poverty,* for example, redirects blame for the disproportionate numbers of women-headed households living below the poverty line *away from* the economic aggressions of the Reagan era and *back onto* poor women themselves. Why not *the Reaganomics of poverty?* Relatedly, the designation *welfare mothers* reduces the life histories of real women to one feature of their lives. In both instances, women are pathologized; women become the "problem" deserving of analysis. Otherwise put, blame the victim. Language abets this turnabout.

Homophobia may be another example of a term whose uncritical deployment effectively reinforces the hegemony of white, masculinist, heterosexist values. I have been referring throughout to *homophobia* as if it were clear what that term means, as if its application to the range of phenomena commonly identified as instances of homophobia were unproblematic. I want to suggest that *homophobia* may not be the most useful way either to name or to conceptualize the diverse practices—from physical violence to verbal insinuations—that seek to deny or efface outright the existence and integrity of same-sex love.

I begin with the word itself. The term may be caught in a circuit of "blaming the victim" similar to the one sketched out above. *Homophobia,* which literally means "fear of the same," might seem to displace the burden of responsibility onto its targets. An analysis of homophobia may all to easily become an investigation into what it is about gay men and lesbians that "makes" heterosexuals hate us so. This move shifts attention away from what it is about the institution of compulsory heterosexuality that not only directs but approves the hatred of lesbians, gay males, and bisexual persons.

Additionally, *phobia* inscribes the oppression of gay men and lesbians within the same clinical discourse that named us *inverts* and, later, *homosexuals.* Because gay men and lesbians have, historically, been made "objects" of scientific study and experimentation, a healthy skepticism toward clinical terms might seem advisable here. Also, it is worth considering how, within this psychoanalytic discourse, phobias categorically represent an *irrational fear and/or hatred.*

I find unhelpful, at best, any account of homophobia that would consider the root causes of lesbian hating irrational, incomprehensible, or otherwise insusceptible to careful, reasoned analysis. Such a claim, however convenient, overlooks the manifold ways in which compulsory heterosexuality functions as an institution. It denies the ways in which sexism and heterosexism are mutually reinforcing. It says that the oppression of gay males and lesbians has nothing in common with the oppression of any other targeted class of individuals. Further, it "naturalizes" the hatred of same-sex love by pronouncing this hatred and fear as a somehow inescapable feature of the human psyche. But is it not rather the case that the hatred of lesbians and gay males issues not from the subterranean order of the psyche but from the unexamined premises of the social realm?

One of these premises is that women exist for men or not at all. Yet it is worth remarking that the converse is not true: it is just not the case that the social identity of men is held to depend on their connection to some woman. Men *do* exist as socially and politically autonomous beings. In fact, this may be considered one of the defining characteristics of a man's social gender: his independence or his autonomy; he lacks nothing and no one. Woman, of course, *is* lack: of a penis (the infamous Freudian penis envy), of autonomous moral agency, of social position, of political and economic power.

Because women and men suffer under different expectations of what is proper behavior for them as "feminine" and "masculine," respectively, because gender roles are enforced differently for women than for men, because women and men are not social and political equals in Western culture (consider how small a percentage of the U.S. Congress is *not* white and male), it is not unreasonable to expect that *homophobia* should mean differently for women than for men. Certainly, the institution of compulsory heterosexuality has different implications for women and men.[5] Further, it must be asked whether the term *homophobia* properly designates the same constellation of forces across time and cultures.

History Lesson

It is a striking feature of Western cultural history that sexism and misogyny seem to be transhistorical phenomena. This is not to claim either that the specific forms and meanings of female subordination have not changed over time or that conceptual models for interpreting women's oppression are meaningful transculturally. Here great care must be taken to avoid a fall into totalizing theories that diminish or deny outright differences between and within cultures. Such caution is especially called for in feminist theory, where, as Judith Butler says, "the very notion of 'patriarchy' has threatened to become a universalizing concept that overrides or reduces distinct articulation of gender asymmetry in different cultural contexts."[6] For now, I wish to make only the limited point that we do not know of any period in Western history when women have not been socially and politically subordinate to men.

On the other hand, we *do* know of periods in Western history when homophobia (at least, homophobia directed at men) would *not* appear to have been operable. The cultural devaluation of male same-sex relationships in contemporary U.S. society finds no precise parallel among the ancient Greeks, for example, whose social and political institutions not only encouraged but even celebrated certain forms of male homoeroticism.[7] There are terminological problems here, however. Because the concepts *heterosexuality* and *homosexuality* are of recent coinage, it may be anachronistic, if not simply illogical, to search for evidence of homophobia and heterosexism before the nineteenth century.[8] This brief history and its attendant oversimplifications risk an updated version of the popular and highly romanticized (mis)interpretation of classical Greek culture as not merely gay positive but positively gay. I proceed despite, and in awareness of, the risks of the schematic overview. One such risk is mistaking the absence of homophobia strictly speaking for something approximating sexual tolerance. Accordingly, this brief history of Greek sexuality is intended to indicate this much: the cultural meaning and interpretation of sex, gender, and the erotic—how they are mapped across the body politic and onto the physical bodies of social subjects—have shifted over time.

In classical Greece, it was social ranking that determined the appropriateness of certain sexual configurations, not the biological sex of the participants. Hierarchies of sex, age, and class determined an individual's social power and, significantly, *his* social gender. A sexual act licit under some circumstances might be illicit under other: for example, a citizen male could penetrate his social subordinates (women of any age, boys, foreigners, or slaves of either sex), but it was considered shameful for him to be penetrated in turn.[9] To be penetrated was to take on the social gender of women, who were as a class the "natural" inferiors of men. Women were even categorically excluded from citizenship.

Classical Greece, then, provides an example of a society open to certain forms of male same-sex attachments but closed to any social parity between women and men. In fact, the positive appreciation for male same-sex erotic attachments in classical Greek culture seems inseparable from the low status of women.[10] The stigmatization of the *kinaidos,* the "effeminate" man, further indicates how Greek attitudes toward women helped determine the parameters of the socially and sexually permissible. In turn, the regulation of sexual and erotic expression was a means of policing gender boundaries.[11]

This suggests a tentative relation between sexism and heterosexism: the cultural enforcement of gender roles and male dominance are necessary but *in*-sufficient conditions for homophobia. Homophobia is one possible effect of misogyny, but it is not a systematic requirement of institutionalized sexual inequalities. The experience of classical Greece, with its very different social attitudes toward male homosexuality, "denaturalizes" and so historicizes the relation between sexism and homophobia. Although it seems impossible to conceive a homophobic culture that is not also sexist, the converse is not true: ritualized male homosexuality in

certain cultural contexts does not appear incompatible with pa-
triarchal social organization.[12] In fact, in certain cultures, it may
even seem to reinforce the cultural devaluation of women.

In claiming this, I am in no way arguing that male homosexuality "causes" or "produces" misogyny and sexism. Such an assertion would in fact be a stunning reformulation of the contemporary
analysis of homophobia as a weapon of sexism. Sexism provides the
social context within which the hatred of lesbians and gay men may
flourish; in its turn, homophobia reinforces gender asymmetries.
As Suzanne Pharr argues, "Without the existence of sexism, there
would be no homophobia."[13] On this reading, homophobia would
seem to be part of the structure of sexism. This does not mean,
however, that the oppression of women and the oppression of lesbians and gay men are identical—only that they are interstructured. It is important here to resist any conceptual approach that
would fully assimilate lesbian and gay male experiences of oppression to women's. Similar caution must be exercised with respect to
differences between lesbian and gay male experiences of oppression.

Multiplying Homophobias

If, as I am suggesting, the generic term *homophobia* assimi-
lates the experiences of gay men and lesbians, then it might be
more analytically helpful to speak of *homophobias* plural, each with
its own characteristic motivations in, and implications for, the het-
erosocial order.[14] Four types of homophobia may be mapped along
gender lines: (1) the homophobia of men toward other men; (2) the
homophobia of men toward women; (3) the homophobia of women
toward other women; and (4) the homophobia of women toward
men. On each tier, heterosexual persons may be victims of homophobia if they transgress accepted gender roles; for example, a
woman who refuses the sexual advances of a man, a feminist activist, and an adolescent girl who excels in athletics and disdains so-
called feminine dress (the tomboy of legend) are all easy targets for
lesbian baiting. Additionally, because gay males and lesbians may
internalize their experience of oppression and even redirect their

stigmatization outward against other gays and lesbians, I have not written the homophobia of heterosexual men or the homophobia or heterosexual women. The categories *men* and *women* as used above may thus include lesbian, gay, bisexual, and heterosexual persons. Finally, these four homophobias also multiply rapidly once variables of age, race, class, and ethnicity are figured in.

Societal pressures to marry and have children, for example, mean different things for women than for men; these pressures also differ across class and racial lines. Consider the easy slide from *unmarried woman* to the pejorative *spinster.* Yet there is no equivalent derogatory expression for an unmarried man; he is a bachelor. Additionally, a woman involved in women's political groups is often called *radical* or *man hater,* both code words for *lesbian.* Yet a man involved in principally male political groups is called *Congressman* or *Senator.* None of this is meant to deny any commonalities in the experiences lesbians and gay men have of homophobic oppression. It is, however, to resist the assimilation of lesbian existence into a presumptively gender-neutral homosexual experience. What, after all, could be less gender neutral than lesbian hating?

Getting Specific

I want to indicate briefly some specific ways in which gender stereotyping structures lesbian-baiting:

1. A woman's assumption of male prerogatives of dress or manner generates charges of "mannishness." That is to say, she is euphemized: lesbian.
2. Women working in nontraditional occupations are easy targets for lesbian baiting. The U.S. Navy, for example, calls "the stereotypical female homosexual in the Navy . . . among the command's top professionals" and in the same breath claims that "senior and aggressive female sailors [create] a predator-type environment" for "young, often more vulnerable female sailors." These top professionals are charged and discharged: lesbians.[15]
3. If a woman resists male control, heterosexual advances, or man-made definitions of "appropriate" female behavior, she is threat-

ened with loss of male approval and protection. In short, she is called a lesbian.

4. When women demand equal rights, denounce male aggression, choose to work in women-only environments, or seek to create women-only space, they are written off as bitter, angry, man-hating radical feminists. In a word, they are called lesbians.

In each example given above, any woman who challenges accepted conventions of female behavior or "femininity" is threatened with loss of male approval. In a society organized around the myth of the (white, middle-class) heterosexual family, this loss represents her potential or effective removal from a social, political, and sexual economy predicated on male access to women. This is compulsory heterosexuality. And it is inseparable from the institutionalization of sexist ideology and practice.

It is important to be quite clear on what sexism means for women, on its brutal facts. Nationwide, a woman is beaten every fifteen seconds; annually, three to four million women are battered by their husbands, ex-husbands, or male lovers.[16] In Massachusetts, a woman is murdered by her male lover every twenty-two days. Nor is the Massachusetts statistic somehow an aberration (I here bracket the question whether the term *aberration* has any meaning in *this* context). Of the five thousand women murdered annually in the United States, approximately one-third are killed by their male lovers. The FBI, an organization hardly known for a feminist politics, estimates that one out of three American women will be raped in her lifetime.

So ordinary is violence against women that the 1990 Federal Hate Crimes Statistics Act, which directs the Justice Department to collect annual statistics on crimes motivated by the victim's race, religion, ethnicity, or sexual orientation, overlooked the most obvious form of hate crimes: violence against women. Gender was specifically excluded as a category of analysis; women as a class were rendered invisible. Women comprise some 52 percent of the U.S. population. Counting hate crimes against women would thus represent a serious systemic indictment of American society. It would mean granting that half the population is, as a class, at serious risk of a hate crime. It would mean recognizing violence against women for what it is, namely, the most direct expression of cultural misogyny. Such an admission might even be a conceptual impossibility. It is possible to see and name what is always there? It is possible to isolate from the system what just *is* the system?

The system is compulsory heterosexuality. Women whose primary ties are not to men, whose emotional, political, and/or sexual energies are primarily or exclusively directed toward other women, whose occupation places them in a traditionally male domain (from the armed forces to the board room), who do not shy away from the self-definition *feminist*, or who are insufficiently "deferential" to male authority may experience intimidation and harassment. This sexist intimidation, with its woman-hating intimations of "lesbianism," turns in on its target; women may thus internalize the cultural hatred of women. This internalization is another form of violence. It makes women doubt themselves and each other; it makes women turn away from life-sustaining alliances with women, alliances whose political possibilities hold so much promise for all women.

Fear and distrust among women, then, is another effect of the interstructuring of sexism and lesbian hating. Where woman hating is endemic to a culture, lesbian hating, understood as the hatred of women making their lives with other women, is sure to follow. Sometimes the costs may be assigned a dollar value: when lesbian baiting proves an easy way to discredit women's organizations; when the "promotion of homosexuality" (whatever that means) provides sufficient grounds to revoke or deny government funds to shelters for battered women; when major women sports figures lose lucrative promotional contracts because of homophobic innuendo (to cite three quantifiable cases). But the costs to all women in energies diffused, talent and commitment wasted outright, and lives lost amid silence, denials, and invisibility are immeasurable.

While all women may suffer under the institution of compulsory heterosexuality and its sanctification of the married couple, lesbians encounter particular challenges and potential dangers. In the face of widespread cultural hatred of lesbians and gays, lesbians cannot fall back on heterosexual privileges. However well meaning heterosexual feminists may be when they place themselves onto the lesbian continuum or when they self-identify as "theoretical bisexuals" or "political lesbians," they do not really know the risks of a *lived* lesbian identity.

Nor do they similarly experience the contradictions of multiple political identities. As lesbians in feminist organizations we may be asked to keep silent about our lives for the "good of the organization." We may engage in self-censorship in order to make our politics more palatable to heterosexual feminists. Lesbians may even convince themselves of the political necessity of speaking around the *L*-word to protect feminism's "reputation" from the lavender menace. Self-censorship and disavowal, even and especially in the name of progressive politics, do not prevent the cultural conflation of lesbianism and feminism. Where feminism already connotes lesbianism, circumlocution does not avoid the issue. On the contrary, it promotes it. Additionally, denying the connotation admits its force: it says how *lesbian* attracts the force of an accusation; and it tells how feminists are all suspect. Young women who disclaim the name *feminist* at the same moment they pledge their faith to the stated aims of feminism (e.g., the Equal Rights Amendment, reproductive rights, state-supported child care, equal pay for equal work, health benefits for all women) speak to the effectiveness of lesbian baiting as a means of undercutting the revolutionary political possibilities of women working together for social change.

Conversely, as women in gay rights groups, lesbians may be reinscribed in a male-dominated political hierarchy where our specific histories and oppressions as women and as lesbians are discounted, ignored, or assimilated into a universal gay (male) experience. Women's rights and gay rights should not be seen as disjunctive options. It is critical that lesbians working in feminist organizations foreground our unique experiences as lesbians living and surviving in heterosexist culture. Political feminism still has much to learn about inclusivity and the particularity of experience. Relatedly, it is vital to the expansion of the gay, lesbian, and bisexual rights movement that lesbian-feminists engaged in antihomophobia activism foreground our commonalities with our heterosexual sisters. The fiction of gender neutrality must not obscure the profound links between sexism and the hatred of lesbians and gays. Each of us—from the multiple perspectives of our varied and over-lapping communities—must train her sights to see the complex mapping of power within and across the categories of sex and gen-der, race, class, and sexual orientation.

Toward a Theory of Oppression

Racism and anti-Semitism, classism, sexism, heterosexism— these "isms," which do not exhaust the structural possibilities of prejudice, are the contours, the defining terms, of oppression in contemporary American society. The term *oppression* here does not signal some static and polarized condition of dominance and submission. The dualistic model of "oppressor" and "oppressed," "dominant" and "dominated," with all it implies—the passive, di-sempowered victim who has no history of her own or whose story tells of no resistance—seems to me misleading. I want to move beyond modeling oppression on vertical lines, unidirectional in their distribution of power. These linear models, meant to expose hierarchies of power, might in practice (certainly in theory) recon-stitute and reinforce hierarchies.

Double oppression, for example, which corrects for universal-izing theory on one front, might seem to mislead on another. For *double oppression* suggests a vertical stacking of oppressions, one atop the other, with privilege of place going to that oppression of oppressions under which all others may be subsumed. This image, of a doubling and tripling of oppressions, seems to demand a quan-titative analysis of oppressions, as if all that is required to rate the various oppressions is the right moral calculus. It seems to me that a very different paradigm of oppression is needed, one that focuses attention on the interstructuring of oppressions without assigning priority of position, one that recognizes the interconnections be-tween and among oppressions without requiring their contiguity at every point, one that imagines otherwise.

Oppression is a process; it is constituted within and through a complicated and dynamic network of asymmetrical power relations. Oppression is all about power: the power to enforce a particular worldview; the power to deny equal access to housing, employment opportunities, and health care; the power alternately to define and to efface difference; the power to maim, physically, mentally, and emotionally; and, importantly, the power to set the very terms of power. This list of oppression's powers is by no means exhaustive. It does not, for example, exhaust the possibility of other, fundamentally revolutionary expressions of power. There is as yet the power and the will to risk, to resist, to love and live, with a fierceness of integrity and dignity despite and at great costs.

Because oppression is a system of relations, it is both theoretically inadequate and politically self-defeating to treat particular manifestations of oppression in isolation. It is theoretically inadequate because the forms that oppression takes in contemporary American society are not free standing; they are "interstructured." It is politically self-defeating because treating each oppression as a discrete phenomenon complete unto itself is divisive, separating potential allies in the struggle for social justice from one another. Oppression, after all, works best when it convinces "us" that "we" are somehow fundamentally different from "them." We thus replay the politics of "us versus them" whenever we deny the interconnection between and among oppressions. But we do not heal these divisions by forcing identifications across communities. The colonial urge to assimilate or homologize creates its own half truths. Coalition politics survives not despite but *because* of differences.

And who are we? We are everyone participating, in her or his own way, in movements for social justice and genuine political inclusiveness. We are antiracists; womanists and feminists; gay, lesbian, and bisexual rights activists; AIDS workers and PWAs; disabled rights activists; environmentalists; and war resisters. "We are," as the old saying goes, "everywhere," even if we are not everywhere the same.

NOTES

Thanks are due to the friends, colleagues, and teachers whose observations, critical questions, and thoughtful conversations have enabled this essay: Warren J. Blumenfeld was the model of editorial patience during my footnoting frenzies; Julia Lieblich read an early draft and was liberal in her encouragements, considerate in her criticisms; David Lamberth was, as ever, an engaging and insightful interlocutor; lively discussions with Heidi Rubin demonstrated the not inconsiderable pleasures of high theory, so called; and Blake Vermeule's friendship and intellectual engagements have been the occasion of rich exchange. Above all, I am grateful to D. A. Miller and David Halperin, whose examples of politically committed, acutely sensitive scholarship I might hope to emulate.

1. This much anthologized piece was originally published in *Signs* (5, no. 4 [Summer 1980]: 631–60).

2. Adrienne Rich, "Transcendental Étude," in *The Dream of a Common Language* (New York: Norton, 1978), 75.

3. Adrienne Rich, "Twenty-One Love Poems, XIX," in *The Dream of a Common Language*, 35.

4. The appeal to the language of gay community and antihomophobia theory in order to establish—to "prove"—male heterosexual identity undermines an interpretation of male heterosexuality as a normative position over and against which the minority discourse of male homosexuality is constituted. The derivative status of male heterosexuality as identity is perhaps indicated here. While the "proof" of female heterosexuality is a woman's relationship to some man, the situation of male heterosexuality is not analogous. It is not, that is, constituted through a man's relationship to some woman. Instead, a man's heterosexuality is asserted negatively: his proof is his *not* being gay. Male heterosexuality is declared by positing and then denying the homosexual possibility. This interpretation gains some support in the protestations of heterosexual male students in the seminar under discussion. These students complained of not knowing the gay code; they asked the professor to tell them the "truth" of gay interpretation. This claim *not* to know was their claim to male heterosexuality. For more on the ways in which male homosexuality, and its denial, may structure male heterosexuality and the realm of the knowable more generally, see Eve Kosofsky Sedgwick's *The Epistemology of the Closet* (Berkeley and Los Angeles: University of California Press, 1990).

5. Whether it even makes sense to speak here of compulsory heterosexuality for men is a separate question, and one worth scrutiny (see n. 4 above).

6. Judith Butler, *Gender Trouble* (New York: Routledge & Kegan Paul, 1990), 35.

7. For excellent examinations of this topic, see David Halperin's *One Hundred Years of Homosexuality* (New York: Routledge & Kegan Paul, 1990) and the late John Winkler's *Constraints of Desire* (New York: Routledge & Kegan Paul, 1990).

8. The words *homosexuality* and *heterosexuality* are attributed to a Ger-

man sodomy-law reform activist Karoly Maria Benkert, who wrote under the pseudonym Karl Maria Kertbeny. Benkert's first private use of the terms dates to a letter of May 1868. The terms first appeared together publicly in a 1889 edition of Krafft-Ebing's *Psychopathia Sexualis*. Given the *New York Times's* continued 1990s use of *homosexual* in preference to *gay or lesbian*, it is perhaps worth noting here that *heterosexuality* was "a love that dared [not] speak its name" until the *Times* came out with it in April 1930! For more on the late Victorian invention of homo- and heterosexuality, see Jonathan N. Katz, "The Invention of Heterosexuality," *Socialist Review* 20, no. 1 January–March 1990: 7–34.

9. *Boys* here means free males past the age of puberty but not yet old enough to be citizens. See Halperin's titular essay in *One Hundred Years of Homosexuality*.

10. Unfortunately, there is scant evidence as to the cultural perception of female same-sex attachments. I have written on the topic of lesbian desire in the Greco-Roman world, in the forthcoming anthology *Tilting the Tower: Lesbian Studies in the Queer '90s*, ed. Linda S. Garber, 2d ed.

11. David Halperin was helpful in pointing out the important "policing" role of the *kinaidos*. Any misinterpretations on these points are my own.

12. See, e.g., Gilbert Herdt, *The Sambia: Ritual and Gender in New Guinea* (New York: Holt, Rinehart & Winston, 1987).

13. Suzanne Pharr, *Homophobia: A Weapon of Sexism* (Little Rock: Chardon, 1988), 26.

14. This reconceptualization of homophobia is not a plea for theoretical correctness over and against the demands of political practice. For strategic purposes, political coalitions may require a more unified view of homophobia.

15. U.S. Navy internal memo, attributed to Vice Admiral Joseph O'Donnell, quoted in *Bay Windows* 8, no. 37 (13–19 September 1990): 1. Women are discharged from the U.S. armed forces for "lesbianism" ten times more frequently than men are discharged for "male homosexuality" (see Benecke and Dodge, this volume).

16. See the special report "Everyday Violence against Women," *Ms.* (September/October 1990), 45.

3

Racism and Homophobia as Reflections on Their Perpetrators

PHILLIP BRIAN HARPER

In 1845, the fugitive slave and abolitionist Frederick Douglass wrote the following words describing his experiences with Mrs. Sophia Auld, mistress of the Baltimore household in which Douglass lived and worked during the 1820s:

> My new mistress proved to be . . . a woman of the kindest heart and finest feelings. She had never had a slave under her control previously to myself. . . . But, alas! this kind heart had but a short time to remain such. The fatal poison of irresponsible power was already in her hands, and soon commenced its infernal work. . . . Slavery proved as injurious to her as it did to me. When I went there, she was a pious, warm, and tender-hearted woman. There was no sorrow or suffering for which she had not a tear. She had bread for the hungry, clothes for the naked, and comfort for every mourner that came within her reach. Slavery soon proved its ability to divest her of these heavenly qualities. Under its influence, the tender heart became stone, and the lamblike disposition gave way to one of tiger-like fierceness.[1]

This passage is remarkable because of its unusual description of what Douglass called the "dehumanizing" effects of slavery. According to Douglass, the victims of those effects are not black slaves alone but also whites whose "superior" position in the slavery context corrupts their humanity.

It is easy to understand why Douglass would think it important

57

to emphasize the negative consequences of slavery for whites as well as for blacks. His *Narrative*, first published by the Anti-Slavery Office during the height of the mid-nineteenth-century abolitionist movement, was really an extension of his oratorical work for the Massachusetts Anti-Slavery Society. Because many northern whites had never witnessed the realities of slavery first-hand, the public addresses by ex-slaves were a necessary feature of abolitionist organizing. It was through these oral narratives that audiences were educated about the horrors of life under the slave system.

Frequently, after making numerous appearances before the public, the slave orators eventually committed their stories to print. There were two primary reasons for this development. One was that the written narrative provided the opportunity for authors to present details of their lives that could not be developed in the more restrictive form of the public address. The relation of these details often proved to be very important since the ex-slaves' ability to give specific, verifiable facts regarding their bondage helped defend them from charges by proslavery forces that they had fabricated their stories. The other reason that ex-slaves turned to the printed word as a means of presenting their life narratives is that they could reach a wider audience through books and pamphlets than through public address.

Frederick Douglass's *Narrative* has long been recognized as the prime example of the published account of the life of a male slave.[2] Douglass had the ability not only to describe the details of his life with great vividness but also to present his experiences as an individual in such a way as to relate them to the effects of slavery on the larger population. This last factor—a key part of the general abolitionist strategy—explains the emphasis Douglass places on slavery's dehumanizing effects on whites. Since the success of the abolitionist movement depended on winning to the cause large numbers of whites, whose numbers and political power were superior to blacks', it was crucial to demonstrate how whites, as well as blacks, were affected by the slave culture.

This anthology strives to achieve the same type of effect that Douglass's *Narrative* did. It aims to demonstrate how prejudicial social attitudes are oppressive to the target group and harmful to those who are not immediate objects of negative sentiment. The parallels between the struggles of blacks and the struggles of lesbians, gay males, and bisexuals have often been recognized within the community of sexual minorities, and the community's struggle for liberation has often been modeled on the fight for racial justice as well as on the feminist struggle. It can be very useful and empowering to recognize the links and parallels between blacks' social position and that of lesbians, gay males, and bisexuals. At the same time, it is very important to acknowledge the differences between the struggles for racial justice and sexual freedom if the two movements are to be useful to each other. (It is also important to remember that any division we draw between the lesbian, gay, and bisexual communities and the African-American community is always artificial, to a large extent, since there are many people who identify both as African-American and as lesbian, gay, or bisexual.) In order to identify some of the crucial differences between blacks' experience of oppression and that experienced by lesbians, gays, and bisexuals, we first have to recognize the different ways that antiblack racism itself is manifested today in comparison with the slave era that Douglass describes.

Slavery was a very clear, concrete manifestation of the racial prejudices that have characterized U.S. society throughout its history. Not only was it an extremely brutal institution, physically and psychically detrimental to its victims, but its brutal qualities were quite evident to anyone who believed in the humanity of people of African descent and who bothered to determine what life was like for those held in bondage. Thus, while it was in place, slavery was the clear target of those in the society who fought against racial injustice. The most insightful and eloquent of the abolitionists were able to argue, as Frederick Douglass did, that slavery was detrimental to whites as well as to blacks and thereby to win increased support for the antislavery cause. If we think about it carefully, though, we will see that the strength of this argument depended on certain facts about slavery that are not necessarily true of all forms of oppression, racial or otherwise.

In the situation with his Baltimore mistress that Douglass describes in his *Narrative,* the dehumanization that Sophia Auld undergoes is a result of the direct control that she has over the slave's every action. Douglass explicitly refers to "the fatal poison of irresponsible power" as the cause of his mistress's moral descent. We know, of course, that, in the society that Douglass describes, *all* whites, slaveowners or not, northern or southern, held power over blacks socially and politically. In the context of slavery, though, the power relationship was made vividly clear because the slave and the master, to a large extent, shared a domestic environment. Because the black slave and the white master lived in close physical proximity to one another, the power that the white held over the black was made evident in countless ways. The most striking of these, of course, was the corporal punishment that was often meted out to slaves for various "offenses" committed against the master. There were other instances, though, in which whites' power became clear; in Douglass's case, it was manifested in his mistress's refusal to allow him to learn to read. In any case, it is clear that, in the slave relationship, the white slaveowner had complete control over what the slave did with his or her person.

The abolition of slavery, while it did not signal an end to racial prejudice, did alter to a large degree the means by which whites exercised control over blacks in southern society.[3] The transitional period in the nature of this control was embodied in the Reconstruction, which lasted from the close of the Civil War in 1865 through 1877, when the last Union troops were withdrawn from southern soil. During Reconstruction, the states of the Southern Confederacy were subject to control by the federal government, which oversaw the modification of those states' (racist) social and legal institutions as preparation for their full readmission to the Union. Through these modifications, blacks were accorded voting rights, formed political organizations, held office in southern state legislatures, and made other significant social and political strides, although these things were by no means easy to achieve. With the Compromise of 1877, the balance tipped again in favor of racist sentiment, as Republican presidential candidate Rutherford B. Hayes negotiated to win the electoral votes of three key states by promising the withdrawal of Union troops from the Confederate states and the consequent "reconciliation" of North and South. This withdrawal effectively restored political autonomy to whites in the South and ensured that the region could establish its own racial policies largely without interference from the government. Slavery was not reinstituted, but many restrictions on blacks' social and economic activity were enacted, with the infamous system of "Jim Crow" laws being solidified during this period. The era was also characterized by a dramatic increase of activity by the Ku Klux Klan and other white supremacist groups that had begun operating as underground organizations during Reconstruction; the violent retaliation that such groups enacted against blacks who appeared in any way to challenge the dominance of the white population is well known.[4]

The violence of the KKK must be recognized, though, as fundamentally different from the control exercised by whites over black slaves: slavery was systemic and legally sanctioned, while the Klan operated outside the law (although often with the tacit approval of the pertinent law enforcement officials). Legally speaking, the means for controlling blacks had shifted from the explicit physical dominance of their persons by individual whites to the restriction of their social, political, and economic activity. The new forms of control, while clearly resulting in consequences that were physically detrimental to large numbers of black people, were not themselves as *directly* physical as the means of control that were common during the slave era had been. This general development, toward less and less directly physical restrictions on blacks' personal freedom, has largely characterized the history of African-Americans from the time of slavery through the present day.

Black people's struggle for civil rights has largely fit itself to this continual development in the nature of racist oppression. The doctrine of "separate but equal," which characterized racial politics in the United States throughout the early twentieth century, was, by the 1950s, subjected to attack by civil rights organizers, who worked both through the legal system and through direct, nonviolent action to address legally sanctioned discrepancies in the treatment of blacks and whites around the country. Restrictions on blacks' freedom were now enforced not so much by individual white citizens, as in the context of slavery, as by a more generalized legal mechanism that supported the suppression of African-American liberty. It was, nonetheless, still relatively easy to identify the objects of black protest: the laws that mandated the inferior status of blacks in all aspects of national life. The objective of civil rights activists through the 1950s and early 1960s was to eliminate these laws from the books, and thus to rectify the compromised legal position that blacks faced in most states.

As the Jim Crow laws and other legal restrictions on blacks' activities began to erode under the pressure of civil rights activism, a new awareness developed among many members of the black community (including Martin Luther King, Jr., who was developing an increasingly radical critique of U.S. society when he was assassinated) that the problems blacks faced were rooted deep in the very ideologies on which the nation was founded. Consequently, the mere passage of civil rights legislation would not be enough to redress the country's racial problems. Even if blacks were to accept the principles generally taken to reflect the "American way," it was clear that they would not be able to take an active part in the further shaping of that ideology without gaining access to a power structure that has historically been dominated by white males. In other words, since the late 1960s, blacks and other racial minorities have been thoroughly educated as to the limits of legislative activism. The strides that civil rights legislation represents (and these advances are themselves always tenuous and subject to revision by a conservative Congress, president, or Supreme Court) are limited to the arenas where legal sanction has an effect. These gains cannot work a great deal of change in the relatively private bastions of national power—in particular, corporate industry and the interrelated social contexts of prep schools, elite universities, and associated clubs in which networks of industry leadership are negotiated. The fabric and operation of these social contexts (and of the many other, less obviously powerful but more pervasive social contexts that constitute the "mainstream" of U.S. life) are governed not so much by official legislation as by personal attitudes—attitudes that themselves underlie many of the racist restrictions characteristic of U.S. legislative history.

This fact explains, to a large degree, the cliché that is well rehearsed among black civil rights activists—that the fight against racism has, paradoxically, grown more difficult rather than less so over the past thirty years. After all, attitudes are much more difficult to change than laws are, and the progress that has been made in the legislative arena has actually made it clear that, fundamentally, what we are fighting against are attitudes. It is in this fact—which we always know on some gut level but which nonetheless has to be demonstrated again and again—that antiracism struggles most closely correspond with the antihomophobia work performed by lesbians, bisexuals, and gay men.

It is probably true that, in the United States at least, the systematic oppression of gays, lesbians, and bisexuals has always been less physicalized than that of blacks. I do not mean to suggest that gay people have not suffered grave physical consequences because of their gayness. Many, if not most of us, have—either through individual acts of "queer bashing" or institutionally, through imprisonment or incarceration in mental hospitals, for instance. These acts of physical violence or restraint have not, however, been *systematic;* they have not been applied across the board to all gays, lesbians, and bisexuals. Indeed, it may well be that the only reason they have not been is that not all gays, lesbians, and bisexuals are easily identifiable as such; by contrast, most, although by no means all, black people are visibly identifiable as being of African descent. Because gay, lesbian, or bisexual identity is of a different nature than African-American identity, the forms of oppression faced by people because they are gay, lesbian, or bisexual will be different from those faced by people because they are black.

This does not mean that people working against homophobia cannot learn from people working against racism, or vice versa. What it means is that we must not lose sight of the specific natures of the different struggles, even while we recognize their similarities and interrelatedness. It also means that we can learn as much from the differences between the antiracism work and antihomophobia work as we can from the similarities between them. This is particularly true, I think, when it comes to considering the effects of the two prejudices on people who are members of neither a

sexual minority nor a racial minority. In order to explain exactly
what I mean, let me return to Frederick Douglass to examine his
argument regarding the detrimental effects of slavery on whites.

Douglass's point was that slavery had a *dehumanizing* effect on
those whites who held slaves (and, by extension, on those who
might not have held slaves but who, by action or inaction, supported the institution of slavery). The brilliance of Douglass's assessment lies in the fact that it recognizes as the primary effect of
slavery on whites the very attribute that white racism ascribed to
blacks; that is, Douglass's analysis reverses the conventional racist
perception that identifies blacks as less than human and whites as
superior to them. If we characterize racist oppression as an attempt
by the dominant group to prove its superiority over the dominated
group, then we can see the ironic power of Douglass's analysis
since he shows us that, by exercising unjust power, the dominant
group actually demonstrates its moral inferiority. Thus, what white
racists try to identify as traits that are external to themselves—in
this case, brutal, inhuman qualities—are actually shown to exist
within their own personalities.[5]

Homophobic activity—violent or otherwise—operates according to a similar, but almost inverse, logic. If it is true (and I think
it is) that homophobia derives, in part, from heterosexuals' fear and
anxiety about their own sexuality—fear about the homosexual desire that might exist within their own psyches—then homophobic
activity represents the homophobe's impulse to *externalize* those
homosexual tendencies, to emphasize to the world that "these
other people are 'sick,' but I'm not, and I'm proving it to you by
demonstrating my hostility toward them." (The acquisition of homophobia is a complex and multifaceted process; this is merely one
aspect.) If we understand part of the nature of homophobic sentiment in this way, then we will understand, as well, that homophobic activity—although clearly most detrimental, on all levels, to
gays, lesbians, and bisexuals themselves—actually represents the
homophobe's self-hatred, his hostility toward something that lies
within himself. (I use the masculine pronoun here because I take
young males to represent the most dangerously homophobic ele-

ment in our society.) The results of this self-hatred, although more subtle than the results of queer bashing on the victim, are nonetheless evident in the ways many heterosexuals repress healthy parts of their personalities because they associate them with homosexuality. This sort of repression is dealt with elsewhere in this book, so I will not go into the issue here. What is worth noting is the similar messages about the dominant groups' sense of itself that are inherent in racism and homophobia. Racism, by representing hostility toward some external group that is perceived as different from and inferior to the majority, actually renders the hostile party morally inferior to the victim of the hostility. Homophobia has the same result, except that it partially originates with the homophobe's negative feelings about something inside his own psyche, which he tries to externalize through homophobic activity.

It is probably easier to see this similarity between the "backfire" effects of racism and homophobia now, in the late twentieth century, than it ever was before. The reason has to do with changes in the nature of racist activity since the end of the slavery era. As legally sanctioned control over blacks' personal freedoms has been eroded, the roots of that immoral control in prejudicial attitudes have become increasingly clear. As a consequence, we have become better able to discern the sociological similarities between racism and homophobia, whose roots in moral attitudes have always been relatively evident since *homosexuality* became a character definition in the late nineteenth century. At this historical juncture, the constraints on blacks' freedoms and on those of gays, lesbians, and bisexuals, while not by any means identical, are more comparable than ever. In a great many locales, explicit discriminatory activity toward members of either group is legally barred, but tacitly sanctioned repression of both blacks and gays continues nonetheless. If we understand the similarities and the subtle differences between the two different types of oppression (and this essay represents only a very tentative first step toward such an understanding), then we can make significant strides in combatting both injustices and thus move our society that much closer toward full democratic freedom.

NOTES

1. *Narrative of the Life of Frederick Douglass, an American Slave, Written by Himself* (1845), edited with an introduction by Houston A Baker, Jr. (New York: Penguin, 1982), 77–78, 81–82.

2. The effects of gender difference made the experiences of black women in slavery distinct from those of black men; Douglass's narrative cannot therefore be considered as representing the life of the female slave. The best example of the female slave's narrative is Harriet A. Jacobs's *Incidents in the Life of a Slave Girl* ([1861], ed. Jean Fagan Yellin [Cambridge, Mass.: Harvard University Press, 1987]).

3. It is worth stating explicitly that antiblack racism has never been a purely southern institution in the United States. The South does, however, offer the clearest examples of the blatant control that characterizes the relation of white to black in the nineteenth century. As my discussion moves chronologically into the twentieth century, the differences between North and South will largely fall away.

4. This history is usefully summarized in Howard Zinn, *A People's History of the United States* (New York: Harper & Row, 1980), 167–205.

5. For further elaboration on this idea, see Joel Kovel, *White Racism* (New York: Columbia University Press, 1984).

4

Moving beyond Binary Thinking

ROBYN OCHS
AND MARCIA DEIHL

All the essays in this anthology address, in some way, how heterosexism and homophobia hurt all of us. Heterosexism denies the reality of bisexuals as well as those people whose identity or behavior is exclusively homosexual. Since homophobia is directed at even the *appearance* of "gayness" in any of us, biphobia and homophobia are often indistinguishable. Indeed, it can be argued that fear of bisexuals is due to homophobia. This is often the case. However, there is an additional component to biphobia that is unlike homophobia and that will be a main focus of this essay. It is our belief that these unique aspects of biphobia harm us all.

Sexual definitions have become polarized. We think of our sexuality in terms of opposites; male/female, staight/gay. This polarization is limiting, causing us to "choose sides" and be loyal to "our team." This focus on the differences between us, rather than on our commonalities, can prevent us from being true to ourselves and to our own feelings and desires. When we do behave in ways that are against the "rules," or when we become friends or lovers with others who violate these rules, we often feel compelled to remain silent about our deviation.

Consider how you would feel if you found out that a close friend identified as bisexual. If you are gay or lesbian, would you feel mistrustful, deserted, or betrayed? If you are heterosexual, would you immediately think either, "Is he/she coming on to me?" (if you are of the same sex) or, "What about AIDS? I can't possibly consider sleeping with him/her now!" (if you are of different sexes). Perhaps your response would be some subtler, "liberal" version. Are these reactions harmful to you? This essay will define *bisexuality* and discuss the ways in which biphobia oppresses bisexuals and how it hurts heterosexuals as well as gays and lesbians.

What Is a Bisexual?

> Everybody knows about bisexuals—they're confused ("just a stage you're going through . . . you'll eventually choose . . . you're not secure in your mature heterosexuality yet . . . you're afraid of the other sex and the same sex is less threatening . . ."); they're sex maniacs ("They will do it with anyone, anytime"); they're shallow ("They can't commit themselves to any one person or even any one sex for a long-term deep relationship . . . they're typical 'swingers' . . . they're fickle . . .").[1]

These descriptions of bisexuals are fairly typical responses. If you ask someone what a bisexual is, they will often envision a married man or woman who has secondary flings with people of the same sex. In the gay and lesbian community, the stereotype is usually associated with betrayal. The 1983 "April Fools" edition of Boston's *Gay Community News* featured a cartoon about a jilted lesbian who had been left by her bisexual lover for a man. The next time, she was prepared with "bisexuality insurance."[2]

This cartoon reflects the common false stereotype that bisexuals are more lacking in compassion when we end relationships than are heterosexuals, lesbians, or gay men. Sometimes bisexuals do leave women for men. We also leave men for women, women for women, and men for men. And, just as often, we are left. Some of us are monogamous and tenacious; others are promiscuous and restless.

There are many types of bisexuals. For some, bisexuality may *be* a phase. Others have always been attracted to both women and men. There are historically "technical" bisexuals, who end up as primarily gay, lesbian, or heterosexual but who may not choose to be known as bisexuals. There are also many people who continue to identify as bisexual despite celibacy or a lifelong monogamous commitment to one partner.

What Is Biphobia?

Biphobia is fear of the other and fear of the space between our categories. Sometimes it manifests itself as homophobia (fear and hatred of homosexuality) and heterosexism (institutional or organizational discrimination against homosexuals), other times as fear on the part of gay and lesbian communities. Our sexual categories have long been founded on the illusion that there are two separate and mutually exclusive sexual identities: heterosexual or homosexual. This ethic states that you are either one or the other, that those who are not like you are very different, and that you need not worry about becoming like them. Biphobia, like homophobia, is prejudice based on negative stereotypes. It is often born of bigotry, but it is sometimes simple ignorance.

ROBYN: I showed a coworker a photograph of a friend with her husband and mentioned that she was a member of my bisexual support group. My coworker responded, "How does her husband feel about sharing her? He must be really tolerant." I asked what she meant. She answered, "Well, tolerating her seeing other people and all that." I informed my coworker that my friend was in a monogamous relationship. She looked confused.

Fear from the Heterosexual World

In the course of our activism, we have come across a number of bisexual men who have described to us their pain and confusion about coming out. One friend told us how afraid he is to come out as bisexual to women he is interested in because many of them will reject him as a potential partner if they know he is bisexual. He said, "What kind of choice is that—honesty or rejection?"

We all lose when we judge a man simply by saying he is bisexual rather than judging him on the basis of who he *is*. If our concern is AIDS, not all bisexual men have engaged in unsafe sex. If our concern is monogamy, not all bisexual men are nonmonogamous. Similarly, not all heterosexual people are at low risk for AIDS, and not all are monogamous. We all lose when we fail to get beyond our stereotypes. We will all gain when we are not punished for our honesty. In a world free of biphobia, we would not have to choose between honesty and rejection.

> ROBYN: I came out to my brother several years ago, and he seems on many levels to accept my bisexual identity. Recently, when I was visiting him, however, he took special care to request that I not discuss being bisexual in front of his roommates.

Bisexuals do exist. Sigmund Freud and Alfred Kinsey agree that there is a spectrum of sexuality from "purely" gay to "purely" straight.[3] Heterosexuals who are brought up in a homophobic environment will often react to bisexuality as they react to homosexuality. But with bisexuality there is the added dimension of potential identification with the "straight half" of a bisexual person. They may be even more threatened because they see that the "other" is not quite as different as they had believed or would prefer. A formerly safe fantasy could turn into a very real possibility.

If homophobic conditioning is keeping some straight people from accepting or acting on their gay fantasies, they will probably be biphobic. If they are living a heterosexual life-style for negative reasons ("It's sick and perverse and sinful to act on any of my homosexual feelings"), they will probably be threatened by others' bisexuality. If they are identifying as heterosexual for positive, inner-directed reasons, their chances of being threatened are lessened. Some of our best allies are secure heterosexual people.

Bisexuality defies old categories and demands new responses. Historically, bisexuals' status has simply been one of nonexistence. In scientific studies and in the media, we are labeled as either heterosexual or homosexual, depending on our external appearance. In a love story about a man and a woman, who considers that one or both of the characters might in fact identify as bisexual? In literature and in popular culture, bisexuality is rarely presented. When it does appear, it is often within a conflict situation, usually involving privileged white men, as in movies like *Sunday Bloody Sunday* and *Torch Song Trilogy*.

The fears expressed about us are largely based on ignorance rooted in our invisibility. Bisexuals, especially bisexual women, who are not middle class or rich, traditionally "beautiful," able bodied, or white are invisible. Thus, it is hardly surprising that, when *Newsweek* finally got around to publishing a feature story on bisexuality, the principal focus was on the secretive married bisexual men who are passing AIDS along to their wives.[4] Bisexuals fare little better in the gay community. We hear in conversation that bisexual women are "really lesbians who want access to heterosexual privilege" and that they are "really heterosexuals who want access to the support and excitement of the lesbian community."

Fear on the Part of the Gay and Lesbian World

MARCIA and ROBYN: A friend of ours had been active in the lesbian community for several years. Then she fell in love with a man. When her lesbian "friends" found out, they ostracized her and held a "funeral" for her.

Sexual minority communities are under siege, especially in this age of AIDS. People under constant siege often band together to form a united front. Consequently, formerly gay and lesbian people who "turn bi" are perceived as regressing into the "safer" haven of heterosexuality and are often met with feelings of betrayal and anger. These reactions are unfair.

A recurring theme in Robyn's lesbian relationships has been the voiced fear on the part of her lover that Robyn would eventually choose to leave her for a man. After all, so much of mainstream society is structured to encourage and support heterosexual relationships. Social life, the media, and the legal institution of marriage (with its economic benefits of corporate health insurance, other "family plans," and inheritance laws) are all based on the configuration of the heterosexual couple. Therefore, how could a lesbian lover possibly "compete" with the odds so stacked against them?

Society's encouragement of heterosexuality and discourage-
ment of homosexuality is very real. However, Robyn also felt that
there was a certain amount of internalized shame due to homophobia at work here too: the feeling that whatever her lover had to
offer her and whatever they had together could not possibly out-
weigh the external benefits of being in a heterosexual relationship.
There is an underlying assumption there that anyone who has the
choice will ultimately choose heterosexuality, that lesbians and gay
men choose homosexual relationships because they are unable to
be heterosexual. However, this assumption is belied by the number of bisexuals who have chosen homosexual relationships.

Some say that bisexuals are only half oppressed. In the words
of one bisexual woman, "I have had rocks thrown at me when I was
out with a woman. I have had my ex-husband threaten to sue me
for custody of my children because I have had lesbian relationships. I have been kicked out of my apartment by a homophobic
landlord. Well, I am *sick and tired* of hearing lesbians tell me that,
because I am bi, I am not oppressed."[5]

The public is becoming more aware that many famous historical figures were gay. Yet many of these "gay" and "lesbian" people
behaved bisexually. Virginia Woolf, Eleanor Roosevelt, Sappho,
Christopher Isherwood, James Baldwin, Vita Sackville-West, Col-
ette, and Kate Millet are embraced by lesbians and gay men;
modern-day bisexuals working common jobs and bearing ordinary
names are not. If we want to add *and bisexual* to a gay and lesbian
organization's title, we are often called intruders.

Like *some* straight people who may be ignoring their gay inner
signals and needs, *some* gay men and lesbians may be repressing
their bisexuality. They may fear the loss of their gay identity and
their closest friends if they act on these desires. Like those who
are secure heterosexuals, people who have chosen positively to be
gay or lesbian tend to be supportive of bisexuality in others.

Biphobia Kills the Spirit

The denial of our existence and the perpetuation of negative
stereotypes prevents many bisexuals from proudly claiming their

identity. Many people are bisexual. Whether they claim that label or not, they behave bisexually as they live their lives in the gay, lesbian, or straight communities. Therefore, any denial of our existence and any outright oppression of us is damaging. Polarized notions of gender and sexuality limit everyone. Margaret Mead documented that societies with the greatest difference between male and female roles exhibit the greatest violence toward women.[6] Societies that have less explicit gender-specific roles tend to be more peaceful and egalitarian in general.

By presenting gender or sexual orientation as polar opposites and pretending that people are only one or the other (exclusively heterosexual, or exclusively homosexual, or exclusively "feminine," or exclusively "masculine"), we are denying the fact that there are many points on the spectrum in between. People are then forced more toward one extreme than is natural for them. This limitation leads to denial of an inner need, which can only hurt the spirit, contributing to a stifled emotional life or, in more extreme cases, to drug use, mental illness, or even suicide. Peter Alsop's song "It's Only a Wee Wee" says it well:

As soon as you're born grown-ups look where you pee,
And then they decide just how you're s'posed to be.
Girls pink and quiet, boys noisy and blue,
Don't it seem like a dumb way to choose what you'll do?

Chorus
It's only a wee-wee, so what's the big deal?
It's only a wee-wee, so what's all the fuss?
It's only a wee-wee and everyone's got one—
There's better things to discuss! . . .

. . . The grown-ups will watch every move that you make,
"Boys must not cry. Girls must bake cake."
It's all very formal and I think it smells,
Let's all be abnormal and act like ourselves![7]

Anyone can be punished for "inappropriate" gender behavior. A woman truck driver of any sexual orientation may be subjected to antilesbian remarks. If a lesbian admits to sleeping with a man, she may be shunned by former friends. If any man—gay, straight, or bisexual—is uninterested in sports, enjoys attending the opera and ballet, happens to lisp, or use his hands flamboyantly, he is in danger of being taunted or even physically attacked. His actual sexuality is less important than his perceived sexuality. When others see how these people are punished, they will restrict their own behavior to avoid censure. Thus, even the "good" members of a community are emotionally limited by the punishment of the overt nonconformists.

If we, as women, walk down the street in the United States holding hands with a man, people will assume that we are straight. If we walk down the street holding hands with a woman, people will assume that we are lesbians, and we may well be subjected to disapproving glances. We aren't shifting; others' perceptions are. We want to be defined not by our behavior but by our essence. We do not get up every day and think, "Should I be straight or gay today?" We are, every day, in all situations, bisexual. Each of us is a living yin-yang symbol, perhaps emphasizing one aspect now but with the seed of the other always present.

If bisexuality were accepted, rigid gender-role expectations would be weakened. Whether one was gay, straight, or bisexual would be less relevant to any activity, way of dressing, or choice of occupation. Bisexuality blurs these gender lines just as much, *not half as much,* as homosexuality does. Plus it adds another choice: the gender of our sexual partners. A movement that calls itself progressive must accept true diversity.

Conclusion

All of us—bisexuals, lesbians, gay men, and heterosexuals—have the right to exist and to choose whom we will love. In answer to the question, "Are you gay or straight?" bisexual activists have begun to challenge this artificial polarization and create a lifetime identity that need not change with the gender of our lovers. Honesty demands flexibility, and by dissolving the barriers created by old static categories, all of us can focus less on our differences and more on our common goals of political empowerment. Bisexuals are not fence sitters. There *is* no fence. Instead of a fence, we see a field, with mostly lesbian and gay people on one side and mostly heterosexual people on the other. Since we *are* men and women, since we *are* "gay" and "straight," we are in the middle. Sometimes we travel toward one end or the other—in a day, in a year, or in a lifetime.

NOTES

1. Marcia Deihl, interview in *Looking at Gay and Lesbian Life*, ed. Warren J. Blumenfeld and Diane Raymond (Boston: Beacon, 1988).

2. *Gay Community News* 10, no. 36 (1 April 1983).

3. S. Freud, "Infantile Sexuality," in *The Basic Writings of Sigmund Freud*, trans. A. A. Brell (New York: Modern Library, 1938). A. Kinsey, W. B. Pomeroy, and C. E. Martin, *Sexual Behavior in the Human Male* (Philadelphia: W. B. Saunders, 1948).

4. "Bisexuals and AIDS: The Dangers of a Double Life," *Newsweek* (13 July 1987), 44.

5. Remarks by a participant in Robyn Ochs' workshop "Bisexuals and Lesbian Women: A Dialogue," conducted at the 1990 Bisexual Conference, San Francisco, 23 June 1990.

6. Margaret Mead, *Sex and Temperament in Three Primitive Societies* (New York: Morrow Quill, 1935).

7. Peter Alsop, "It's Only a Wee Wee" (1981). Permission to quote the lyrics given by Flying Fish Records, Inc.

PART TWO

CHILDREN, FAMILIES, AND HOMOPHOBIA

5

From Silence to Suicide: Measuring a Mother's Loss

B. JAYE MILLER

Dedicated to Bobby and Mary Griffith

I

In the early, predawn hours of 27 August 1983, Bobby Griffith, who had just celebrated his twentieth birthday two months earlier, did a backflip off a freeway overpass in the path of a semi–truck and trailer. He was killed instantly. Later that morning, his mother, Mary, was called from her workplace to receive the news. When she came down to the lobby and saw her older daughter crouched in the corner, crying uncontrollably, she knew that something horrible had happened. For four years, Bobby and his parents had been struggling with the fact of Bobby's homosexuality. Parental pressure, "Christian" counseling, and the antihomosexual attitudes of society had proved too heavy a burden to bear; suicide seemed the only way out.

The tragic story of Bobby and Mary has its own particular character, but it is by no means unique. Each year, many young gay males and lesbians commit suicide. Recent studies estimate that perhaps fully one-third of all completed teen suicides are associated with questions of sexual orientation and that young "homosexuals of both sexes are two to six times more likely to attempt suicide than are (young) heterosexuals."[1] We can only hope that, by retelling and remembering the story of Bobby and Mary, we can better face the situation with which gay, lesbian, and bisexual youths are dealing and learn how to support them. The potential losses are not just to these young people but to their parents as well. The distance from silence to suicide is not so great. Measuring a mother's loss opens our heart to injuries and pain that run like a broad and deep river through our society.

This story centers on the relationship of a mother and her son. Mr. Griffith declined to be interviewed, and, to respect his privacy, his involvement is not addressed. However, in an attempt to avoid the popular myth that children's problems can be traced solely to the mother, it should be emphasized that, as in all families, the conflicts that developed in the Griffith household were complex and arose from many sources. Mary Griffith's objective in going public is to save others the pain that she and her family has experienced. Centering on Mary's role in the story should in no way be seen as ascribing blame to her. The names in this story have not been changed.

II

Until Bobby was about three years old, everything seemed perfectly "normal" in the Griffith family household.[2] In fact, the Griffiths would likely have been seen as the ideal, middle-class American family: four healthy, happy children and a new home in the suburban community of Danville, California, inland, across the foothills from Oakland where Mary and her husband, Robert, had themselves grown up. They met on a blind date shortly after high school and became engaged a month later; following a two-year engagement, they married. The first two children, and a final one born after Bobby, were typical girls and a boy, doing all the things girls and boys are expected to do. Life was easy, straight forward; life was for living. Mary was a caring wife and mother. She became active in her local Presbyterian church, thinking that Christianity was a kind of shell that held the family together and protected her picture-perfect world.

At first, Bobby's birth only confirmed Mary's life, her world, her beliefs and perspectives. He was a quiet and sensitive child, yet also exuberant and life affirming. He was never shy, always outgoing. He had a mind and a way of his own. Mary felt blessed with this special, free-spirited child. But by the time Bobby turned three, Mary began to feel concern and anxiety. Bobby just did not seem like his older brother; he did not care for "boys'" things. He much preferred more gentle activities; he especially liked flowers and playing inside.

One day when Bobby was about three years old, a neighbor called and was very upset. It seems that Bobby had put on one of his sister's little slips and was over at her house kissing everyone, including the other little boys! Mary was afraid; was her son turning into a sissy? She does not recall having ever heard the word *homosexual*, and the idea that Bobby might be homosexual never occurred to her; she was just concerned that her boy did not fit the prescribed patterns. Bobby sometimes got into her makeup and played with the lipstick. Once Mary's mother observed this and became quite upset, telling Mary that she needed to be more careful with her son. Intimidated by her mother and afraid of what her neighbors were saying, Mary was trapped between wanting to let Bobby just be himself and fearing that she must somehow dissuade her son from being a sissy. Most of all, Mary tried to push these concerns from her mind, ignoring what she saw and what people said. But "the problem" persisted.

When Bobby was five, he asked for a doll for Christmas. Feeling desperate, Mary told Bobby that she just did not have the money for such a doll. Knowingly, Bobby questioned, "If you had the money, would you buy me one?" Looking back now, Mary feels angry. What difference would it have made? Why couldn't I give my child the things he wanted? I would never have given a doll to my other son; he wouldn't have known what to do with it. But I couldn't give Bobby a doll even though I know he would have loved it. Mary fears that even then Bobby began to sense that there was something about him that his own mother could not love.

Mary's internal conflicts only intensified. At a parent-teacher conference during Bobby's elementary school years, one of his teachers reported that Bobby seemed to play an awful lot with the little girls in the class. The teacher tried to take the edge off by saying that "perhaps Bobby's going to have the best of both worlds,' but Mary was so anxious that she could not even ask the teacher what she meant. Mary could not figure out what to do. She and her husband and their other children were so "normal." The children all played together well. Her husband took an active interest in the family and the children. She did everything she could think of to be a good wife and mother. She took the children to Sunday School every week; she herself was a Sunday School teacher. She could only wait, hope, and pray.

On the surface, things seemed to be better in junior high and high school for Bobby. There was something of a bigger world. Bobby excelled in art and creative writing. He was a good student and even dated girls. True enough, Mary was concerned about Bobby's long hair and the way he flipped it from side to side. But then lots of boys were wearing their hair long. What difference could it make?

Bobby often seemed unhappy and confused, but Mary was sure that that was just part of being a teenager. *Being a teenager* was a convenient label under which to sweep lingering anxieties. Mary is now convinced that it was exactly during these years that Bobby learned there was another label that applied to him: *homosexual*.

Anita Bryant was popular then and always on television; she was a media personality who spearheaded a successful campaign to repeal a gay rights ordinance in Dade County, Florida, and a national effort under the banner "Save Our Children," aimed against homosexuals across the nation. Mary was into her religion: "My beliefs were my reality." Could Mary's worst fear be true? Could her own son be lost to homosexuality? On one occasion, she even raised with her husband the issue of Bobby's possibly being gay. But they both agreed that he was such a good kid and so faithful about his religious commitments that he just couldn't be "perverted" and "evil" beneath the exterior. Bobby was only having trouble adjusting, trouble growing up. Mary was still worried. Satan was real, and the world was a very dangerous place, especially for young, innocent children. Would her child be snatched away by the Devil?

When Bobby was sixteen, he confided to his brother that he had something terrible to confess, something to share that would make his brother hate him: Bobby was afraid that he was gay. Although he had been sworn to secrecy, his brother pressured his mother while they were out, driving to the store one day: "If Bobby or I turned out to be gay, would you kick us out of the house? Would you still love us?" Mary replied that she would be understanding, and then he told her about his conversation with Bobby. Mary and her husband waited for some time, hoping that Bobby would bring up the subject himself, but when he did not, they confronted him with his brother's story. Bobby ran into the bathroom, crying, too humiliated to talk. But talk they did, until four in the morning. They agreed not to tell anybody else and to seek help.

Mary sought a Christian counselor and went to the public library, where she checked out three books on what parents should know about homosexuality. Unfortunately, these efforts only made matters worse. Condemnation was compounded with guilt. The books and the counselor all agreed: the parents had failed, and now their child was sick and likely to go to hell. Mary and her husband turned in on themselves and each other. Even though they did not fit the pattern of the domineering mother and the absent father that the books said caused homosexuality, they looked back through their life, trying to force the past into this new framework.

Bobby was now more convinced than ever that his life was an abomination to God; in fact, on the therapy application form under "reason for visit," he wrote that he wanted to be the kind of person God wanted him to be. After some four months, however, Bobby pleaded that they stop the counseling. He wasn't getting any better; it just seemed like a waste of time and money. Bobby quit school two months before graduation; he didn't feel like he fit or belonged. He had not been harassed at school. No one knew he was gay; he kept his secret well. But the pressures of keeping his secret and feeling himself to be different had become too much.

During the next two years, Bobby tried several courses of action. He went to a couple of community counseling programs; one that focused on self-esteem really seemed to help him feel stronger and more accepting of his homosexuality. But every effort to affirm his homosexuality was met by Mary's resistance and quotations from the Bible. On the one hand, he tried to accept himself as gay; on the other hand, he feared that God had "given up on him" because he was choosing sin over righteousness.

He attended the local community college in Diablo Valley, studying drama and attending meetings of the gay and lesbian student group there. He went to some parties with his new friends, even ventured into San Francisco. The emphasis, however, in his new circle of friends seemed to be so much on sex and good looks that Bobby had a hard time adjusting to "gay life" as he was experiencing it.

Once he left a book, *How to Love a Gay Person*, out so that his mother would come on it and read it. Mary recalls her immediate sense was that the book was something evil, inspired by Satan. Bobby wanted to believe that gay could be good, but he continued to fear that all gay people were perverted and worthless. He was anxious about growing old alone, anxious about his acne, anxious that he might go bald. He remained confused and in conflict.

In Februry, early in the last year of his life, Bobby decided to move to Portland, Oregon, to live with a favorite cousin for a while. Mary and her husband hoped that a change of environment would be good. Bobby found a job in a convalescent home and really seemed to enjoy helping the old folks, helping the elderly women pick out what dresses they would wear for the day. His cousin, Ambria, was a real Rock of Gibraltar for Bobby. She accepted him as a gay person; she confided after some weeks that she herself was a lesbian.

In June, Bobby made one last trip home. His mother sensed that something terrible had happened. It seemed like some kind of wall or barrier had arisen between Bobby and his mother, between Bobby and the world. He was like a person going through the motions, like someone who had given up on life, given up on love. When he returned to Portland, he reported to Ambria that nothing had changed at home. Mary now tries to imagine what it must feel like for young people to be convinced that no one accepts them, not God, not society, not even their own parents. How alone would such children feel?

In the evening of 26 August, Bobby set out alone for a local gay bar where he and Ambria sometimes went dancing. Nothing seemed wrong; maybe he was a little more quiet than usual. He did not talk to many people that night; he had a drink or two. He left around midnight, but instead of heading for the bus stop, he walked in the opposite direction. Several witnesses, who later called the police, reported that Bobby just stood on the overpass and did a backflip over the edge. They ran over expecting to find Bobby hanging onto the railing. They were sure that it was some sort of stunt, some sort of joke.

III

What had been a source of confusion, conflict, and anxiety had now become a nightmare. The family secret was out. No one in the family could understand what had happened, why it had happened. No one had imagined that Bobby was in so much pain. Each family member felt that he or she had failed Bobby in some way, by not having understood, by not having been more supportive, by not being with Bobby when he was so unhappy. The family had no way of appreciating the pressures faced by a young gay or bisexual person in this society.

Mary's church held a memorial service. The assistant minister spoke of compassion for gay people but concluded that the wages of sin are death. The minister, when he returned from vacationing in Hawaii, sent a form condolence letter to the family. Neither the minister nor the parishioners contacted or supported the family; their uneasiness and anxiety about homosexuality prevented them from even talking to Mary and her husband. Even though Mary had been devoted to and active in the church, it provided no consolation, no place for resolution or rest.

Bobby's death and memorial brought a rude religious awakening for Mary. She struggled with a new trap. Was her son innocent and with God in Heaven? Or had Bobby's name been erased from the Book of Life as promised to the sinful in Revelation? Why had God not cured Bobby? If everyone in the family had prayed and tried as hard as they could, who had failed whom? Mary knew that she had blood on her hands. She came to suspect that others shared part of the blame. If religion had been part of what built the trap imprisoning Mary and her family, religion would have to be part of the path of liberation.

For a full year and a half, Mary struggled alone with her God and his word. She felt that she had to find another way to look at her religion. On her own, she started to regard the Bible as a book among books, to view the men and women of her religious community as people with their own limitations. Before she had been afraid to question; now she knew that she had to. Mainly, she began to rediscover her own conscience, her own mind, the ability to think for herself.

A clear marking point in her religious evolution came with her first conversation with the Reverend Larry Whitsel, minister of the local Metropolitan Community Church, a church that serves a largely gay and lesbian congregation. She was beginning to accept Bobby's homosexuality; after all, he was her son, and she knew firsthand his struggles for self-acceptance. But how would she react to meeting a gay man she did not know? She called the minister several times, hanging up immediately after dialing. Finally, she had the courage to let the phone ring and to set up an appointment. Their first conversation inevitably turned to the story of Sodom and Gomorrah: that constant stumbling block to a more accepting understanding of homosexuality in our culture. Larry argued from a close textual analysis of the original languages that God's displeasure was directed against the selfishness, arrogance, and inhospitality of the people of Sodom and Gomorrah.[3] Little by little, step by step, Mary fought for her intellectual and spiritual freedom. Today, Mary has squared her religious faith with her own sense of love for her son. She is convinced that Bobby was the kind of person God wanted him to be.

IV

Once the Bobby Griffith story has been retold, relived at least in part, what can be learned, what can be salvaged from the loss? Of course, the primary loss, that of a young person who died far earlier than was necessary, can never be regained. By all accounts,

Bobby was a sensitive, bright, talented young man who had a tremendous love of life. But the burden of being gay in a nonaccepting church, in a nonaccepting community, in a nonaccepting family, proved more than he could bear. A mother, a father, and three siblings were deprived of a son and brother. The broader community lost an honest, sincere, and able young citizen. It is of course impossible to calculate the meaning and measure of those losses. The clear and immediate losses are so great that we are tempted to forget about, not even to ask about the more subtle, more hidden losses. But not to inquire further is a loss in itself.

Mary now argues that she feels deprived of her son, not just in death, but from the day he was born. Because of the narrowness and homophobia of the world in which she grew up, of the negative attitudes toward all deviation that she had internalized long before Bobby was born, Mary was unprepared to fully accept and productively support her special son: "I lacked the education. I lacked the knowledge." From early in Bobby's life, Mary found it impossible to relax and just enjoy her son. Instead, every instance of behavior or attitude that spoke of some deviation from the norm frightened her. She was intimidated by her mother's concerns; she was anxious about her neighbors' comments; perhaps most of all she was severely limited by the teachings of her church.

On the other hand, she was torn by the love she had for her son and thus resented outside intrusions. Most of all she was just worried. What was going to happen to her son? How would he manage to grow up? What kind of pressures would he have to face? In those early years, the issue was never explicitly homosexuality as such; rather, the concern focused on how to keep Bobby from being a "sissy." Mary still wonders why little boys being sissies cause such problems in this society. After all, if a little girl is a "tomboy," folks don't seem to be nearly so upset. What difference does any of it make anyway? Why can't we just accept that all kids are different? This whole sissy business seems like such a small thing, but it made Mary's life miserable. She was always concerned, wondering what she might be doing wrong and what she could be doing differently. Bobby had a mind and spirit of his own. Whenever Mary tried to dissuade Bobby from some particular behavior, it didn't work. She was forced to cope with something over which she could have no control.

She now sees all the fear, worry, and confusion as a tremendous waste. A subtle barrier grew up between her and Bobby. She could not feel at ease, or comfortable, or accepting; who Bobby was remained beyond her grasp. As the years progressed, Bobby became more and more of a mystery. By the time he actually told the family that he was gay, Mary was totally unprepared to cope with the situation. She knew nothing about homosexuality, other than what she had been taught in the church and what was reflected in community attitudes. Finally, her son committed suicide: some twenty years of concern, prayer, worry, and anxiety ended in a nightmare.

Mary is convinced that Bobby, even in early childhood, was able to detect her fears. He sensed that there was something about himself that his mother couldn't understand, couldn't accept. What else could Bobby conclude from his mother's reluctance to buy the Christmas doll, from her concerns over the incidences of using makeup and kissing little boys? By junior high and high school, he had learned to hide his inner feelings, often even from himself. When he could no longer keep his emerging sexual feelings from himself, he knew he could not share them with his family. The pressure grew to the point of explosion, and finally the secret, by now made horrible, came out. Bobby was gay. There was nothing within his upbringing that prepared Bobby for his life; the lack of acceptance within the family now infected Bobby himself.

At sixteen, Bobby wrote in his diary:

I can't let anyone find out that I'm not straight. It would be so humiliating. My friends would hate me, I just know it. They might even want to beat me up.

And my family? I've overheard them lots of times talking about gay people. They've said they hate gays, and even God hates gays, too.

It really scares me now, when I hear my family talk that way, because now, they are talking about me.

I guess I'm no good to anyone . . . not even God. Life is so cruel, and unfair. Sometimes I feel like disappearing from the face of this earth.

Homosexuality became a kind of dark cloud for Bobby. Somehow everything else about Bobby was forgotten. Nothing was important except his being gay. Society had only bad things to say about homosexuals: they are all perverts, sex maniacs, and sick. His church conspired by preaching that homosexuality is a moral sin and inspired by the Devil. Bobby was forced to forget about everything else in his life. During the last year and a half, he tried to find some self-acceptance, but the cards were stacked against him. Every step forward was matched by lingering doubts, by constant fears about the future, and above all by an overwhelming sense of failing his family and himself. In the end, the family was robbed of a son and brother, the son robbed of his family, and the child robbed of himself.

Bobby's death opened Mary to the awareness of yet another loss: Mary's loss of herself. Through the years of worry and apprehension, Mary sought comfort and guidance in her church. It seemed the perfect "utopia" for the family, like a bubble protecting their happiness. Little by little, Mary gave more and more weight to what the ministers said and to their interpretation of the Bible. Religion became nothing less than a prison for Mary. She had forgotten about her own conscience, about her own sense of her love. She had no internal place to turn for refuge and certainty. She was prey to the intimidations of others, dependent on what others would think.

It was not easy for Mary to break out of that prison. She could turn to no one for help; she had to do it for herself. For so many years she had believed that there was no good, no health within her, that her best could never be good enough for God. She began to wonder about a God who could be pleased with such an arrangement. Mary searched back in her life for the roots of her own self-awareness, for her own sense of conscience. From there she began to reconstruct her life. She realized that she had to decide for herself how she was going to apply the Bible in her own life, how to construct a religious faith in harmony with her own deepest instincts. Mary now thinks of God as love and understanding. Finally, her religious search has brought her inner peace. Mary has come to accept and like herself.

V

Bobby's and Mary's life stories reveal a fear of homosexuality that is common in our society. They are unique individuals, of course, but the issues they dealt with touch more people than we generally assume. It is widely argued that 10 percent of the overall population have exclusively or predominantly same-sex sexual experiences in their adult lives. Even if we halved that figure to make a highly conservative estimate, that still leaves a gay population of approximately twelve million in the United States alone.

During the last two decades, nothing less than amazing progress has been made by gay, lesbian, and bisexual people in building a sense of self-acceptance and pride. But, for gay, lesbian, and bisexual youths, the issues are much more problematic. Little if anything in most public schools hints at their existence, confirms their right to self-esteem. Even less is done for the parents of these young people. As Bobby's and Mary's stories make clear, suffering in silence brings needless pain and tragedy.

Today, AIDS makes the situation even more acute. Many people still think of AIDS as a "gay disease," even as a punishment from God. Naturally, parents fear that their children might become infected. Without a national program educating youths about HIV transmission and about safe-sex practices, their fears are not unfounded. The broad media coverage given to AIDS and homosexuality in recent years has forced young people to consider the possibility of their own homosexuality earlier than ever before. Now, gay, lesbian, and bisexual youths recognize and often want to act on their sexual feelings and attractions. All this occurs at a time of heightened parental concerns and intense social bigotry. In short, despite the recent progress toward gay, lesbian, and bisexual pride, the tensions and stakes are as high as ever.

Mary repeatedly speaks of the need for education. It is a question not just of making a more accepting and supportive world for young people of all sexual orientations but of educating future parents. Mary recalls nothing in her own education that prepared her for dealing with Bobby, nothing that told her about the broad and natural differences among people. Thus, in addition to the enormous numbers of gays, lesbians, and bisexuals, we must also consider the even larger number of parents of gays and lesbians. And, of course, we must include grandparents, aunts, uncles, etc., to speak only of direct family relationships. Clearly, we must imagine that the issue of homosexuality and bisexuality directly touches the lives of a huge segment of our population; nearly every family has its "homosexual secret." Within every ethnic, class, and religious group, the particular approaches and issues vary. But there is little in our society that helps families understand, discuss, and accept the homosexuality of their own members. It is often within the family that the silence is first enforced.

Families generally think of homosexuality and bisexuality as a failing, a disgrace, something to hide from others. Most people do not want to admit that homosexuality knows no boundaries, favors no race, class, or religion. As long as one imagines homosexuality as someone else's business, as affecting only other people, one protects oneself from truly considering the matter. Many parents who pride themselves on being accepting are astonished at their own reactions when it becomes a question of their own children's "sexual deviance." We never know how a shoe feels until we actually try it on.

Finally, a better understanding and acceptance of homosexuality and bisexuality is also in the interests of those people whose family life may not be touched directly by the issue. Undoubtedly, these people will meet and know homosexuals in their own lives, whether in school, in the neighborhood, at work, or in their churches and social clubs. How much better that everyone could feel at ease with and not prejudge others. As Mary's life makes clear, whenever we feel uncomfortable with homosexuality and the issues it raises, we are likely to seek security in beliefs and behaviors that set us apart, cut us off from human contact, alienate us even from ourselves.

Postscript

In recent years, Mary Griffith has spoken on local and national television and has become a leading figure in PFLAG, Parents and Friends of Lesbians and Gays, a national organization with chapters in some eighty major cities in the United States.[4] PFLAG is primarily a support system for parents whose children are gay, lesbian, or bisexual.[5] Given the continuing silence about homosexuality and the family, PFLAG groups can be of tremendous consolation to parents who imagine that they are totally alone. PFLAG often sponsors or has referrals for social and support groups for gay, lesbian, and bisexual youths.[6] PFLAG has also been one of the most significant national, state, and regional organizations supporting gay and lesbian rights; few can speak more convincingly of the need for public education about homosexuality and of the importance of civil and social rights for gays and lesbians than members of PFLAG. Along with the Contra Costa County chapter of the Bay Area Network of Gay and Lesbian Educators (BANGLE), Mary's local chapter of PFLAG in Diablo Valley has established a "Bobby Griffith Memorial Scholarship" to be offered to graduating seniors in the schools of Contra Costa County.[7] In the first year of competition (1990), four PFLAG/BANGLE "Bobby Griffith" scholarships were given out in the San Francisco Bay Area. The purpose of the scholarships is to support gay, lesbian, and bisexual youths by increasing visibility and support in the public schools.

NOTES

1. In recent years, several studies have appeared on the special pressures faced by gay, lesbian, and bisexual youths. Perhaps the most useful, thorough, and authoritative is Paul Gibson's "Gay Male and Lesbian Youth Suicide," in *Report of the Secretary's Task Force on Youth Suicide* vol. 3 (Washington, D.C.: U.S. Department of Health and Human Services, January 1989). Gibson argues that "suicide is the leading cause of death among gay male, lesbian, bisexual, and transsexual youth." He provides an overview of sexual minority youths, the problems they face, and the coping mechanisms they use, including the abuse of drugs and alcohol. His piece includes an excellent summary of current research and a helpful bibliography of relevant sources. Unfortunately, this pioneering piece caused such controversy in the U.S.

Congress that considerable pressures were mobilized to repress the publication of the report and to silence those who are trying to help us face the facts and find ways to support sexual minority youths.

2. Bobby's and Mary's stories have been published in a number of San Francisco Bay Area newspapers and documented on local television programs. In addition to consulting those sources, the primary material for my telling of their stories is drawn from two lengthy interviews I conducted with Mary during October and November 1989. I have severely limited my use of quotation marks so that the text can be easily read. But I have used Mary's own words and expressions, varying from her story only where necessary for the flow of the text.

3. Father John McNeill's recent *Taking a Chance on God* (Boston: Beacon, 1988) summarizes the research leading to the reinterpretation of Sodom and Gomorrah. Along with his earlier *The Church and the Homosexual* (Boston: Beacon, 1988) and the Reverend Troy Perry's *The Lord Is My Shepherd, and He Knows That I'm Gay* (Austin, Tex.: Liberty Press, 1987), numerous studies provide a positive reconciliation of homosexuality with the Scriptures and with basic Christian beliefs.

4. The location, meeting time, and contact person for local PFLAG groups can be obtained from the national family support headquarters, which can be reached by mail (P.O. Box 20308, Denver, Colorado 80218) or by telephone (303–321–2270). In addition to the regular group meetings, there are also contact persons in less urban areas whom one can also contact by phone or letter.

5. PFLAG has compiled a forty-page "Bibliography on Homosexuality and Related Issues" that provides an excellent guide to literature, national organizations, and book stores. PFLAG pamphlets recommend the following books as beginning points for reading and study: *Now That You Know,* by Betty Fairchild and Nancy Hayward (New York: Harcourt Brace, 1979); *Loving Someone Gay,* by Don Clark (New York: New American Library, 1978); *Positively Gay,* by B. Berzon and R. Leighton (Berkeley: Celestial Arts, 1984); *A Family Matter,* by Charles Silverstein (New York: McGraw-Hill, 1977); *Is the Homosexual My Neighbor?* by L. Scanzoni and V. Mollenkott (New York: Harper & Row, 1978); *Word Is Out,* by Nancy and Casey Adair (San Francisco: New Glide, 1978); and *Gay—What You Should Know about Homosexuality,* by Morton Hunt (New York: Farrar Straus Giroux, 1988).

6. The books most commonly suggested for these youths include *One Teenager in Ten: Writings by Gay and Lesbian Youth,* ed. Ann Heron (Boston: Alyson, 1983); *Young, Gay, and Proud: A Resource Book for Gay and Lesbian Youth,* ed. Sasha Alyson (Boston: Alyson, 1980); and *Coming Out to Parents,* by Mary V. Borhek (New York: Pilgrim, 1983).

7. Those who wish to contribute to the scholarship should send their donations to the Bobby Griffith Memorial Scholarship Fund, c/o Wells

Fargo Bank, Clayton Valley Office, 4599 Clayton Road, Concord, California 94521 (account 6173–256074). Those who wish more information about the scholarship and how similar efforts might be established in other communities should write Diablo Valley PFLAG, 1304 Rudgear Road, Walnut Creek, California 94596.

6

"It Has Nothing to Do with Me"

DIANE ELZE

I remember in fifth grade we had this thing called the "fag test." What would happen is that a kid would go up to another kid and scratch him on the hand as hard as he could, and if it made a scar, or if it bled, that meant he was a fag. —A seventeen-year-old

He said it so adamantly, this eighteen-year-old working-class man. "It has nothing to do with me. It has nothing to do with me," he said, glancing quickly at his friends for their nods of approval, his body tensing, when I asked him how he feels when he witnesses homophobic name-calling directed at other young people.

I sighed. Well, I never thought interviewing a group of heterosexually identified adolescents about homophobia would be easy.

"It has nothing to do with me." When I left him and the others that day, his words rang in my ears, a perfect encapsulation of what we are up against when we try to challenge homophobia and other forms of oppression. How do I teach him that it has everything to do with him?

I remember the young boys squirming in their seats when I popped the hot question. "What could be wonderful about having a friend who is gay?" I asked, during a workshop on prejudice with a group of fifth- and sixth-grade students. Oh, how they squirmed, their hands tightly gripping their pencils or the sides of their chairs, their faces growing flushed, their heads nervously moving from side to side, hoping their friends knew they were not taking this question seriously.

95

Earlier, we explored the language of racism, sexism, homophobia, classism, and ableism, and, in small groups, the students shared how they had been victimized by different forms of prejudice, particularly by classism, as so many came from rural poor and working-class Maine families. With much honesty, they also shared how they had victimized others.

They responded enthusiastically to questions like, "What could be wonderful about having a friend from Cambodia or Vietnam?" and, "What could be wonderful about having a friend who uses a wheelchair?" They talked of learning about each other's cultures, enriching each other's lives, helping their friend fight for access to school programs. But when asked, "What could be wonderful about having a friend who is gay?" many moments of silence followed.

"I know this is very difficult," I said, my voice soft and encouraging. "We're used to hearing only bad and untrue things about gay people. Now, really think hard. What could be wonderful about having a friend who is gay?"

The young boys continued squirming. Several more minutes lapsed. Finally, a fifth-grade girl raised her hand. "I might learn that I wouldn't have to be afraid," she said. I thanked her for her heartfelt response and then felt very sad at how difficult that question was for them.

"What gives?" I asked Bill, an OUTRIGHT member, after he and several other young men missed their prescheduled interview with me for the second time, highly atypical behavior among these young gay activists who are usually, if anything, *too* committed, eager to risk their jobs or a school detention to attend the next speaking engagement. "How can you tell who is the gay or lesbian youth?" they'll sometimes joke. "It's the workaholic who's always falling asleep in class." For this essay, I wanted their perspective on how homophobia hurts heterosexual youths.

"I just don't want to talk about it," Bill said, shrugging his shoulders and looking confused, searching himself for exactly why he felt troubled. "I don't care if it hurts them," he finally said, anger in his voice.

I scold myself for not anticipating this. Bill, nineteen years old, has been repeatedly bashed, verbally and physically, in his small rural high school, his wounds too raw for him to theorize how such homophobia could harm the perpetrators.

This essay is a collection of voices. The voices belong to young men and women between fourteen and twenty years of age, heterosexual, gay, and lesbian. The young people represented here are white, the majority from poor and working-class families. Their voices tell us about the many ways homophobia hurts them. Their words also show us how homophobia and sexism are inextricably linked. As they go about their lives in school, at work, and in their neighborhoods, young people risk the label *queer* or *fag* should their behavior fall outside rigid gender-role expectations. Their voices tell us how much work we still must do.

"I'd Have Sex Just to Prove I Was Straight."

> *I think homophobia forces a lot of people to be sexually active. Even young people who know they're straight feel like they have to show it to prevent themselves from being called* queer.
>
> —*A sixteen-year-old woman*

Young people have sex for many reasons: fun and pleasure, rebellion, to defy parents and other authority figures, for love, money, status among their peers, out of boredom, because they are under the influence of alcohol or other drugs, for attention, affection, and intimacy, and to prove they are "normal" (i.e., heterosexual). In a society that stigmatizes homosexuality and withholds from young people accurate information on sexuality, including the development of sexual orientation, heterosexual sex provides anxious teenagers with a means to prove their heterosexuality.

We bombard adolescents with conflicting messages about sexuality and sexual decision making. Family, religious institutions, peers, videos, music, and advertising scream at teenagers everything from "Abstinence Makes the Heart Grow Fonder" to "Sex Is the Gateway to Nirvana." We fail to empower young people to integrate the joys of sex into their lives, protecting and caring for themselves at the same time.

Hence, teenage sexual activity can have serious consequences. Only 24 percent of unmarried sexually active teenage women, ages fifteen to nineteen, consistently use any form of birth control, and only 21 percent of those using contraception report condom use. Each year, one teenager in six, or 2.5 million teens, contracts a sexually transmitted disease. Over 20 percent of people with AIDS are in their twenties, most of whom were probably infected as teenagers.[1] The Center for Disease Control reported 1,429 cases of AIDS among teens by March 1990.[2]

Some young women we interviewed had this to say about the pressures to be sexually active:

> In the locker room we'd talk about how many of us were virgins, how this guy was in bed, what party you were going to that night, and who you were going to be with. After softball or basketball practice, everybody would be showering and then doing up their hair and putting on their makeup to get ready for their man.

> The thing to do was to go out and get laid.

> In my high school, we were expected to have a boyfriend who would give you his letter jacket or his high school ring, and be the happy couple, and get married with a Catholic wedding right after graduation.

For gay and lesbian youths, heterosexual sexual activity serves as a refuge, although sometimes an anguished one, from the label *fag, queer, lezzie,* or *dyke.* They may use heterosexual relationships to mask their sexual orientation or to attempt to force themselves to change.

> YOUNG LESBIAN, AGE TWENTY: When I first noticed I was having these "odd feelings" toward women, probably in seventh grade, I tried to hide them for a long time. By the time I was in high school, I was very sexually active with men. I'd have sex at parties just to

prove I was straight. I grew up in a very Catholic community. To have sex before marriage was a sin, but to screw another woman was to get in big trouble and commit a mortal sin. I'd go to parties and get real drunk. I couldn't have sex with a man when I was sober. I wasn't into makeup or stuff like that, but I could get by because I was fucking men. Looking at me, everyone thought *dyke,* and I had that against me, so I started doing anything I could to make them think I was straight.

YOUNG GAY MAN, AGE SEVENTEEN: I just fucked someone to prove that I was OK. I'd go to a party and go into a bedroom with someone, and I was OK.

YOUNG LESBIAN, AGE SIXTEEN: Some young women I know become really sexually active to avoid being called a lesbian, and they're straight. I think homophobia forces a lot of people to be sexually active. Even young people who know they're straight feel they have to show it to prevent themselves from being called *queer.*

YOUNG LESBIAN, AGE SIXTEEN: I remember a friend of mine who was sleeping with a lot of men. I overheard someone asking her why she was going to screw this one guy who was a real loser, and she said, "If I don't, people will think I'm a dyke." She was only thirteen at the time.

This pressure to prove one's heterosexuality places young people at risk for pregnancy and sexually transmitted diseases. In addition, AIDS-phobia has fueled homophobia, and homophobia allows teens to ignore their own risk for HIV infection. A common misconception among heterosexual teens is that AIDS affects only people who are gay and IV drug users, a belief that places heterosexual teens at risk.

Many gay and lesbian high school students in OUTRIGHT have admitted that they dread the day AIDS education is scheduled for their health class, as it provides students with one more opportunity to engage in verbal gay bashing, much of which goes unchallenged by the teacher.

YOUNG GAY MAN, AGE EIGHTEEN: When we do any kind of AIDS education, I brace myself for days of hearing "fag this" and "fag that," and it's never handled very well by the teachers. All the teachers say is that anyone can get AIDS, but they don't say that it's wrong to use the word *fag* or that homosexuality is normal, and they don't talk about how calling people names is the pits.

YOUNG LESBIAN, AGE TWENTY: I didn't ever really think about getting pregnant. I didn't do anything about it. I never used any type of birth control. I thought it would be cool to have a kid because that would mean I was definitely not gay. . . . And I never worried about STDs.

YOUNG GAY MAN, AGE NINETEEN: Just look at the graffiti in any high school bathroom, especially right after we talk about AIDS. If anybody wonders whether homophobia is a problem, they just have to look in there.

YOUNG MAN, AGE EIGHTEEN: AIDS scares people. It's the first thing people think of when they think of homosexuals.

While the young heterosexual men denied that homophobia played a role in their sexual decision making and in the sexual decision making of their friends, their denial was strongly challenged by the young heterosexual women in the interview group.

YOUNG WOMAN, AGE SEVENTEEN: Guys try to prove how manly they are by how much they score, how many girls they conquer. If they can brag about how many girls they've slept with, if they can score a lot, no one would ever think they are gay.

YOUNG WOMAN, AGE EIGHTEEN: If a guy goes out on a date with some girl, and his friends ask him if he scored last night, if he says no, they'd say stuff like, "Oh, you're not good enough," or, "You must be a faggot." If it happens over and over and over, they might even think he never went out on a date with her and that he must be gay.

Young women realize how such different prescriptions for acceptable male and female sexual behavior lead to violence against women. A film in the "Acquaintance Rape Prevention" series addresses the relation between peer pressure, gender roles, and acquaintance rape. *Just One of the Boys* shows a sexually inexperienced young man wondering what to do when two of his football teammates urge him to participate in the rape of a young woman with a "bad reputation." "What if they find out?" he says to himself, as they shout for him to come on. Find out what? That he is inexperienced? That he is, therefore, a *sissy*, a *fag*, a *wimp?*

> YOUNG WOMAN, AGE SEVENTEEN: I think some guys prove themselves, prove their sexuality, their masculinity, by raping women.

> YOUNG LESBIAN, AGE EIGHTEEN: I have so many friends who have been date raped. I know someone who was raped in front of a male friend of hers, and he didn't do anything about it. She said he just looked away and allowed it to happen. I'm sure he was afraid of being called *queer.*

"He Talks Like a Girl"

> LAURA: *Being caring and sensitive is not macho.*
> BARB: *That's why I'm attracted to more feminine men.*
> SUSAN: *Men with emotions.*
> LAURA: *Yeah, normal.*
> —An exchange among three seventeen- and eighteen-year-old women

Homophobia serves to squeeze young men and women into rigid gender roles, limiting their aspirations, squelching their dreams of what they can be, isolating those youths whose behaviors defy traditional ideals of "masculine" and "feminine," and fostering violence against gay and lesbian youths and those perceived to be gay or lesbian. A spirited debate about gender roles naturally evolved in our discussions about homophobia. This dialogue also illustrates how both heterosexual and gay and lesbian youths are victimized by homophobia and become potential targets of violence.

> DIANE: Who gets called *queer* or *fag* in school?
> TAMMY, AGE THIRTEEN: People who look different, who aren't as

smart as other people. Someone who is unpopular. Boys who are more feminine get called *fairy* or *fag*, and kids don't hang around with them. They avoid them. Sometimes people get called *fag* because of the way they talk, like if a boy's voice squeaks, and no one will hang around with them.

MARK, AGE FOURTEEN: Lots of kids, but most of the time it's only joking. You do something goofy and people will call you *queer*.

DIANE: Who gets called that seriously?

TOM, AGE FIFTEEN: A guy at our high school on the cheerleading team. He does the cheers with the girls. He gets called names constantly, every game. He's about as feminine as you can get. The only thing he doesn't have is a skirt.

JIM, AGE EIGHTEEN: Does that make him gay?

TOM: No, but everybody calls him a fag.

PHIL, AGE SIXTEEN: He's a sick puppy. Who wants to watch a boy cheerleader? It's mostly girls who go out for cheerleading. I've never seen a guy out there cheerleading before. I wouldn't look at him, for one thing. It's pretty sickening.

DIANE: Tom, you used the word *feminine*. How is he feminine?

TOM: The way he walks. The way he acts. You should see him cheerleading. He's right at home. I've never seen him walk down the halls at school. He doesn't dare show his face.

ALICE, AGE SIXTEEN: He hangs out with a couple boys, and he doesn't really seem to be a fag, but everybody thinks he is because he does all girl things. He walks like a girl.

DIANE: How do girls walk? Can you describe that to me?

TOM: Hands out to the side. Real soft.

ALICE: Like this. [She demonstrates, making quick, small steps with her feet and holding her arms out to the side.]

DIANE: Is that how you usually walk, Alice?

ALICE: No. [Laughter.]

JIM: You mustn't be a girl, huh?!

DIANE: Where does that leave us, then?

Among the heterosexual youths we interviewed, adherence to gender-stereotyped norms of behavior extends to perceptions of appropriate career options. Both sexes lose. Young women receive some affirmation for pursuing nontraditional jobs, but they are under tremendous pressure to pursue traditional female occupations. Young men, however, garner no status in jobs historically assigned to women and are more likely to be labeled *queer.* Homophobia also limits the aspirations of gay and lesbian youths, as they believe a meaningful career cannot coexist with their sexual orientation.

TAMMY: There was this guy. He was my uncle's friend, and he was really nice, and you never would have thought he was gay. He dresses like a man, he has a job, and he acts like a man, talks like a man. He has a man's job.

JIM: What's a man's job?

TAMMY: You don't see many women out there selling cars, do you?

JIM: Sure you do. Sure you do.

TAMMY: Construction workers.

MARK: Construction worker. That's a man's job.

JIM AND ALICE: [In unison.] No, it doesn't matter. It doesn't matter.

DIANE: If you saw a woman carrying a big sledgehammer, Mark, what would you think about her?

MARK: Dyke. Dyke.

JIM: I think it would be cool.

TAMMY: Yeah, I think it would be cool, if they did whatever they wanted to do.

MARK: If she was walking like this [demonstrates], acting all big and tough like a man, I'd think *dyke.*

JIM: There's no difference between a man's job and a woman's job. Women are doing just as much as men. Chemists, technicians, machine operators, laborers. I'm a hand sewer. There are women hand sewers, construction workers, everything.

MARK: Well, if I saw a woman driving a truck, I'd think *dyke,* just because of the way she acts and what she does for a living.

TAMMY: I think a woman has guts if she does what she wants to do, like if she wants to be a construction worker, and I think a man has guts if he wants to do what he wants to do and doesn't care what other people think.

DIANE: Why does it take guts? What is gutsy about that?

TAMMY: Because they might get called *queer,* and people would think they are no good. My sister is a secretary, and I know a guy who is a secretary, and he gets called a *fag* and everything. I know a lot of men who are secretaries. If they go anywhere, they're all supposedly *fairies* because it's a woman's job.

When gay and lesbian youths acknowledge their sexual orientation, a fairly typical response, especially among those youths who have experienced isolation and the absence of any positive information about gays, is illustrated by the experience of this eighteen-year-old lesbian:

When I came out, I thought my life was over. I thought I'd never be happy now that I was gay. I thought I could never have a house, or children, or a relationship, or a good job.

"They'd Call You *Sissy*"

No one feels free enough to be real with each other, and people keep each other at a distance.

—A seventeen-year-old

Homophobia interferes with the development of physical and emotional intimacy between same-sex friends. Young people fear being stigmatized as *queer.* Young men feel terror at the thought of a male friend touching them in an intimate way. Friendships also become strained between gay and lesbian youths and their heterosexual peers, as gay youths often approach their friendships expecting rejection.

YOUNG LESBIAN, AGE TWENTY: Before I got into junior high, my friends and I would always be touching each other, hugging each other, and holding hands. That's what little girls do. When we got into junior high, that changed. You never saw much of that. No one ever did that in public anymore. No one touched each other. Everyone stopped hugging each other. We wouldn't brush each other's hair. We'd never hold hands.

YOUNG WOMAN, AGE SEVENTEEN: I know a lot of young men who are gay. Homophobia played a role in how they treated me in a different sense. My gay friends started out fearing I'd be homophobic. They'd assume I wouldn't understand how they felt or that I'd have a negative reaction. And they'd play it up in a way. I have a friend whom I met when he thought he was straight. We were never sexually involved, but we'd kiss and play around. I didn't see him for about a year, and friends told me he came out. I ran into him, and he was "Mr. Homosexual" with me, and talked down to me, like, "Oh, you could never understand me."

YOUNG LESBIAN, AGE EIGHTEEN: Yeah, and everyone assumes everyone else is going to be homophobic, and they play off each other and feed each other, and everyone acts homophobicly because that's what they all expect.

YOUNG WOMAN, AGE SEVENTEEN: I think it's so great to see a man hugging another man, and you just don't see it very often. They'll punch each other on the arm, and do macho stuff like that. It's more accepted for women to be affectionate with each other than it is for men, and I think it's very hard for men to even imagine themselves with another man. The thought horrifies them, and they get instantly defensive.

YOUNG LESBIAN, AGE EIGHTEEN: There was a popular movie last year, *Bill and Ted's Excellent Adventure,* and it was a pretty good movie, really hilarious. In one scene, however, one of them had fallen down the stairs, and the other was very concerned, and ran over to make sure he was all right, and they hugged each other, and then both backed off, and looked at each other, and yelled "fag" at each other. I was really pissed.

YOUNG WOMAN, AGE SEVENTEEN: I've always been physically affectionate with my friends—hugging, kissing them on the cheek, walking arm in arm down the street. I've experienced people assuming we're lesbians because of what we're doing. I've been called *dyke* by people on the street when they saw us being physically affectionate. I've had some friends get nervous and push me off, not wanting to touch anymore.

YOUNG LESBIAN, AGE SEVENTEEN: Young people who are really prejudiced against homosexuals are really prejudiced against a lot of different people. If you open yourself to one prejudice, a thousand others seep in. Many kids I know who are prejudiced against gay people are also prejudiced against people of color and people who dress a certain way. That really hurts people. They become really close-minded.

The young heterosexual men with whom I spoke could not conceive of expressing physical affection with their male friends. As we would expect, however, it is more acceptable for young women to be affectionate with their female friends, although anxiety is present, and self-censorship occurs.

DIANE: Mark and Tom, do you have a best buddy?

MARK AND TOM: Yes.

DIANE: Would you feel free to walk from one end of Congress Street to the other with your arm around him?

TOM: If you paid me money to do it.

DIANE: How much money would it take?

JIM: You don't have enough.

MARK: It depends. If my friend went away for a long time. . . . No, I wouldn't do it then, either. I'd shake his hand.

JIM: I wouldn't do it. But I wouldn't be afraid to do it. What would make me do it in the first place? He's my friend, but I don't show affection. I'd shake his hand. That's good enough for me.

DIANE: How come you don't hug your friends?

JIM: I do.

DIANE: Your male friends?

JIM: [Makes a noise like a buzzer.] Wrong answer. Girls.

DIANE: How come you don't hug your male friends?

JIM: Because they are friends. How do you greet a person? You say hello and shake their hand. Am I wrong? I rest my case. There's nothing more to it than that.

PAM: I disagree with him. I hug my female friends. If I hadn't seen my girlfriends in a month or two, I would hug them. It's easier for girls to do it. It's more acceptable for girls because you find more guys who are gay. Guys are more afraid of people thinking they're gay.

TAMMY: I disagree with Jim, too. Whenever I see a friend from another grade in the hallway at school, we'll give each other a hug. And whenever I see my cousin, she'll always ask for a hug because she misses me. I know she's my cousin, and I know she's not gay, but sometimes when she kisses me on the cheek I feel really weird. People look and laugh at us. She doesn't care, but I feel a little weird.

TOM: You hear girls all the time saying, "Oh, she looks great today. Isn't she pretty!" But if a guy says that, you're gay right there. If you say one of your male friends looks good today, someone will say, "Hey, you homo."

The verbal and physical abuse directed at those who do not conform to gender-role expectations victimizes both gay and heterosexual youths, and gay and lesbian youths may participate in their own oppression by perpetrating or silently witnessing the abuse of others.

YOUNG LESBIAN, AGE EIGHTEEN: I didn't know women could be homosexual. I knew that being gay was wrong for guys. I used to be just one of the guys. I was an active participant in creating homophobia. If a guy didn't play football, which was a big thing in my neighborhood, or if a guy wore mittens to play ice football, we'd all go, "Oh, you sissy, you fag," and we'd start pushing him around and tackling him extra hard. . . . If you could fight, people would take back calling you a sissy. If you couldn't, you'd be tagged a sissy for the rest of the time you lived in the neighborhood. I got picked to go after this one guy. The guys would never let him live down the fact that a girl kicked his butt.

YOUNG LESBIAN, AGE SEVENTEEN: I was like one of the guys in my neighborhood, too. I played ice hockey. It was a really big thing in my family to play ice hockey, and my brother wouldn't play, and he was the only male child. My grandfather really regarded my brother as a sissy. He called him a sissy to his face. So I started to play ice hockey. My brother would sit on the sidelines, and we'd call him a sissy and harass him. We'd call him a faggot.

YOUNG LESBIAN, AGE EIGHTEEN: I suffered a lot of harassment in high school. The woman who harassed me the most my freshman year was a very big, very tall, very masculine-looking woman. She would just rag on me about being a dyke. Others did the same thing to her. She didn't belong to the nice preppy group, and she was targeted by them.

YOUNG LESBIAN, AGE EIGHTEEN: In gym class, we'd tease boys who couldn't throw a ball, of course. We'd call them fags. In high school there were kids who everyone thought were gay, and other kids were very violent toward them, toward one kid in particular. I don't remember ever seeing him with anyone as a friend.

YOUNG LESBIAN, AGE EIGHTEEN: In high school I had these two girlfriends, and we were always together, but there were these rumors that I was a lesbian and in love with one of them. I knew I was a lesbian at the time, but I wasn't in love with my friend. A lot of people stopped talking to me. I stopped going to school halfway into my senior year and eventually applied to a private program for kids having trouble with public school.

"If He Touches Me, I'll Bash Him"

I was in a rehab for adolescents. The health teacher asked us what we'd do if we found out our best friend was gay. There had been a movie on TV about it. Well, the kids in the rehab said things like they'd beat on the person. Then the teacher asked what we'd do if one of the kids in the rehab was gay. People's answers were really scary. "I'd beat on him." "I'd kick

him out." One guy even said he'd kill the person. A
gay resident left after that. He was just coming out
about his sexuality and got really freaked out.

—A twenty-year-old

Sadly, the heterosexual adolescents we interviewed found it difficult to imagine befriending someone who is gay or lesbian. During
this discussion, additional myths they held about homosexuality
emerged—that gay and lesbian people possess uncontrollable sexual urges and are attracted to everyone of the same sex, that close
relationships with gay and lesbian people will transform them into
homosexuals, that homosexuality is deviant and unnatural, and
that gay and lesbian people have nothing in common with them.

Not only are they afraid to establish intimacy with same-sex
friends, but for the young heterosexual men touching that fear of
getting close quickly leads to articulations of violence against any
man who would approach them in a physically intimate manner.
The terror of being touched lies right under the surface.

DIANE: Can you imagine having a friend who is gay or lesbian?
[Lengthy silence, nervous giggles.]

JIM: It depends. If that person is your only friend, you have nothing to worry about. But if you have more friends than that, there
goes your reputation.

PHIL: I'd be afraid they'd be looking at me. I'd definitely have a
hard time. I don't want some guy looking at me.

JIM: I'd be afraid they'd be undressing me in their mind, and I'd
have that instant uneasy feeling.

PAM: But let's say they're your friend and they know you're not
gay.

MARK: If it's your friend and they're queer, they probably want
you to be queer.

LORI: I'd be very uncomfortable, like among my peers. I'd be
afraid they'd think I was gay, too.

JIM: Yeah, it would make you feel like nobody would look up to
you the same way as they did before, knowing that you have that gay
friend.

TOM: I definitely couldn't have a friend who was gay. If someone hit on me, I could see how I could definitely fly off the wall and hurt someone.

MARK: He better not touch me if he's homo. If he's attracted to me, he's not my friend anymore. Well, he could still be my friend, but he'd have to stay away from me. If he did touch me, he wouldn't live to see the next day.

PHIL: Same thing. As long as they didn't touch me, it would be all right. If he ever hit on me, that would be a big problem.

TOM: I'd definitely want to bash him if he touched me.

PHIL: Definitely.

DIANE: What if a woman hit on you whom you weren't interested in at all?

TOM: I wouldn't be offended if a female hit on me who was a friend. I might tell her off.

PHIL: At least they'd have the sexes right.

MARK: Yeah, at least they'd have the sexes right. I'd tell her to stay away from me. I'd never hit a girl. If she was a nice person, I'd say, "You're a nice person, but you're just not for me. I don't want you touching me."

LORI: I wouldn't feel as threatened if a woman hit on me. Guys are bigger.

JIM: If you have a friend who you know for a fact is gay, then you worry. You're always going to be wondering if the two of you joke around physically. Maybe they don't know when to draw the line. Maybe you don't know when to draw the line, and that's when you have to call it quits. You're always going to worry about whether they are really joking.

TAMMY: If I had a friend and I found out she was a lesbian, it really wouldn't change my opinion of her. I would still hang around with her unless she started throwing passes at me, and then I'd back off.

"We Want Them to Do Something"

Can it happen that a heterosexual guy will wake up and say, "Oh, I think I'm tired of the opposite sex.

*I'm going to find me a man"? That's a scary concept.
I hope that can't happen.* —An eighteen-year-old male

*What do we want teachers to do? I want them to stop
allowing gay and lesbian kids to be verbally abused
in class, right in front of their noses, and to think
about the fact that we're sitting right there, but they
just don't know it.* —A sixteen-year-old lesbian

"You can't do anything about it," Pam said, during our discussion of gender roles and homophobia. "It will always be like that."

Tammy seconded her remarks. "You can't change it. There's nothing you can do. It's always going to happen," she said.

Our task is to show these young people a different way—not an easy assignment, but one we must take on if we believe in stopping young people from being needlessly hurt.

Gay and lesbian students are being oppressed by name-calling, physical violence, and, perhaps most insidious of all, damaging myths about who they are and what they can be as gay men and lesbians. Heterosexual students are being hurt by name-calling and physical violence, should they defy gender-role stereotypes, and, perhaps most insidious of all, damaging myths about who they are and what they can be as men and women.

Parents and professionals working with youths possess a great deal of power to transform homophobia into understanding and appreciation of gay and lesbian people, to transform anxiety and ignorance about issues of sexuality into self-esteem and self-confidence, and to help young women and men aspire to greatness as compassionate people capable of establishing intimacy with other human beings.

Just ask any gay or lesbian youth. These youths can teach us how to create safe environments for young people. They are experts at knowing what does not feel safe. Safe environments allow self-esteem to flourish, environments free from racist, sexist, ableist, classist, and homophobic oppression. I have learned this from gay and lesbian youths.

"My English teacher stopped a homophobic joke once," one

young gay man shared. "Man, I thought I'd get down on my knees and kiss her feet on the spot. It made me feel like I wasn't all alone. I even thought about coming out to her, but I didn't. But it helped just the same."

Young people know that we teach them as much by our silences as we do with our words. They hear the ear-splitting messages in our silence about gay and lesbian youths in health and sexuality education, our silence when the homophobic or sexist joke is made by the student in the front row, our silence when the new poster about gay and lesbian youths is pulled off the wall in the school nurse's office, our silence when the presentation by a gay and lesbian youth group during "Teen Issues Week" is suddenly canceled.

The interviews with heterosexual youths illustrate how homophobia is rooted in ignorance and untruths. Myths about homosexuality abound, and most school health education curricula do little to dispel the stereotypes. The words of the eighteen-year-old quoted above illustrate the lack of knowledge shared by so many young people about the nature of sexual orientation. This young man feared that he could wake up one morning and find himself turned into a homosexual, against his will, a victim of some mysterious, supernatural force.

During a workshop on gay and lesbian youths for high school peer counselors, a student wrote the following note to the OUTRIGHT participants in the question-and-answer period: "Your presence here today has done more to show me that homosexual people are people just like me than anything else ever could." We need to do more of the same thing, and at an earlier age.

I have a little friend who is five years old. We spend an evening together every week, and my partner sometimes joins me. One night, my little friend and I got into one of our many intense conversations, this one about families. He told me all about the different kinds of families the children in his day-care center come from. I asked him if he knew that it was against the law for my partner and me to get married. (He knew what "against the law" meant because we once had a lengthy conversation about my stay in the D.C. jail following the 1987 civil disobedience action at the U.S. Supreme Court. "Sometimes people should do things that are against the law," I taught him, with pride.) Uncertain, he wrinkled his brow and asked me why. I explained that the law allowed only men and women to marry each other, not two women or two men. His face suddenly brightened, as if a light went on in his very big brain, and he said, with excitement, "We talked about that at school, Auntie Elze [his pet name for me], and my teacher told us that was going to change soon, and if you'd like me to, I'll ask her when, and I'll call you and let you know tomorrow."

Oh, how I laughed, and I gave him a very big hug, and I told him I would look forward to his phone call.

"It has everything to do with me," I hope he will say at eighteen, when he witnesses someone being victimized by prejudice.

NOTES

This article was developed with the invaluable assistance of members of OUTRIGHT, the Portland Alliance of Gay and Lesbian Youth, and the People's Regional Opportunity Program Peer Leaders, who contributed their own words and the words of their peers. Their names, and the names of other young people interviewed, have been changed to protect their privacy. I interviewed small groups of gay, lesbian, and heterosexually identified teenagers, and a few of the young people also interviewed some of their peers. Established in 1987, OUTRIGHT is Maine's first support group for gay, lesbian, and bisexual youths. The PROP Peer Leader Program, also established in 1987, is a nationally acclaimed substance abuse prevention program training young people from Portland's public housing projects to be peer leaders.

1. Center for Population Options, "Adolescents, AIDS, and the Human Immunodeficiency Virus," a fact sheet, April 1989, Washington, D.C.

2. Barbara Kantrowitz, "The Dangers of Doing It," *Newsweek* (special issue, Summer/Fall 1990), 56–57.

7
"In the Best Interests of the Child": Thoughts on Homophobia and Parenting

DIANE RAYMOND

In the midst of the controversy in Massachusetts over a Department of Social Services decision to deny gays and lesbians rights to foster parenting, an article by Donna Scalcione (1987) in *Bay Windows* opened with the following: "I wish everyone knew what nine-year-old Jennifer knows. When asked to define the word 'lesbian' or 'gay' Jennifer says, 'It's like a man and a woman being together—it's just two women or two men. They have a relationship like all the other people do. It's no different" (p. 1). This article goes on to discuss the complications that plague the lives of children of lesbians, gay men, and bisexuals. Scalcione concludes that what these children learn is "that the gender of the person you love doesn't matter; that what *is* important is how you treat each other" (p. 12).

The Kinsey Institute has estimated that one-third of all lesbians and one-fifth of all gay men have been married; half these gays and lesbians are parents. Further, at least twenty thousand women are inseminated yearly; no one knows what percentage of those women are lesbians. Finally, although in most states an openly gay man or lesbian will not be allowed to adopt a child, gays and lesbians do succeed in adopting, often posing as "single" parents.[1] Thus, although we have no accurate statistics, one thing is certain: gays and lesbians have and do parent children. We can probably safely assume that most of those children are heterosexual. Conversely,

114

just as gays and lesbians may have heterosexual children, so may heterosexual parents have gay children.

In this essay, I want to explore the ways in which homophobia undermines parenting. I will argue that homophobia harms not only in the more obvious cases where there are gay children and/ or gay parents but even in those "mainstream" heterosexual families with heterosexual children. If I am right about this, then it follows that *anyone* who wants to be a good parent (and here one might interpret *parent* rather more broadly to refer to any adult in a fairly regular caretaking role) should take the personal and social costs of homophobia seriously; this stance commits one to a range of implications that I shall discuss in my conclusion.

Homophobia and Gay, Lesbian, and Bisexual Parents

Issues relating to parenting provoke deeply felt and often contradictory feelings. Although we tend to be somewhat cynical about the merits of the nuclear family, the mind fairly reels at the prospect of posing a viable alternative. We valorize the biological aspects of parenting: the popular media document case after case of adoptive child in search of "natural" parent and of upper-class couples' costly pursuits of the latest technology that will enable them to have "their own" (biological) children.

The phenomenon of *gay* parenting defies many of our most deeply felt cultural norms about the family. While the gay man or lesbian who first comes out may be called "selfish" for his or her rejection of heterosexuality (and, it is usually assumed, of future opportunities for parenting), the gay or lesbian who announces an intention to have children is also, ironically, considered "selfish." Norman Podhoretz, for example, wrote in one Father's Day column that "a man who decides to live as a homosexual is abdicating his place as a father" (quoted in "Gays and Parents" 1981, 21). The stereotype that gay sexuality (particularly gay male sexuality) is hedonistic and rooted in immediate gratification flies in the face of our images of parenting as requiring responsibility and a willingness to make personal sacrifices. In contrast, the lesbian, simply because she is usually seen first as a woman,[2] has the dominant culture's a priori seal of approval for her desire to mother; indeed, in general, a woman who refuses to actualize her biological potential to give birth is seen as a social anomaly. But the lesbian, in part because she refuses to be dependent on a man, is a suspect candidate for mothering. This has also been said about heterosexual single mothers.

Some critics of gay and lesbian parenting have argued that the "choice" to be gay or lesbian carries with it a willingness to give up children. This "life-style," critics claim, is incompatible with the "best interests of children." For those who see homosexuality only as *sexuality*, as private "bedroom" behavior, gays and lesbians cannot possibly be fit parents. Sociobiologist E. O. Wilson has actually maintained that gays and lesbians may possess a gene for altruism that makes them forgo biological parenting in the interests of species survival. Even liberals who generally defend the civil rights of gays and lesbians may be uncomfortable with the idea of those same gays and lesbians parenting or with the idea of gays and lesbians in intimate settings with other people's children.

The harmful effects of homophobia on families with gay and lesbian parents are by now clear. The children of gays and lesbians often live schizophrenic lives wherein they must keep secrets from teachers, friends, and parents of friends. At times, vindictive ex-husbands and ex-wives may use the threat of public exposure in order to prevent custody disputes. Although some openly gay men and women have won custody of their children and there seem increasingly to be positive outcomes (where 1 percent of lesbians won custody in 1970, the figure grew to 15 percent in 1986), such results are never certain; often the decision is idiosyncratic, dependent on the judge's level of tolerance. In one case, for example, two lesbians, lovers for ten years, were each sued by their ex-husbands. The judge in one trial noted that, although the woman's life-style was "unconventional," there was not a "scintilla of evidence from which the court could infer that [her] sexual orientation was adversely affecting [the children]" ("Gays and Parents" 1981, 21); her lover, however, lost custody of her children in a separate decision. In custody cases, judges commonly limit visitation when there is a live-in same-sex lover; gays often have to choose between visibility and their children; gay friends may be barred when the children are visiting, and a lesbian or gay man with children may be forced to give up her or his activist work in order to steer clear of the limelight. One cannot overstate the devastating psychological effect of these stresses and disruptions on the children of lesbians and gay men.

In other cases, the children of gays and lesbians may be harassed at school; teachers and other adult authorities might even be unwilling to come to their defense. Interestingly, even opponents of gay parents acknowledge this phenomenon; ironically, such homophobia is often cited as a *rationale* for denying gays and lesbians the right to parent or access to their children. A paradigm example of "blaming the victim" (Ryan 1988), this response—while expressing sympathetic concern for the tribulations endured—demands that gays and lesbians adapt to homophobia by *not* having children. Losing the right to parent, in this view, is the price one pays for one's social deviance. Gays and lesbians, it is argued, are "selfish" in that they are putting their own desire for children over the children's safety and well-being. Yet this is no different from suggesting that, because we live in a racist society, people of color have an obligation not to bring children into the world. Although, no doubt, good parents wish to prevent harm from befalling their children, this argument misguidedly puts the responsibility for homophobia on gays and lesbians. Further, this argument not only resigns itself to the inevitability of homophobia but even cooperates with the ideology of which homophobia is a part. For gays and lesbians not to have children, as this view advocates, is to increase the invisibility of gays and lesbians and not to take any positive steps to eliminate homophobia and heterosexism.

Further, some critics of gay parenting have argued that gay parents might produce gay children; or could pressure a child to a same-sex sexual orientation; or, minimally, would needlessly confuse the child with their oppositional sexualities. These critics would reject my analogy between sexual orientation and race, arguing perhaps that people of color "cannot help" the color of their skin. In contrast, one might claim, gays "can help" their sexual orientation; or, if one cannot change one's sexual orientation, one can choose not to act on one's attractions, or, minimally, one can choose not to subject children to one's life-style.

Gays and lesbians have responded to these sorts of claims with some troubling and self-defeating arguments. They have, for example, countered that they have as little control over sexuality as others have over race. Further, they claim, homosexuality is innate—a "given"—and environmental factors cannot affect it any more than do attempts to change hand preference. Mark Perigard (1985), for example, writes, "Children raised by homosexuals, according to more than one study, show no more likelihood of becoming gay than those raised by straight parents. Sexual orientation is not handed down from parent to child as easily as the alphabet or how to tie one's shoes" (p. 23). And a gay father wrote, "Society has been the one that has tried to make us look different or that says I am going to convince [my son] John to be gay, but you don't recruit homosexuals. Either they are or they aren't. We're not a religion" (quoted in Scalcione 1987, 12). Yet, if it is true (as Perigard grants) that we may never know the source of sexual orientation, then it would make sense—within a homophobic framework—to "play it safe" and refuse to let gays and lesbians parent or to deny custody to them. No matter what some people's earliest experiences of their own same-sex attractions might be like, no one can be sure that there are not subtle and mysterious situational forces that can reinforce or even create those attractions.

My objective here is hardly to provide the homophobe with more ammunition. Rather, my point is to suggest that gays and lesbians who declare themselves the defenseless results of immutable (and noncontagious!) forces unwittingly feed the fires of homophobia. Some gays and lesbians should parent because some gays and lesbians make good parents and some gays and lesbians want to be parents. Children of gays and lesbians *may* be more likely to be gay; why should that matter, unless we are uncomfortable with the prospect of more gays and lesbians? Do we think that such "gayness" would be forced on those children? If we view it thus, then it would follow that all sexuality is forced, for no one can know what is one's "natural" sexuality. Indeed, I would argue that the notion of a "natural," spontaneous sexuality is a myth.

Homophobia also has disastrous consequences for gay, lesbian, or bisexual children. Homophobia is intimately connected with more authoritarian thinking and greater sex-role rigidity. Parents of gay children may believe that they are doing what is best for their children by trying to mold their sexuality; they may argue that, given that heterosexuality is the norm, a gay child will have a much more difficult time negotiating his or her way through the world. In one well-known case, the parents of a lesbian had her kidnapped and repeatedly raped in order to "deprogram" her.[3] In other cases, parents have cut off financial support; have sent the child to homophobic psychiatrists or even had the child institutionalized; or have refused to see the child. Jewish parents of gay children have been known to "sit shiva" when the child comes out to them, a ritual that proclaims publicly, "This child is dead to me." Perhaps most tragic are cases like that of Bobby Griffith who, at age twenty, jumped off a freeway overpass into the path of a truck; his parents, strict fundamentalist Christians, could not accept their son's sexual orientation.[4]

The "coming-out process," we now know, is a multistage process in which the gay, lesbian, or bisexual must come to grips with his or her emerging sexuality. Some argue that "coming out" is in fact a lifelong process in which one acknowledges both to oneself and to others the fact of one's sexual orientation. The development of "gay identity" evolves over time, and some may never reach the stage of full acceptance. Regardless, though, there is no question that coming out is a painful process and that homophobia adds to (indeed, may even be *responsible* for) the psychic struggle. The silencing effects of homophobia make it difficult to unearth the history of gays and lesbians who have made contributions to our culture; finding adult role models may be especially problematic for young gays.

Adoption agencies have in some cases allowed openly gay men to adopt openly gay adolescents. But this requires that the adoptee in question have a clear and definite sense of his or her sexual identity; given that the denial stage of the coming-out process can be quite prolonged, and given that lesbians tend to "come out" later on average than gay men (age twenty-two compared to age seventeen), this approach excludes many candidates who might benefit from gay or lesbian adoptive parents. Further, insisting that gays can adopt *only* gay children assumes that gays cannot be good role models for anyone other than another gay; further, it negates whatever appropriate talents, skills, and interests the gay or lesbian has while objectifying him or her as a purely sexual being.

Because of homophobia, our culture assumes that a gay or lesbian parent is likely to confuse or, worse, abuse a heterosexual child. Yet studies suggest that the children of gay parents not only are not confused or harmed by their parents' sexuality but actually *learn* from it. Children of gays and lesbians seem to exhibit a greater understanding of and tolerance for differences in the culture. Children who live in homes where there are gays and lesbians very quickly learn the lie of homophobia: "When children discover that many of the people they love and admire are gay or lesbian, it makes it more difficult to convince them of the lie that homosexual expression arises out of some sort of sick, sinful, or self-hating orientation" (MacKinnon 1985, 1).

Thus, the argument that gays should be allowed to parent because they do not "influence" their children colludes with homophobia. In its defensiveness, the argument fails to question the assumption that the "influence" of gays and lesbians, if there were any, would be negative. It also seems patently absurd in the face of all the data, anecdotal as well as quantitative, that make very clear the powerful roles parents play in the lives of their children.

Even in the domain of sexual practices, if we accept that sexuality is at all fluid and that our choices are not totally constrained and predetermined, then it follows that gay parents *may* even influence sexuality. Indeed, at the very least, the child of gays learns that gay and lesbian sexualities *exist* and that they are available personal choices. Further, to argue that gays and lesbians are "just like" everyone else but for the (trivial) fact of sexual orientation is also to ignore the reality of the actual differences in gay and lesbian life and to divorce sexuality from its social context. Virtually any gay or lesbian can recite how his or her life is *forced* into difference by the existence of homophobia: the fears about coming out, the lack of role models in popular culture, the rejections by family members and friends, the absence of legal protections, and so on. The fact that those differences result from oppression does not make them any less real or give them any less significance for those who live them. Whether there would be a "gay culture" without homophobia is an interesting (and uncomfirmable) question; at least for the time being, however, gay and lesbian parents are *not* "just like everyone else," as the Scalcione piece excerpted above maintains. Indeed, that is what all the fuss is about.

Homophobia and All Parents

The gay or lesbian parent is a constant challenge to the negative stereotypes of homosexuality endorsed and reinforced by the culture. Homophobia acts as a form of social control to ensure that we do not question our assumptions about sexual norms; such rigidity ultimately makes us hate others and hate ourselves, regardless of our sexuality: "Our culture stands in desperate need of more honest and humane sexual values. Openly gay and lesbian people, through their own struggles and experience, are in a unique position to lead the way out of society's current wilderness" (MacKinnon 1985, 1).

Although it seems fairly clear how homophobia undermines parenting where the adults or the children are gay, it may not be so clear how homophobia is antithetical to good parenting more generally. I now want to turn to this question.

We have already seen that homophobia tends to be linked with greater sex-role rigidity. The homophobe finds comfort and security in the existence of socially mandated dichotomous divisions of labor and personal characteristics. These divisions have the advantage of clarity and predictability, but they guarantee that individual men and women will inevitably become only partial selves. Studies reveal, for example, that women who score very high on "femininity" scales and men who score very high on "masculinity" scales are quite skilled at certain sex-linked activities (e.g., mothering for women and mechanical ability for men) but that these rigid gender roles actually in the final analysis disempower these individuals. It seems in fact that those individuals who score highest on an "androgyny" scale—that is, those who are able to blend the best qualities of each stereotyped gender role—are most effective overall.

Contrary to the popular stereotypes, gays and lesbians do not seem to be as restricted by gender roles as are heterosexuals. While the popular ideology suggests that gays and lesbians role-play in their relationships (with one in the "butch" and the other in the "femme" role), in fact "the very nature of gay relationships— man loving man, woman loving woman—challenges the old structures and provides an impetus for further change" (Blumenfeld and Raymond, 1988, 375).

Gays and lesbians, active in the earlier feminist and the gay liberation movements, were among the first to challenge the rigidity of gender roles and gender-role expectations. Where lesbians cannot count on men for the traditional male contributions to relationships (including economic support) and gay men cannot count on women for emotional support and the fulfillment of other traditionally "feminine" duties, lesbians and gay men—however they ultimately do assign relationship responsibilities—cannot take gender roles for granted. Heterosexual couples, even the most aware, can easily lapse into traditional gender-role behavior. Although not much empirical research has been conducted to confirm these observations, one study suggests that lesbians are less bound by traditional gender divisions of labor, and another reveals that lesbian relationships tend to be more egalitarian than heterosexual relationships. As one gay man told researchers: "My lover and I have constantly shifting roles, depending on the needs of the moment. If ever I felt we were getting locked into any roles . . . I would run to escape this relationship" (quoted in Blumenfeld and Raymond, 1988, 376).

Gays and lesbians provide role models that teach children an invaluable social lesson: that one need not be imprisoned by one's biological sex. This is the fear of the homophobe, and it is a legitimate fear. Contrary to those gay apologists who claim that we are "no different from anyone else," the gay man or lesbian *is* a threat to gender. Homophobia is a means of social control that ultimately restricts *all* parenting, for it forces every one of us into rigid gender roles for fear that we or our children will be labeled *queer*. It is especially onerous for the boy or man who must distance himself from all intimate relationships (including, perhaps primarily, that with his mother), must labor to control any sign of weakness, and must forge sexual bonds with women while at the same time feeling something akin to contempt for them. While lesbians and gay men are often stereotyped as hating the other sex, it may be that heterosexual men and women—dependent on one another for intimate relationships yet socialized so as to make successful relationships almost impossible—live with a keen sense of disappointment in the other sex. How can children—regardless of their eventual sexual orientation—*not* be harmed by this polarization?

Homophobia is also connected to what have been termed *sex-negative* attitudes about the body and about sexuality. Homophobic parents not only are rigid about the assignment of gender roles and their insistence on the immutability of the nuclear family but also tend to manifest more guilt or negativity about sexuality. There has been ample discussion of how homophobia has undermined efforts in this country to educate communities—including heterosexual communities—about safer sex practices. In other countries, more "sex-positive" than our own, sexually explicit safer-sex campaigns have used humor (rather than scare tactics) and nonjudgmental language to emphasize the importance of safer sex. The widespread phenomena of teenage pregnancy and sexually transmitted diseases, including AIDS, in this country testify to our failure to educate positively about sexuality.

"Most people, whether gay or straight, have grown up internalizing powerful negative messages about their own sexuality" (MacKinnon 1985, 4), and although gays are not immune from internalized homophobia, gays and lesbians who decide to become parents have had to work through many of their own ambivalent feelings about their sexuality. Similarly, although I would not argue that all gays and lesbians accept sexual openness, the gay and lesbian communities have been far more supportive of open and honest discussions of sexuality. The fact that gays and lesbians are sexual "outlaws" has meant that those same gays and lesbians have had to examine sexuality from the "margins." While homophobes fear open discussions of sexuality, such discussions can only help to combat the fear and misinformation that are so common in our culture and that have such disastrous repercussions. Parents—gay *and* straight—who reject homophobia are also rejecting sex-negative attitudes that ultimately teach children to hate their bodies, their desires, and, consequently, themselves.

Another stereotype of gays and lesbians is that they are promiscuous and do not stay in committed relationships. Although more often aimed at gay men (especially as another victim-blaming technique more common since the outbreak of AIDS), this charge has been used to trivialize *all* same-sex relationships. The real meaning of this criticism is not always clear; indeed, depending on the specific context, it can imply at least three different objections: that gays and lesbians are not in relationships at all; that gays and lesbians, while in relationships, are not in committed (monogamous?) relationships and thus at best continue to maintain a series of superficial relationships; or that same-sex relationships are somehow, in principle, not "real" relationships at all, no matter what form they may take. While the first claim is clearly meant as an empirical observation and can most obviously and most easily be proved wrong, the second's use of the term *superficial* renders its judgment more subjective but empirically based nonetheless; the third point, however, rests on an a priori assumption about what a "real" relationship is and is therefore fully normative.

While many defenders of gay and lesbian life-styles have countered with available statistics documenting longevity in those relationships,[5] this response misses the fact that, despite appearances, empirical data are [not really] in dispute; indeed, more likely than not, the homophobe, when challenged with such data, will simply shift from position 1 to position 2 and/or position 3. Once again, I would suggest that to attempt to counter such claims with contrary evidence is inadequate and may even be defensive. Nor is it enough to enumerate the many ways in which gay and lesbian relationships are undermined by the culture at large; given the homophobic laws and cultural practices that prohibit and restrict same-sex relationships and the heterosexist policies that legitimize and reinforce heterosexual bonds, it may border on miraculous that *any* homosexual relationships survive at all. But all this fails to articulate the more positive vision of relationships and "families" that were once such a compelling part of the gay liberation movement.

Why do we come to value longevity in relationships when we know of so many examples of unhealthy long-term relationships? Why do we assume that children are happier in families of long-term relationships? One might instead confront those very assumptions and explore the benefits of ending destructive or mutually unsatisfying relationships. As we have seen, the lesbian and gay communities have served to challenge the assumptions of heterosexism and homophobia. But they can also challenge the assumptions that we tend to share about love, romance, and commitment. Just as we should continue to question the concept of gender itself, so should we examine our assumptions about long-term relationships. Gays and lesbians who seek to create relationships that do no more than mirror heterosexual bonds have failed to realize the more truly transformative potential in these more marginalized relationships.

The feminist and gay and lesbian liberation movements of the 1960s and 1970s altered the consciousnesses of many men and women, heterosexual and homosexual. More concretely, these movements "expanded the possibilities" that exist "in many areas of our lives: work, love, sex, parenting and politics" (Haber 1979, 417). There is already a powerful trend among heterosexuals toward single-parent families; this phenomenon is on the rise not only because of the high divorce rate (which tends to leave women the primary custodial parents) but also because more women are having children outside marriage. The very fact that such children have borne the social stigma of "illegitimacy" testifies to the weight of heterosexist hegemony. One recalls how Senator Patrick Moynihan bemoaned this earlier trend in the black community and argued that this so-called black matriarchy not only was unhealthy for black children but also tended to emasculate black men. Currently, popular magazines like *People* and talk shows like "The Oprah Winfrey Show" sensationalize the desire of older (heterosexual) single women to be in relationships, and they pathologize the phenomena of single parenting, alternative families, even divorce.

In contrast, I would argue that the trends toward single-parent families should be encouraged as one way to break down gendered familial patterns. Rather than privilege long-term relationships, gays and lesbians (along with single parents and others) can fight for the social programs necessary to allow women to be independent. This agenda must include, but is certainly not limited to, child care, a support allowance for adults with children, a nonjudgmental welfare system, and a "gender-neutral wage structure" (Lorber 1989, 64). Traditionally, our economic structure has buttressed the nuclear family and in particular has made women dependent on men. This is one example of Adrienne Rich's "compulsory heterosexuality" (see Rich 1980), and it continues to function to keep women in destructive and even abusive relationships. Gays and lesbians, in addition to challenging sex-role rigidity, can also work to undermine traditional assumptions about the family itself. One has to wonder how much of our panic at the growing number of households headed by women is, at bottom, evidence of a more subtle form of homophobia; can we trust single mothers of sons to teach them how to be "real men"? It is not usually the fact that two are more productive than one that leads to advocacy of dual parenting; if that were the case, the actual sex of the parents should be irrelevant. Rather, our unarticulated assumption that the presence of a mother *and* a father is necessary to teach and reinforce gender-role behavior seems to ground most discussions of parenting; how else will little girls learn what it means to be a woman and little boys what it means to be a man?[6]

Conclusion

In an editorial piece in response to the Massachusetts foster-care debate, *Boston Globe* columnist Ellen Goodman (1985) wrote the following:

This tale isn't about gay rights, it is about children's needs. In the best of all possible worlds, each child would have its own caring mother and father. In the best of all possible worlds, no child would have to adjust to a parent who was this "different." But then, in the best of all possible worlds, no child would be abused or neglected or ever, ever in need of foster care. . . . In the public mind, perhaps, the state can choose between [gay foster parents] Babets and Jean, or Ozzie and Harriet. But in real life, the choices are often meager and not every foster parent has altrustic motives. How many of the critics of these two gay men have volunteered to be foster parents themselves?

This excerpt is shocking not only because Ellen Goodman is usually thought of as a friend of "choice" but also because of the assumptions that underlie it. Imagine that we *could* have a world in which we were able to have "Ozzie and Harriet" parents. This sort of family would clearly have Goodman's vote, despite all the available evidence from "survivors" of such families who have testified to these families' oppressive characteristics. Further, to argue that we must tolerate (rather than *accept,* rather than *embrace*) gay parents because we have no better options is to presuppose that available heterosexual parents *would* be better. Indeed, one could consistently argue, that, if there are no available heterosexual parents, such children might be better left in caring institutional settings. To suggest that some arrangements could be much worse is surely to damn gays and lesbians with faint praise, if it is to praise at all. Finally, to argue in puerile *tu quoque* fashion that one is not allowed to criticize foster parents unless one is willing to volunteer oneself is absurd—in almost no other context would we accept such an inane argument. Goodman also mentions in this piece that she is "uncomfortable with those gay women who *deliberately* go out to 'get' children of their own through artificial insemination" (my emphasis). Thus, we see quite graphically the implications of a position that refuses to confront homophobia in all its manifestations.

Goodman's analysis was not so very different from much of what appeared—in both the lesbian and gay and in the mainstream presses—about this case. Indeed, given that she rejected the Department of Social Services decision to remove the children, her stance was far more liberal than many others that challenged the "rights" of gays and lesbians to parent. But I have tried to argue in this essay that, although its consequences are always damaging, homophobia is often very subtle and very deep seated; and it is especially complex in the arena of parenting, a domain already highly emotionally charged.

Any good person begins with a desire to avoid inflicting unnecessary harm on others. Likewise, a good parent begins with a desire to avoid inflicting harm on one's children. There is no question that in most ways it is easier today to be heterosexual than to be homosexual. It is not melodramatic to suggest that the heterosexual man or woman has the weight of the dominant culture behind him or her. Thus, it makes sense that a good parent, in seeking to protect his or her child (or in extrapolating to the welfare of all children), would encourage heterosexuality, discourage same-sex attachments, and reinforce "appropriate" gender-role behavior. In response, gays and lesbians and their supporters have sought to emphasize the qualities that make us all similar rather than those that challenge and subvert the status quo. In some ways (in that mythical "ideal world"?), one can understand how *in*-significant a characteristic one's sexual orientation might be. But sexuality, as it is socially constructed today, *does* matter, for it (like race, gender, religion, class, age, etc.) frames our social lives.

All parents—heterosexual as well as homosexual—stand to lose in the maintenance of homophobia. The losses that lesbians and gays and their children experience are far more obvious, more graphic, and easier to recount. But heterosexual parents and heterosexual children also lose. As homophobia is connected to rigid sex roles, heterosexuals lose the potential to stretch beyond the limits of gender definitions. As homophobia is tied to revulsion toward the body and the hatred of sexuality, heterosexuals learn to despise themselves and their own bodies. Further, the fear that one may be gay or lesbian forces the containment of same-sex erotic desire, which in turn constrains all same-sex attachments, sexual or otherwise. It keeps fathers from their sons, mothers from their daughters, and all of us from sexual "experimentation" of any sort because homophobia would have us believe that the labels we fear are immutable characterological stains. Finally, homophobia robs us of the opportunities for learning that gay and lesbian parenting provides and of the possibility for dialogue that explores and confronts some of the assumptions we share. Why have we failed to open up to *all* children the option to be gay or lesbian? Why have we hesitated to examine the values in "deliberately" having children? Why have we tended to privilege biology? Must women experience parenting differently from men? Why have we assumed that the traditional nuclear family is the best of which we are capable? In the context of homophobia, such questions are terrifying. Of what are we afraid?

NOTES

My thanks to Marlene Gerber Fried, with whom I discussed many of these issues. Although she probably does not agree with everything I have written here, I benefited enormously from our conversations.

1. Another issue for lesbians and gays is whether the same-sex partner is allowed to adopt the lesbian's or gay's biological child legally. To date, twelve "children in the world . . . have two legal parents of the same sex," mostly a result of the fact that "a few relatively gay-sympathetic jurisdictions are beginning to be able to circumvent state policies that prohibit gay couples from adopting each other's children" (Chasnoff 1990, 4).

2. Indeed, the lesbians first prosecuted in this country were found guilty of wearing men's clothing, that is, of attempting to "pass" and thereby assume male privilege.

3. In 1981, nineteen-year-old Stephanie Riethmiller was held captive for seven days in a secluded cabin in Alabama. During that time, her captors, hired for $8,000 by her parents, raped her nightly and preached to her constantly on the sins of homosexuality. Her mother remained in the next room throughout the time. The jury later failed to bring in a guilty verdict against the kidnappers.

4. Mary Griffith has since established "The Bobby Griffith Memorial Scholarship," given to deserving lesbian and gay high school students (see Miller, this volume).

5. And there can be no doubt that whatever statistics we do possess underestimate actual numbers of same-sex relationships. Because of homophobia, such relationships are often invisible. Also, more pragmatically, given that gays lack a legally recognized institution comparable to heterosexual marriage, by what criteria does one determine what constitutes a relationship qualified for tallying?

6. Sadly, many gays respond to this particular question by promising that their children watch enough television to learn what these cultural signifiers mean, or that there is a significant person in their lives, of the other sex from their parent, who can model appropriate behaviors.

REFERENCES

Blumenfeld, Warren, and Diane Raymond. *Looking at Gay and Lesbian Life*. Boston: Beacon, 1988.

Chasnoff, Debra. "Let's Get National." *Out/Look* 3, no. 2 (Fall 1990): 3–5.

"Gays and Parents." *Village Voice* (1 July 1981), 19–25.

Goodman, Ellen. "DSS (Department of Social Services) and Child Care." *Boston Globe* (12 May 1985), 7, 21.

Haber, Barbara. "Is Personal Life Still a Political Issue?" *Feminist Studies* 5, no. 3 (Fall 1979): 417–30.

Lorber, Judith. "Dismantling Noah's Ark." In *Gender in Intimate Relations*, ed. Barbara Risman and Pepper Schwartz, 58–67. Belmont, Calif.: Wadsworth, 1989.

MacKinnon, Catharine A. "The Need for Gay Parents." *The Guide* (June 1985): 1.

Perigard, Mark. "Sweeping away the Myths on Gays and Foster Care." *Boston Sunday Globe* (6 June 1985), 23.

Rich, Adrienne. "Compulsory Heterosexuality and Lesbian Existence." *Signs: Journal of Women in Culture and Society* 5, no. 4 (1980): 631–60.

Ryan, William. "Blaming the Victim." In *Racism and Sexism*, ed. Paula S. Rothenberg, 324–33. New York: St. Martin's, 1988.

Scalcione, Donna. "One Parent in Ten." *Bay Windows*, 5, no. 11 (19–25 March 1987), 1, 12.

8

Homophobia, Homosexuality, and Heterosexual Marriage

JEAN S. GOCHROS

My husband's coming out of his closet. Now I'm the one who's in it!

My in-laws are ashamed of him and won't speak to me. They say I caused his homosexuality. I not only lost my husband, I lost my whole close family.

I told a psychiatrist I thought my husband might be gay and asked him how to broach the subject tactfully. . . . He said sarcastically, "What's the matter? Can't you say 'Cocksucker'?" Then he carried on such a diatribe about women in general and me in particular—I finally walked out.

Recently a number of people in my office went through divorces, often because of a spouse's infidelity. When that happened with most of the women, we would all gather around, offer support, and say to ourselves, "No wonder she's been acting so bitchy lately. She's been going through hell!" But when one woman told us she and her husband were divorcing because of his homosexual infidelities, we gave her no support at all, and we said to ourselves, "Wouldn't you know she'd have a husband like that? She's so bitchy!"

Since the start of the gay liberation movement in the late 1960s, more and more homosexually oriented men and women have begun to come out of their closets. What we may not realize, however, is how many kinds of closets exist or how restricting and painful they can be for their inhabitants. One of those closets holds couples like those in the vignettes above, in which one partner is gay or bisexual. Little has been written about these relationships, and, until recently, what little information existed dealt mainly with the problems of gay husbands. It either ignored the needs and feelings of spouses or dismissed them in a paragraph suggesting that such wives are neurotic and unable to cope with the results of their own "self-deception."

No one knows how many couples are in this situation. Alfred Kinsey's 1948 research found that 15 percent of white married American men between the ages of twenty-one and forty-five had had some amount of homosexual experience during marriage. Over 3 percent had had as much homosexual as heterosexual interest and experience. His study did not include nonwhites or men who had become homosexually active only after divorce or the death of their wives. It did, however, include hundreds of single men who had had sexual affairs with older married men not participating in the study. Hence, Kinsey estimated the number of married men with some degree of homosexual orientation as far higher than he could document (approaching 18–20 percent). His study is still considered the most comprehensive and reliable available.

Differing definitions of homosexuality and people's fears about participating in studies prevent truly accurate estimates. Yet not only do more recent American and European studies of gay or bisexual men generally support Kinsey's findings, but they also suggest that even his 20 percent estimate is too low. A Kinsey Institute (Reinisch 1989) review of various studies notes that 70 percent of self-identified gay men report having had sex (ranging form one-night stands to full marriages) with women and sex (again ranging from one-night stands to long-term, albeit clandestine, relationships) with one to five married men. In the end, a "conservative" estimate is of four to five million gay or bisexual American men who marry at some point in their lives. To date, there is no research that provides any reasonable estimate for their counterparts, lesbian or bisexual women in heterosexual marriages. For various reasons, even Kinsey's estimate (which was lower than for men) is suspect. My hunch is that, if we were to have more reliable research, we would find the numbers relatively equal to that of men—making a grand total of at least ten million Americans.

Does that sound incredible? In 1970 it would have seemed so. Today there is considerable evidence for such figures. As one wife married to a gay husband said to me, "This may be the best kept secret in America." In the past few years, AIDS has made that secret an unusually important and frightening one.

This essay, then, is about the effects of homophobia not simply on homosexual or bisexual persons but on their spouses, their children, and their families. It is based partly on my clinical experience as a therapist, partly on an intensive study of wives of gay and bisexual men, and partly on the letters and phone calls I continually receive in response to my book on the subject (Gochros 1989).

I am focusing on couples in which the husband is the homosexual/bisexual partner simply because that is the situation that is most researched. Many of the statements made about this situation, however, can also be applied to families in which the husband is the straight partner.

Why Are We Talking about Homophobia?

A logical question at this point is, What does this situation have to do with homophobia? More specifically, What does homophobia have to do with the straight people in the situation? The answer can be found in the questions and comments I hear about my research. For example:

1. Why would gay or bisexual men marry? I bet they're either deliberately using the marriage as a front or pretending they're bisexual because they can't face the fact that they're gay.

2. What kind of women marry such men? I bet the wives were abused as children and had such low self-esteem that they re-

peated the abuse by marrying someone who couldn't possibly meet any of their needs. Or they're afraid of sex or too ugly to get a straight man, or maybe they're latent lesbians.

3. How could a wife not know? I bet they deny reality.

4. How do wives react to learning that their husbands are gay? What kind of women stay with such men? I bet they fall apart, or commit suicide, or divorce immediately and become very vindictive. Any why on earth would anyone stay in a marriage without sex? They must have very low self-esteem.

5. Are the children in danger? I suppose they become gay too.

Such assumptions contain myths and stereotypes that stem from both sexism and homophobia. Yet any stereotype contains kernels of truth. This essay attempts to sift through the stereotypes, the truths, and the reasons behind both.

Why Do Gay and Bisexual Men Marry?

It should come as no shock to anyone that it can be difficult to be gay in our society. Adolescents, even when not openly harassed, often suffer from stigmatization both deliberately and unintentionally by teachers, the clergy, people in the helping professions, peers, parents, and mass media. At best, gay, lesbian, and bisexual teenagers have few good role models, support groups, or understanding parents or parent figures to offset the barrage of messages that society sends them to make them feel immoral, sick, worthless, unlovable, and—for teenagers the worst sin of all—different.

Adults may find more emotional support systems, but they are also subject to real or potential rejection, loss of job and shelter, and legal exclusion from society's most sacred institutions: marriage, parenthood, and often organized religion. Despite changes in our society, not only prejudice and discrimination still abound, but fear of stigmatization is often as powerful as reality.

Using Marriage as a Front

It is both true and understandable, then, that some men and women do indeed deliberately use marriage as a "front" in order to obtain at least a reasonable facsimile of their presumed "right" as citizens to "life, liberty, and the pursuit of happiness." Unless they either come out to or are found out by their spouses, they may go to their graves with their secret intact.

I am often asked, "How can they live with themselves?" Usually, the answer is, "With difficulty!" Not only is there constant fear of discovery, but there is also an internal mixture of guilt, self-hate, and anger at a society that makes such pretense (seem) necessary. And if the spouse does learn, or if the person decides to come out on his or her own, the emotional conflict can have serious consequences. (The names and other identifying characteristics in the stories below have been changed.)

George, for example, was a top business executive, involved in community organizations and the proverbial pillar of the church. He and Laura married because of a one-time sexual relationship that made her pregnant. He subsequently avoided sex with her rather than tell her that he was gay. She in turn coped with having found him having sex with a male guest at a party by wiping it out of her mind. Even when she later faced the truth and confronted him, he denied it. He became increasingly depressed and alcoholic. Laura sought psychiatric help for him when he drunkenly exhibited himself to another man at a bar, was brought home forcibly, and spent the rest of the night flagellating himself with the drapery cord, crying, "Oh, God—why did you make me this way?" Despite divorce and honesty with his psychiatrist, he has never admitted the truth to Laura.

Sometimes the answer to, "How do they live with themselves?" is, "Very easily." Phil, for example, told his wife of many years that he had never loved her, always knew he was gay, and married only to aid his career. He had always planned to divorce as soon as he became financially able and had encouraged her return to school only so that she could be self-supporting when he left her. The only real concern he had shown in their entire marriage was his disclosure of his homosexuality when he learned that he had contracted syphilis.

Such dishonesty may have nothing to do with either homophobia or homosexuality. It may simply be a function of individual personality. Many gay, lesbian, and bisexual people, however, think or have been told by others (including professional therapists and clergy) that marriage will "cure" them and that they should not tell their spouses. We shall see later how such homophobic views not only are destructive to gays, lesbians, and bisexuals but also hurt the heterosexual spouses.

Inability to Face One's Own Homosexuality

Contrary to the stereotype, deliberately "using" marriage as a "front" is probably *not* the most common way of coping with homophobia. Many people, however, having absorbed society's homophobia, have internalized so much shame that they cannot bring themselves to face their homosexuality. We have no way of knowing how many couples are in this situation with no ill results. We do know, however, that many marriages with sexual difficulties, physical and/or emotional spouse abuse, or even simply unfulfilling marriages arise from such denial.

Joe, for example, is sure that his one-night stands, which occur two to three times a week, mean nothing more than that he is more "horny" than his wife and can satisfy physical urges without being unfaithful. Jim attributes his occasional homosexual affairs to alcohol and has an on-again off-again relationship with Alcoholics Anonymous. Ed suffers from "sexual addiction." He attends a Sex Anonymous group and insists that he cannot be truly homosexual because he feels "disgusted" after each homosexual experience. John is a "Don Juan" who sees his wife as so uninterested and unresponsive that he is driven to meeting his sexual needs elsewhere. He does not see his frequent choice of men rather than women as having anything to do with homosexuality or bisexuality. As he puts it, "Any port in a storm will do." Charles says his encounters do not express his "true self" but are caused by the Devil. He does not need counseling; he just needs to pray harder.

Richard, a gay and formerly married pastoral counselor, explains this reasoning as "compartmentalization," an extension of the denial all people use for emotional survival in facing real or potential dangers such as life-threatening illnesses, dangerous sports, driving, or even crossing streets. Aided and abetted by religious precepts, when the danger is one that threatens social acceptance or one's sense of moral integrity, people compartmentalize their feelings and ascribe the ones in the "unwanted" compartment to outside forces like the Devil or a specific situation outside their control. One might call this an "outside agitator" explanation for one's unacceptable thoughts or behaviors.

While not a deliberate lie, such logic can, unfortunately, compromise one's moral integrity. If the amount of denial and moral impairment is small, the person lives with guilt that itself impairs marital relationships. If denial really works and there is little or no guilt about—say—infidelity, that insensitivity to others' feelings and rights may impair the marriage in many ways. Again, our knowledge is limited by the fact that we have little access to spouses who do not know the truth and who do not enter our offices. But those families who come for counseling or participate in research report serious problems whether or not the homosexuality is known.

Bisexuality, Love, Heterosexuality, and All That Jazz

Although I have spent a lot of time on complicated "fronts" and "denials," the major reason gay—or, more accurately, bisexual— men give for marrying is simply love. Michael Ross (1983) found that the most frequent and usually the primary reason given for marriage was having fallen in love, even with husbands (or former husbands) who had acknowledged their homosexual feelings and who had been entirely or almost entirely homosexually active before marriage, and no matter what other reasons (such as the desire for children, social acceptance, etc.) contributed to the decision. This holds true with most of the men and women I have interviewed, even including one or two men who had deliberately lied and been unfaithful from the beginning of their marriage to the end.

This finding brings us to the third but probably largest category of men and women who may have hidden homosexual feelings from themselves or their spouses but who do not fit the categories mentioned earlier. They are probably more accurately considered bisexual, and their experiences vary greatly.

Bisexuality and Biphobia

Homosexuality and heterosexuality are not static "either-or" states, nor can they be defined simply in terms of erotic desires or behaviors. They are complex constellations of feelings and behaviors that may change in amount, intensity, and form, coexisting in a delicate balancing act throughout life, with many combinations and permutations. Kinsey (1948), for example, found that almost 40 percent of white American male adults had had at least one homosexual experience ending in orgasm but that most of these people considered themselves heterosexual. Only about 10 percent had exclusively or primarily homosexual relationships. Labels, then, can be misleading. People can like different kinds of food at the same time, for example, their tastes varying from day to day, week to week, year to year, and without labeling themselves as the foods they eat at a given point. They do not eat only one thing, eliminating all others for the remainder of their lives.

Klein (1978) notes that a person might have concurrent homosexual and heterosexual relationships or sequential ones, might enjoy one aspect of a homosexual relationship, another aspect of a heterosexual one. Homosexual needs might be strong at one point, weak at another. A person with a low heterosexual sex drive might have an equally low homosexual sex drive, and vice versa. For some, homosexuality means love and emotional intimacy, not erotic desire.

Uncomfortable as our society has been with homosexuality, however, we tend to be even more uncomfortable with ambiguity. We can make our peace with differences that are well defined, labeled, and contained, for we can find clear-cut rules for understanding and dealing with *them* and go on about *our* business. Bisexuals, however, are ambiguous people who fit no category, who ruin our concepts of how life should be, and who threaten our ability to separate *them* from *us*. As we shall see later, biphobia will prove to be as big a factor as homophobia in creating problems for people in mixed-orientation marriages.

To sum up, while some people may use marriage as a "front" or bisexuality to deny their true homosexuality, many do not experience homosexual desires until later in life. Others are vaguely aware of homosexual feelings but forget them, consider them just part of adolescent experimentation or curiosity, or do not think about them enough to get in touch with them. Overridden by heterosexual feelings, often they are so vague that they remain unrecognized and are acted on only in such socially acceptable ways as football players patting each others' bottoms' or one man admiring another's manly physique. Prejudice continues to force repression and denial here, but it is weaker. Sexual arousal strong enough to create erections or homosexual fantasies breaks through, but possibly not for some time. Indeed, some men get in touch with such feelings only after the death of their wives. For some, homosexuality has little to do with erotic sex but is mainly emotional; their strongest attachment is to men rather than women even though little or no erotic activity is involved.

This honest lack of awareness may be even more true of married bisexual women. They have no erections to help them define erotic feelings and are able to have heterosexual intercourse without arousal. Because of society's sex-role expectations, women's sexual desires are more apt to grow out of, rather than lead into, emotional love. Hence, they may be less able to pinpoint erotic feelings and less willing to have "quicky" recreational sex.

Marcia, for example, told me that never in her life had it occurred to her that she could be physically attracted to another woman until her fifties, long after a divorce initiated by her husband. She and her present lover had had a close friendship for years. It had come as a shock to both of them that their socially accepted nonerotic hugs had begun to take on an erotic tone. She has never had such feelings toward any other woman.

Finally, many men and women enter marriage acknowledging the homosexual part of their lives but sure that it has been or will be "cured" by their heterosexual love. Often, professionals have advised them not to frighten their partners by talking about their past. Sometimes they are completely honest, yet neither partner is really prepared for the possible future resurgence of homosexual feelings. In either situation, no matter what happens in the future, the marriage has been entered for the same mixture of reasons that *any* marriage is entered: for love, the desire for companionship, security, family, social acceptance.

Coming Out

Just as in adolescence, the married person facing either new or renewed homosexual feelings has many reasons to try to repress those feelings, and usually tries to do so. Coming out to oneself, then, is usually a slow and painful process. Deciding what to do about a marriage can be even more difficult, particularly when the partners are still in love and want to remain married. The partner coming out asks, Can my spouse understand? Will I be thrown out? Will I lose my children? Will my spouse be vindictive? Suicidal? Almost all the husbands and wives in this situation whom I have interviewed have agonized over such questions. Too often they are too filled with their own homophobia to believe that their fears may be exaggerated. Unable either to contain their homosexuality or to be honest, the continued infidelity and dishonesty stemming from that homophobia not only hurts the wives but ensures the very situation husbands most fear.

How Homophobia Continues to Hurt the Spouse

True, learning that one's spouse is gay or bisexual is difficult. True, spouses need not be told about a one-time experience in adolescence. But the assumption that what spouses don't know won't hurt them is simply incorrect, if for no other reason than that it is harmful to people either to be deliberately "used," to have their trust betrayed, or to be deliberately kept uninformed about forces that potentially or actually affect their lives. Moreover, people who are spending most of their energy lying to others or repressing their own sexual feelings are not apt to be highly ethical in other aspects of their marital relationships, nor are they apt to be sensitive to the spouse's needs and feelings in any area.

The period during which gay/bisexual partners are facing their feelings and agonizing over what to do about them is frequently harder on the spouse than is the actual disclosure. I call this period a *predisclosure buildup.* Depending on the situation, a spouse may be aware of growing tension but unable to define the problem. Husbands, for example, may at best be withdrawn, remote, depressed, and irritable, at worst violent and abusive. Formerly good marriages and good sexual relationships can be destroyed during this period.

Typically, straight wives are blamed and tend to blame themselves for the growing problems in the marriage. They may suspect "another woman," but if they suspect the truth, they are in an even worse spot. Homophobia has turned honest questions about one's sexual orientation into accusations. Straight men in our society do not take kindly to being asked if they are gay. Straight spouses, then, report feeling disloyal and "crazy" for even thinking such a thing. Actually to ask about it means running the risk of unfairly hurting a loved one and making the situation worse instead of better. Several wives have reported seeking professional help at such a time and receiving such homophobic (and often antifemale) responses from the counselor that their own self-esteem and ability to cope with the situation was even further impaired. While wives' questions may result in disclosure of homosexuality or bisexuality, often they are met with angry evasiveness ("Are you crazy? How could you think such a thing?") or lies.

If it is difficult to cope with reality, however, it is more difficult to cope with not knowing what reality is. Faced with problems that seemingly have no definable cause and hence no viable solution, straight spouses themselves lose self-esteem and become anywhere from mildly to severely depressed. Contrary to their husbands' fears, many straight wives report being most suicidal just prior to learning the truth and almost relieved when the disclosure is finally made. Wives who have been divorced by their husbands for no reason or an inadequate one, who suspect homosexuality but have no way to confirm it, are apt to be in great emotional distress, for they have no way to evaluate the past, free themselves of self-blame, and get on with their lives.

How Do Spouses React to Disclosure?

What happens when a straight spouse learns the truth? It depends on the situation and the gay partner's behavior more than on the spouse's beliefs about homosexuality. To the extent that the revelation reveals long-standing and serious, deliberate infidelity, little or no concern for the spouse's feelings, needs or rights, or lack of commitment to the marriage, the straight spouse immediately suffers all the hurt and anger one might expect with any marital infidelity and all the grief one might expect with any such loss. Loss and betrayal of trust are the immediate issues, not sexual orientation.

However, when the gay/bisexual husband has been essentially honest, coming to grips with his feelings and telling his wife the truth as soon as possible, when he is showing love for her and concern for and sensitivity to her feelings, and particularly when he is committed emotionally and sexually to the marriage, she is apt to be understanding and empathic. That scenario has characterized well over half the couples I have counseled. The immediate consequence of what I call *positive disclosures* (as opposed to more negative ones) is often an immediate honeymoon period. Tension and depression decrease, and the self-esteem of both partners increases. They recommit to each other, and an immediately improved sexual relationship results. Often a new contract is made to allow for meeting homosexual needs.

By rights, this should be the end of the chapter. If the gay partner has been a real "heel," we should see a bitter but speedy divorce. If he or she has been a caring "good guy" but honestly unable to maintain a heterosexual marriage, we should see a poignant, grief filled, speedy, but amicable divorce. If the disclosure has been a positive one, we should see a honeymoon. Whatever happens, both partners should receive competent counseling as needed and emotional support from family, friends, and colleagues. Readjustment should take place as in any similar hetero-

sexual marital situation, and perhaps more easily: since a heterosexual spouse cannot be expected to change gender, such wives
need not (and often do not) expect to run in a competition and
hence need lose no self-esteem in the event of divorce. Unfortunately, life seldom unfolds the way it "should." If homophobia has
created problems earlier, it now begins, with considerable help
from sex-role stereotyping, to take its most bitter toll on straight
spouses, who after the divorce are left stigmatized and isolated,
feeling confused and lost.

Stigma, Isolation, Confusion, and Sense of Loss

These four problem areas go hand in hand, are interwoven,
feed on one another, and come in many forms. For example, homophobia may prevent one or both partners from truly coming to
grips with a degree of homosexuality that makes marriage untenable. Contracts are made that cannot be kept, promises of fidelity
are broken, and new and increasingly negative disclosures ensue.
The straight partner becomes increasingly confused. This in turn
further erodes self-confidence. Eventually, the marriage dissolves
with a maximum, rather than a minimum, of pain and bitterness.

Conversely, couples in which one partner is bisexual may become caught in the political crossfire between the biphobic gay
community and equally biphobic and homophobic straight society.
Despite changing attitudes, biphobia continues to be a potent
force. For example, given any good reason to do so, straight
spouses tend to be willing to consider more flexible marital contracts. Yet they are often given no such reason or any choice in the
matter. Their bisexual partners, feeling forced to choose between
two stereotypical life-styles and knowing that they can no longer
maintain the one, adopt the other, leaving their spouses with an
unnecessary sense of loss, rejection, and helplessness. When I
asked a gay psychologist what his major task with bisexual husbands was, he told me,

> Relieving . . . stigma. The husbands are often really homophobic,
> although they don't realize it. They dichotomize and act in ways that

they think gays are supposed to act. I try to help them realize that
their behaviors are stereotypes and have nothing at all to do with
gayness. There's nothing sadder to me than to see fifty-year-old men
suddenly start dressing like twenty-year-olds, trying to change their
entire personality and project a gay swinger image, and, for no reason whatsoever except for their own stereotypes and guilt, insist on
riding off into the sunset and leaving long and perfectly happy marriages.

Isolation and Stigmatization of the Heterosexual Partner

One would expect that it would be the gay partners who are
isolated and stigmatized. And so they are. But once the gay partners disclose their secret to their spouses, the burden of stigma
descends immediately and heavily on the straight spouses. Indeed,
gay partners who disclosed their secret only after finding a support
system to help them often report that the disclosure (when coupled
with a spouse's positive response) has all but released them from
the sense of stigma. In such cases, it is often the straight partner
who is left to carry the bulk of that burden. How can that be?

It works this way. If society stigmatizes and subjugates people
who do not conform to expected norms, it has slowly been able to
tolerate and at times even accept them. What it finds almost impossible to understand, however, is why someone "normal" would
voluntarily stand up for, identify with, and even go so far as to love
and marry a "deviant."

A parent loving and fighting for the rights of a mentally disabled child? A wife loving and staying with a husband who returns
from a war disabled? Such devotion is understandable, even pra-
iseworthy. But healthy young people dating and even marrying
paraplegics—who, according to our stereotypes, are asexual? A
white person in a majority white society marrying a black person?
A Christian converting to Judaism? Why would people place themselves in such stigmatized positions?

Society finds only one "rational" reason. Such people must
have something wrong with them. They are themselves inferior or
sick. They suffer from low self-esteem; they are martyrs; they are

closeted members of the group; they are afraid to be with "health-ier" people; they are for some reason unacceptable to others and unable to do any better; they themselves have caused the other person's "deformity." The list of reasons goes on, changing to fit the stereotypes about the minority in question.

And so it is with this situation, as suggested in the statements and assumptions cited at the beginning of this chapter. For ex-ample, no matter whether the disclosure and response have been positive or negative, straight wives (who, after all, are part of straight society) report quickly being overwhelmed with a barrage of conflicting thoughts, reflecting, in large measure, such atti-tudes. How did I get in this situation? What does it say about me that I'm in this situation? What will it say about me if I stay? If I leave? Why did he choose me? Why did I choose him? Am I myself a latent lesbian? Wasn't I sexy enough? Am I too masculine? Too feminine? How could I not know? Am I stupid? If I stay or I'm willing to change the contract to meet his needs, am I being flex-ible and understanding or just another sucker who's denying real-ity? If I leave, feel anger, or refuse to change our contract, am I assertive or homophobic and rigid? Why can't I make up my mind? What's wrong with me? *What would others think of me if they knew?*

These are only a few of the questions straight wives ask them-selves. Some of them are not so different from those wives ask when their heterosexual husbands are unfaithful. But here isola-tion sets in. Wives with unfaithful heterosexual husbands have books and articles to read, understanding confidantes, and knowl-edgeable professionals to turn to. Despite confusion and humilia-tion, they know or learn quickly that they are not alone.

Until recently, however, there was practically no literature on mixed-orientation marriages to be found either for the couples themselves or for their therapists to read. In my own research (Gochros 1989), wives reported that, when they asked themselves, "Who can I turn to and what will people think of me?" the answers they gave themselves convinced them that they were unique and alone, that they and their husbands would become the objects of pity and scorn, and that they would lose the support system they already had if their secret were to be revealed. Hence, the internal dialogue continued, with wives feeling increasingly isolated and confused. The gay community had at least helped the husbands face their homosexual feelings. It had not helped the wives.

Despite better help available, wives are often still too fearful to utilize that help. For example, they were often told, "Well, if you weren't so assertive . . . ," "If you weren't working . . . ," They were asked, "What's it like living with a man who can't have sex with you?" "How could you stay with someone like that?" "How could you not know? I knew it all along!" "Why can't you just be understanding? He's your husband!" "If you're unhappy, why don't you just leave?" "If you love your husband and he wants to stay married, why are you so unhappy?" "What's the problem? It sounds pretty simple to me." "You should be happy it isn't another woman." "Wow! And I thought I had it bad. At least my husband was normal." And so on.

Professionals' responses were hardly more enlightened. Many women reported being immediately asked such questions as, "How long have you been attracted to gay men?" "Was there spouse abuse, child abuse, or sexual abuse in your family?" Many therapists have stated to me incorrect and unyieldingly biased notions about wives of gay men, even when they had never treated such women. The gay community has also often been harmful instead of helpful, labeling wives *fag hags* and husbands who elect to stay married *cowards*.

As for the husbands, even the caring ones were often so unable to cope with their guilt about having hurt their wives and so busy trying to liberate themselves from their own sense of shame about homosexuality that they did not even realize what was actually happening with the wives, much less provide help. Hence, an ironic set of syndromes came into play, combining male chauvinism and what I call *liberation ethics*. Husbands assumed that it was their right, either as males or as an oppressed minority, to meet their needs as they saw fit and that their wives' duty, as females or symbolic oppressors, was to support them regardless. Heretofore thoughtful and loving men became completely insensitive to their wives' feelings, needs, and rights. For example, misinterpreting grief, confusion, or anger as homophobia, they accused their wives of being crybabies, of being aggressive, of laying "guilt trips" on them, of removing themselves both emotionally and physically.

When dealing with "normal" marriage problems, any reputable therapist would be able to separate issues and help the couple avoid such traps. Social stereotypes have clouded the issues involved in this particular marriage problem, and many therapists add to rather than alleviate the stigmatization. Although both partners suffer, husbands at least have access to literature on the subject and support from the gay community. Straight wives, however, have been left alone to cope in days, weeks, or months with the same sense of stigma and isolation that husbands have taken many years even to face, much less overcome. Out of 103 wives I interviewed, not one did not cite stigmatization and isolation as either the worst or one of the worst problems she faced.

Of course the situation has improved greatly since the time of my study. Support groups have sprung up across the country, therapists have become more understanding, television talk shows have at least made the situation more visible, and some excellent books have recently appeared. Those books, however, are often found mainly in gay or feminist bookstores and are neither well publicized nor circulated. Straight partners are often unaware of the literature or are too embarrassed to go into such shops or to ask in more traditional bookstores. The orchestrated hostility of talk-show audiences could certainly deter husbands from being honest or wives from confiding in others. I continually receive letters from people without access to support groups or therapists. And attitudes still have a long way to grow.

For example, there is growing evidence that, like earlier interracial and interfaith marriages, many of these pioneer marriages in which one partner is gay can work and be happy given competent help and a supportive environment. Yet, like an earlier couple in my research, one couple recently reported that, after asking their marriage counselor if he thought such marriages were viable, they were told absolutely not, that he had never seen one work, that he knew of no other therapist who would disagree with him, but that if they still wished counseling from him they were welcome to try.

(One can only hope that they had the good sense to find another, more supportive and knowledgeable counselor.)

Do straight husbands of lesbian or bisexual wives fare any better? Myths abound that they are completely unable to cope with the situation and respond with violence. There is little way to know. Such husbands are almost totally ignored, with neither research nor advocates to speak for them. Most of the husbands I have seen, however, have been as supportive and flexible as their female counterparts and for the most part have received the same insensitivity as straight wives. The labels may be different: the wives may be called *bitches* and the husbands *wimps*. The effect, however, is the same. It is almost as if gay/bisexual partners (and the gay community) still maintain a self-deprecating and Woody Allen stance that "anyone who would have me for a partner can't be worth having."

Whether or not marriages stay together, straight spouses are left with a sense of confusion and loss. They are confused about what is real and what is not, what homosexuality means to the partner, how to evaluate not only the past but also the future. Ironically, San Francisco provides an analogy—not because of its gay community, but because mixed-orientation marriages and San Francisco are both earthquake zones. One can never know what the future will bring, but earthquakes are always a danger. Will they be big or small? Was that sound a tremor or just imagination? Wives express this uncertainty in such questions as, "Was my marriage a sham?" "If he never loved me and I never perceived it, how do I know it won't happen again?" "How can I trust that he really loves me?" "How do I trust my own perceptions?" Loss of a past relationship or a loved one is difficult. But to lose faith in one's own perceptions is to lose one's sense of self and one's future.

Children

Whether they are told or not, children can hardly help but be caught in the crossfire since divorce on the grounds of one partner's homosexuality or bisexuality often involves bitter custody suits. Teenagers and young adults report torn loyalties, feeling stigmatized, panicking whenever they experience the sexual difficulties that commonly occur in achieving adulthood, and feeling forced to cope alone with their own conflicts and with the homophobic jokes and comments they hear from their peers.

The Impact of AIDS

Just when such gay/bisexual men began to think it was safe to come out of the closet, a new *Jaws* appeared to send them scurrying back in. Its name is *AIDS*. It is a masterpiece of understatement to note that both the fear and the actuality of losing one's husband or still-loved ex-husband, one's children, even one's own life to such a debilitating and fatal disease is devastating.

Interestingly enough, AIDS has not seemed to change either husbands' or wives' reactions to each other—it has simply highlighted the problems that already exist and given infidelity more serious consequences. Women's reaction to the news of both bisexuality and infection continues to depend on the way the husband has dealt with the situation, not on their own homophobia. In four years of working directly with patients at risk for AIDS, I have still met comparatively few true "heels" and many caring, responsible husbands whose wives (and sometimes ex-wives) have responded to them in caring, responsible ways. To date there seems no reason for panic. The number of AIDS infections from bisexual spouses or partners is amazingly low.

Yet such low figures are so amazing that I cannot help but suspect that homophobia has contributed to poor research. Reports of a rise in deaths from "respiratory" ailments of middle-aged divorced or widowed women in AIDS-prone cities only (Kaspar 1989) lead me to wonder if we have simply been so blind to the possibilities that we have not asked the right questions. Until recently, men being tested for the HIV virus were not asked their marital status, nor was there much effort to distinguish between several possible factors in the Center for Disease Control's category *heterosexually transmitted infection*. The major factor in women's infection appears to be intravenous drug use. But many women, even if asked about their husbands' sexual orientation, would not know the correct answer.

If I see many men who are honest and act responsibly about

infection or potential infection and few who knowingly risk wom-
en's lives, I also see the equivalent of the same pre-AIDS "good
guys" taking the same pre-AIDS disastrous routes discussed earlier. Whether they spread AIDS or not, they are setting the next
generation up for a repeat of history. In panic, they tell me that
they are seeking religious conversions to cure their homosexual
urges, are desperately seeking a woman to marry so as to avoid
AIDS, and are being tested to make sure they are "clean for a
woman" as their way of taking responsibility. I see men who, afraid
to start using condoms, use any excuse possible to avoid sex and
any affection that might lead to sex with their wives while awaiting
HIV test results.

There is anecdotal evidence that one can predict how men will
cope with HIV infection by the way in which they have coped with
homosexuality. My own experience supports that evidence and
suggests that acknowledging homosexuality is often the biggest
hurdle. I see men who would divorce or kill themselves and who
confess to heterosexual affairs, hiring prostitutes, and using drugs
rather than admit to their wives that they have had homosexual
experiences. We have already seen how such deception hurts
wives even when AIDS is not a factor. Despite changing attitudes,
if one or both partners develop AIDS, society's general inability to
deal with homosexuality in marriage creates even more serious
problems.

For example, helping professionals who work with HIV-
infected people (therapists, support group leaders, physicians,
etc.) are generally supportive of gays and are often gay themselves.
Their skillful and vigorous leadership helps frightened people discuss such sensitive issues as sex, death, and suicide. Yet many are
reluctant to provide the same help when a husband is known to be
or suspected of being gay or bisexual. Not only do they fail to
broach the subject; they may not even realize that help is needed
or wanted with this problem. They assume that AIDS itself takes
priority and that discussion of problems with sexual orientation is
unnecessary unless specifically requested.

I find, however, that failure to deal with homosexuality actually
impedes and sometimes prevents people's ability to cope with

AIDS. *Not* to open doors for closeted people is like a doctor refusing to notice or discuss patients' obviously broken legs until the patients themselves have provided their own diagnoses and insisted on help. This form of homophobia is especially tragic when it affects AIDS counseling, for it negates the sense of acceptance that most AIDS professionals try to convey. The implicit message here is that to practice homosexuality during marriage is worse than AIDS or death and that to be a homosexual or bisexual spouse and to have married, or that to have married a gay/bisexual man, is literally an unspeakable crime. As one young mother with AIDS said to me, "What makes me feel most angry and isolated is that nobody will mention homosexuality. I can read. I know that not *all* women in my support group were infected from transfusions. I think my husband was lying. But I don't know why he lied or why he suddenly rejected me. I don't know, if he was gay, if I caused it. I feel like such a fool, I hate to face each day. And if nobody else can talk about homosexuality, how can I?"

Given enough time, such a wife may somehow be able to heal her emotional hurt herself. But when she has AIDS, she may not have the luxury of time. By the time that young mother and her family had been offered the help needed to face the almost certain bisexuality of her deceased husband, to address their concerns, to separate appropriate grief and anger from homophobia, and to get on with the business of coping with AIDS and enjoying what was left of her life, she had only two months left to live.

Summary

Homophobia has created both direct and indirect problems not only for gay, lesbian, and bisexual men and women who marry but also for their straight spouses, their children, and their families. Far more than simply creating untenable marriages that end in divorce, it has created such a complex set of intrapsychic and interpersonal problems for both partners that this essay has barely begun to enumerate them.

Homophobia may interfere with a couple's ability to form an honest, caring, and intimate marital relationship even if the issue of homosexuality is never raised. Prior to disclosure, it may create guilt and fear, damaging straight partners' self-esteem as they helplessly try to grapple with undefined problems. Following disclosure, it stigmatizes straight partners, creating self-doubt and guilt, loss of self-identity and self-trust. Whether because of anticipated or actual homophobic and sexist reactions from others, straight partners become isolated, forced into a closet within a closet. They become increasingly confused and depressed and either have no access to or are afraid to join a support system.

Finally, even professional counselors, lacking information and often homophobic or sexist themselves, are often unable to provide the competent help they provide others and may unwittingly add to the sense of stigmatization. Without the support available to other couples, without information or guidelines for behavior, often caught in the crossfire between opposing political forces and still struggling with guilt themselves, it is not surprising that many gay, lesbian, and bisexual spouses often fail even to recognize, much less respond sensitively to, their straight spouses' or childrens' needs. Hence, many good marriages fail because of society's unwillingness and inability to provide adequate help. What is surprising is that some marriages work and even flourish despite the hostile environment.

Solutions

Finding solutions to complex problems is not easy, but we can do much to provide a more supportive environment for such couples. Whether we are men or women, straight, gay, or "somewhere in between," whether we act as individuals or collectively, we are all part of a racist, sexist, and homophobic world. Like it or not, we all inherit and to some extent maintain the hurtful attitudes of such a world; we are all both victims and oppressors. We all bear responsibility for trying to understand others and change ourselves. What can we do?

We can try to understand the plight of both partners in this situation and to use that new understanding to help create better solutions. We can share our own feelings, needs, and confusions, truly listen to one another and help ease others' pain with empathy rather than pity or criticism. Professional "helpers" can become more knowledgeable about and innovative in finding ways to share expertise and to collaborate in providing services. The mass media can become more concerned in its news coverage and more flexible in its policies on public service announcements. Television talk-show hosts can refrain from exploiting homophobia to stir audience interest. Gay organizations can be more responsive to such couples and to straight spouses. We can all, individually or as a group, speak out and do more to counteract the upsurge of oppressive forces in our society today. And we can all open closet doors simply by our own willingness to learn, to grow, and to share our new insights with our children, friends, families, and colleagues.

REFERENCES

Gochros, J. *When Husbands Come Out of the Closet*. New York: Haworth, 1989.

Kaspar, B. "Women and AIDS: A Psychosocial Perspective." *Affilia* 4 no. 4 (1989): 2–22.

Kinsey, A., W. Pomeroy, and C. Martin. *Sexual Behavior in the Human Male*. Philadelphia: W. B. Saunders, 1948.

Klein, Fred. *The Bisexual Option*. New York: Arbor, 1978.

Reinisch, J. "The Prevalence of AIDS Risk Related to Sexual Behaviors among White Middle-Class Urban American Adults: A Survey of Research from Kinsey to the Present." Paper presented at the V International Conference on AIDS, Montreal, 1989.

Ross, M. *The Married Homosexual Man*. London: Routledge & Kegan Paul, 1983.

PART THREE

OTHER SOCIETAL MANIFESTATIONS OF HOMOPHOBIA

9

Appearances

CARMEN VÁZQUEZ

North of Market Street and east of Twin Peaks, where you can see the white fog mushroom above San Francisco's hills, is a place called the Castro. Gay men, lesbians, and bisexuals stroll leisurely up and down the bustling street. They jaywalk with abandon. Night and day they fill the cafés and bars, and on weekends they line up for a double feature of vintage classics at their ornate and beloved Castro theater.

The 24 bus line brings people into and out of the Castro. People from all walks of life ride the electric-powered coaches. They come from the opulence of San Francisco's Marina and the squalor of Bayview projects. The very gay Castro is in the middle of its route. Every day, boys in pairs or gangs from either end of the city board the bus for a ride through the Castro and a bit of fun. Sometimes their fun is fulfilled with passionately obscene derision: "Fucking cocksucking faggots." "Dyke cunts." "Diseased butt fuckers." Sometimes, their fun is brutal.

Brian boarded the 24 Divisadero and handed his transfer to the driver one late June night. Epithets were fired at him the moment he turned for a seat. He slid his slight frame into an empty seat next to an old woman with silver blue hair who clutched her handbag and stared straight ahead. Brian stuffed his hands into the pockets of his worn brown bomber jacket and stared with her. He heard the flip of a skateboard in the back. The taunting shouts grew louder. "Faggot!" From the corner of his eye, he saw a beer bottle hurtling past the window and crash on the street. A man in his forties, wearing a Giants baseball cap and warmup jacket, yelled at the driver to stop the bus and get the hoodlums off. The bus driver ignored him and pulled out.

Brian dug his hands deeper into his pockets and clenched his jaw. It was just five stops to the top of the hill. When he got up to move toward the exit, the skate board slammed into his gut and one kick followed another until every boy had got his kick in. Despite the pleas of the passengers, the driver never called the police.

Brian spent a week in a hospital bed, afraid that he would never walk again. A lawsuit filed by Brian against the city states, "As claimant lay crumpled and bleeding on the floor of the bus, the bus driver tried to force claimant off the bus so that the driver could get off work and go home. Claimant was severely beaten by a gang of young men on the #24 Divisadero Bus who perceived that he was gay."

On the south side of Market Street, night brings a chill wind and rough trade. On a brisk November night, men with sculptured torsos and thighs wrapped in leather walked with precision. The clamor of steel on the heels of their boots echoed in the darkness. Young men and women walked by the men in leather, who smiled in silence. They admired the studded bracelets on Mickey's wrists, the shine of his flowing hair, and the rise of his laughter. They were, each of them, eager to be among the safety of like company where they could dance with abandon to the pulse of hard rock, the hypnotism of disco, or the measured steps of country soul. They looked forward to a few drinks, flirting with strangers, finding Mr. or Ms. Right or, maybe, someone to spend the night with.

At the end of the street, a lone black street lamp shone through the mist. The men in leather walked under the light and disappeared into the next street. As they reached the corner, Mickey and his friends could hear the raucous sounds of the Garden spill onto the street. They shimmied and rocked down the block and through the doors.

The Garden was packed with men and women in sweat-stained shirts. Blue smoke stung the eyes. The sour and sweet smell of beer hung in the air. Strobe lights pulsed over the dancers. Mickey pulled off his wash-faded black denim jacket and wrapped it around his waist. An iridescent blue tank top hung easy on his shoulders. Impatient with the wait for a drink, Mickey steered his girlfriend onto the crowded dance floor.

Reeling to the music and immersed in the pleasure of his rhythms, Mickey never saw the ice pick plunge into his neck. It was just a bump with a drunk yelling, "Lame-assed faggot." "Faggot. Faggot. Faggot. Punk faggot." Mickey thought it was a punch to the neck. He ran after the roaring drunk man for seven steps, then lurched and fell on the dance floor, blood gushing everywhere. His girlfriend screamed. The dance floor spun black.

Mickey was rushed to San Francisco General Hospital, where thirty-six stitches were used by trauma staff to close the wound on his neck. Doctors said the pick used in the attack against him was millimeters away from his spinal cord. His assailant, charged with attempted murder, pleaded innocent.

Mickey and Brian were unfortunate stand-ins for any gay man. Mickey was thin and wiry, a great dancer clad in black denim, earrings dangling from his ear. Brian was slight of build, wore a leather jacket, and boarded a bus in the Castro. Dress like a homo, dance like a homo, must be a homo. The homophobic fury directed at lesbians, gay men, and bisexuals in America most often finds its target. Ironclad evidence of sexual orientation, however, is not necessary for someone to qualify as a potential victim of deadly fury. Appearances will do.

The incidents described above are based on actual events reported to the San Francisco Police and Community United Against Violence (CUAV), an agency serving victims of antilesbian and antigay violence where I worked for four years. The names of the victims have been changed. Both men assaulted were straight.

Incidents of antilesbian and antigay violence are not uncommon or limited to San Francisco. A *San Francisco Examiner* survey estimates that over one million hate-motivated physical assaults take place each year against lesbians, gays, and bisexuals. The National Gay and Lesbian Task Force conducted a survey in 1984 that found that 94 percent of all lesbians and gay men surveyed reported being physically assaulted, threatened, or harassed in an antigay incident at one time or another. The great majority of these incidents go unreported.

To my knowledge, no agency other than CUAV keeps track of incidents of antigay violence involving heterosexuals as victims. An average of 3 percent of the over three hundred victims seen by CUAV each year identify as heterosexuals. This may or may not be an accurate gauge of the actual prevalence of antigay violence directed at heterosexuals. Most law enforcement agencies, including those in San Francisco, have no way of documenting this form of assault other than under a generic "harassment" code. The actual incidence of violence directed at heterosexuals that is motivated by homophobia is probably much higher than CUAV's six to nine victims a year. Despite the official paucity of data, however, it is a fact that incidents of antigay and antilesbian violence in which straight men and women are victimized do occur. Shelters for battered women are filled with stories of lesbian baiting of staff and of women whose husbands and boyfriends repeatedly called them "dykes" or "whores" as they beat them.[1] I have personally experienced verbal abuse while in the company of a straight friend, who was assumed to be my lover.

Why does it happen? I have no definitive answers to that question. Understanding homophobic violence is no less complex than understanding racial violence. The institutional and ideological reinforcements of homophobia are myriad and deeply woven into our culture. I offer one perspective that I hope will contribute to a better understanding of how homophobia works and why it threatens all that we value as humane.

At the simplest level, looking or behaving like the stereotypical gay man or lesbian is reason enough to provoke a homophobic assault. Beneath the veneer of the effeminate gay male or the butch dyke, however, is a more basic trigger for homophobic violence. I call it *gender betrayal*.

The clearest expression I have heard of this sense of gender betrayal comes from Doug Barr, who was acquitted of murder in an incident of gay bashing in San Francisco that resulted in the death of John O'Connell, a gay man. Barr is currently serving a prison sentence for related assaults on the same night that O'Connell was killed. He was interviewed for a special report on homophobia produced by ABC's "20/20" (10 April 1986). When asked what he and his friends thought of gay men, he said, "We hate homosexuals. They degrade our manhood. We was brought up in a high school where guys are football players, mean and macho. Homosexuals are sissies who wear dresses. I'd rather be seen as a football player."

Doug Barr's perspective is one shared by many young men. I have made about three hundred presentations to high school students in San Francisco, to boards of directors and staff of nonprofit organizations, and at conferences and workshops on the topic of homophobia or "being lesbian or gay." Over and over again, I have asked, "Why do gay men and lesbians bother you?" The most popular response to the question is, "Because they act like girls," or, "Because they think they're men." I have even been told, quite explicitly, "I don't care what they do in bed, but they shouldn't act like that."

They shouldn't act like that. Women who are not identified by their relationship to a man, who value their female friendships, who like and are knowledgeable about sports, or work as blue-collar laborers and wear what they wish are very likely to be "lesbian baited" at some point in their lives. Men who are not pursuing sexual conquests of women at every available opportunity, who disdain sports, who choose to stay at home and be a househusband, who are employed as hairdressers, designers, or housecleaners, or who dress in any way remotely resembling traditional female attire (an earring will do) are very likely to experience the taunts and sometimes the brutality of "fag bashing."

The straitjacket of gender roles suffocates many lesbians, gay men, and bisexuals, forcing them into closets without an exit and threatening our very existence when we tear the closet open. It also, however, threatens all heterosexuals unwilling to be bound by their assigned gender identity. Why, then, does it persist?

Suzanne Pharr's examination of homophobia as a phenomenon based in sexism and misogyny offers a succinct and logical explanation for the virulence of homophobia in Western civilization:

It is not by chance that when children approach puberty and increased sexual awareness they begin to taunt each other by calling these names: "queer," "faggot," "pervert." It is at puberty that the full force of society's pressure to conform to heterosexuality and prepare for marriage is brought to bear. Children know what we have taught them, and we have given clear messages that those who deviate from standard expectations are to be made to get back in line. . . .

To be named as lesbian threatens all women, not just lesbians, with great loss. And any woman who steps out of role risks being called a lesbian. To understand how this is a threat to all women, one must understand that any woman can be called a lesbian and there is no real way she can defend herself: there is no real way to credential one's sexuality. ("The Children's Hour," a Lillian Hellman play, makes this point when a student asserts two teachers are lesbians and they have no way to disprove it.) She may be married or divorced, have children, dress in the most feminine manner, have sex with men, be celibate—but there are lesbians who do all these things. *Lesbians look like all women and all women look like lesbians.*[2]

I would add that gay men look like all men and all men look like gay men. There is no guaranteed method for identifying sexual orientation. Those small or outrageous deviations we sometimes take from the idealized mystique of "real men" and "real women" place all of us—lesbians, gay men, bisexuals, and heterosexuals alike—at risk of violence, derision, isolation, and hatred.

It is a frightening reality. Dorothy Ehrlich, executive director of the Northern California American Civil Liberties Union (ACLU), was the victim of a verbal assault in the Castro several years ago. Dorothy lives with her husband, Gary, and her two children, Jill and Paul, in one of those worn and comfortable Victorian homes that grace so many San Francisco neighborhoods. Their home is several blocks from the Castro, but Dorothy recalls the many times she and Gary could hear, from the safety of their bedroom, shouts of "faggot" and men running in the streets.

When Jill was an infant, Gary and Dorothy had occasion to experience for themselves how frightening even the threat of homophobic violence can be. One foggy, chilly night they decided to go for a walk in the Castro. Dorothy is a small woman whom some might call petite; she wore her hair short at the time and delights in the comfort of jeans and oversized wool jackets. Gary is very tall and lean, a bespectacled and bearded cross between a professor and a basketball player who wears jean jackets and tweed jackets with the exact same slouch. On this night they were crossing Castro Street, huddled close together with Jill in Dorothy's arms. As they reached the corner, their backs to the street, they heard a truck rev its engine and roar up Castro, the dreaded "faggot" spewing from young men they could not see in the fog. They looked around them for the intended victims, but there was no one else on the corner with them. They who were the target that night: Dorothy and Gary and Jill. They were walking on "gay turf," and it was reason enough to make them a target. "It was so frightening," Dorothy said. "So frightening and unreal."

But it is real. The "20/20" report on homophobia ends with the story of Tom and Jan Matarrase, who are married, have a child, and lived in Brooklyn, New York, at the time of their encounter with homophobic violence. On camera, Tom and Jan are walking down a street in Brooklyn lined with brown townhouses and black wrought-iron gates. It is snowing, and, with hands entwined, they walk slowly down the street where they were assaulted. Tom is wearing a khaki trenchcoat, slacks, and loafers. Snowflakes melt into the tight dark curls on his head. Jan is almost his height, her short bobbed hair moving softly as she walks. She is wearing a black leather jacket, a red scarf, and burnt orange cords. The broadness of her hips and softness of her face belie the tomboy flavor of her carriage and clothes, and it is hard to believe that she was mistaken for a gay man. But she was.

They were walking home, holding hands and engrossed with each other. On the other side of the street, Jan saw a group of boys moving toward them. As the gang approached, Jan heard a distinct taunt meant for her and Tom: "Aw, look at the cute gay couple." Tom and Jan quickened their step, but it was too late. Before they could say anything, Tom was being punched in the face and slammed against a car. Jan ran toward Tom and the car, screaming desperately that Tom was her husband. Fists pummeled her face as well. Outnumbered and in fear for their lives, Tom yelled at Jan to please open her jacket and show their assailants that she was a woman. The beating subsided only when Jan was able to show her breasts.

For the "20/20" interview, Jan and Tom sat in the warmth of their living room, their infant son in Jan's lap. The interviewer asked them how they felt when people said they looked like a gay couple. "We used to laugh," they said. "But now we realize how heavy the implications are. Now we know what the gay community goes through. We had no idea how widespread it was. It's on every level."

Sadly, it *is* on every level. Enforced heterosexism and the pressure to conform to aggressive masculine and passive feminine roles place fag bashers and lesbian baiters in the same psychic prison with their victims, gay or straight. Until all children are free to realize their full potential, until all women and men are free from the stigma, threats, alienation, or violence that come from stepping outside their roles, we are all at risk.

The economic and ideological underpinnings of enforced heterosexism and sexism or any other form of systematic oppression are formidable foes and far too complex for the scope of this essay. It is important to remember, however, that bigots are natural allies and that poverty or the fear of it has the power to seduce us all into conformity. In Castro graffiti, *faggot* appears right next to *nigger* and *kike*. Race betrayal or any threat to the sanctimony of light-skinned privilege engenders no less a rage than gender betrayal, most especially when we have a great stake in the elusive privilege of proper gender roles or the right skin color. *Queer lover* and *fag hag* are cut from the same mold that gave us *nigger lover*, a mold forged by fears of change and a loss of privilege.

Unfortunately, our sacrifices to conformity rarely guarantee the privilege or protection we were promised. Lesbians, gay men, and bisexuals who have tried to pass know that. Heterosexuals who have been perceived to be gay know that. Those of us with a vision of tomorrow that goes beyond tolerance to a genuine celebration of humanity's diversity have innumerable fronts to fight on. Homophobia is one of them.

But how will this front be won? With a lot of help, and not easily. Challenges to homophobia and the rigidity of gender roles must go beyond the visible lesbian and gay movement. Lesbians, gay men, and bisexuals alone cannot defuse the power of stigmatization and the license it gives to frighten, wound, or kill. Literally millions of us are needed on this front, straight and gay alike. We invite any heterosexual unwilling to live with the damage that "real men" or "real women" messages wreak on them, on their children, and on lesbians, gay men, and bisexuals to join us. We ask that you not let queer jokes go unchallenged at work, at home, in the media, or anywhere. We ask that you foster in your children a genuine respect for themselves and their right to be who and what they wish to be, regardless of their gender. We ask that you embrace your daughter's desire to swing a bat or be a carpenter, that you nurture your son's efforts to express affection and sentiment. We ask that you teach your children how painful and destructive words like *faggot* or *bulldyke* are. We ask that you invite your lesbian, gay, and bisexual friends and relatives into the routine of your lives without demanding silence or discretion from them. We invite you to study our history, read the literature written by our people, patronize our businesses, come into our homes and neighborhoods. We ask that you give us your vote when we need it to protect our privacy or to elect open lesbians, gay men, and bisexuals to office. We ask that you stand with us in public demonstrations to demand our right to live as free people, without fear. We ask that you respect our dignity by acting to end the poison of homophobia.

Until individuals are free to choose their roles and be bound only by the limits of their own imagination, *faggot, dyke,* and *pervert* will continue to be playground words and adult weapons that hurt and limit far many more people than their intended victims. Whether we like it or not, the romance of virile men and dainty women, of Mother, Father, Dick, Jane, Sally, and Spot is doomed to extinction and dangerous in a world that can no longer meet the expectations conjured by history. There is much to be won and so little to lose in the realization of a world where the dignity of each person is worthy of celebration and protection. The struggle to end homophobia can and must be won, for all our sakes. Personhood is imminent.

NOTE

1. See Suzanne Pharr, *Homophobia: A Weapon of Sexism* (Inverness, Calif.: Chardon, 1988).
2. Ibid., 17–19.

10

Lesbian Baiting as Sexual Harassment: Women in the Military

MICHELLE M. BENECKE
AND KIRSTIN S. DODGE

Military men, from the bottom ranks to the top, don't want women in their midst and the most expedient way to get rid of women—whether they can be gay women or married heterosexuals with children—is to pin them with the label "lesbian."

—*LISA M. KEEN*, Washington Blade (*10 March 1989*)

I thank God every day that I'm a male Marine in this male Marine Corps. . . . If a woman Marine is a little too friendly, she's a slut. If she doesn't smile at all, she's a dyke. I personally believe that a woman Marine in the normal course of a day confronts more stress and more bullshit than a male Marine would in twenty years.

—*CAPTAIN GUY RICHARDSON*, The Progressive (*March 1989*)

Where sexism and homophobia meet, you get a viciousness the likes of which you have never seen.

—*SANDRA LOWE*, Yale University (*28 October 1989*)

For most people, the assertion that homophobia and sexism are prevalent in the military comes as no surprise. Less well known is the degree to which these prejudices combine with the military policy barring homosexuals from the services to cultivate

167

and justify the harassment and intimidation of military women, lesbian and straight. The threat of being called a lesbian and the professional consequences of this label force military women to remain silent when they are harassed, to modify the way they dress, speak, and act, and to refrain from building too strong or obvious bonds of solidarity with one another.

"Lesbian baiting" is the practice of pressuring and harassing women through calling, or threatening to call them, lesbians. The consequences of lesbian baiting can be severe for military women. The military bars homosexuals from service, stating,

> Homosexuality is incompatible with military service. The presence in the military environment of persons who engage in homosexual conduct or who, by their statements, demonstrate a propensity to engage in homosexual conduct, seriously impairs the accomplishment of the military mission. The presence of such members adversely affects the ability of the Military Services to maintain discipline, good order, and morale; to foster mutual trust and confidence among servicemembers, to ensure the integrity of the system of rank and command; to facilitate assignment and worldwide deployment of servicemembers who frequently must live and work under close conditions affording minimal privacy; to recruit and retain members of the Military Services; to maintain the public acceptability of military service; and to prevent breaches of security.[1]

The military criminalizes homosexual conduct,[2] and women who are alleged to be lesbians face the real possibility not only of having their professional reputations tarnished but also of losing their careers and even their liberty.

During the 1980s, a wave of antilesbian investigations swept through ships and military installations. These included investigations on board the USS *Norton Sound,* resulting in the discharge of eight women sailors in 1980; the hospital ship *Sanctuary* and the USS *Dixon;* the Army's ouster of eight female military police officers from the U.S. Military Academy at West Point in 1986; the investigation of thirty women, including every African-American woman, on board the destroyer-tender USS *Yellowstone,* which re-

sulted in the discharge of eight women; and the 1988 investigation
of five of the thirteen female crewmembers on board the USS
Grapple. One of the most infamous investigations took place at the
Marine recruit installation at Parris Island, South Carolina, where
over half the 246 women at the base were questioned about alleged
homosexual activities.[3] Sixty-five women were eventually discharged or chose to resign or accept voluntary discharges rather
than face extensive investigations, the possibility of criminal
charges, and the emotional and financial costs of salvaging their
careers.[4] Three women were actually imprisoned for engaging in
homosexual activities.[5]

While the DOD policy on homosexuality does not distinguish
between male and female servicemembers, recent reports indicate
that women are discharged from the military services at a rate ten
times that of men.[6] The different investigative methods used to
target women and men may account for this disparity. Men are
typically investigated on a case-by-case basis, and allegations of
male homosexuality tend to be handled quietly, with efforts made
to usher the men involved out of the service as quickly as possible.[7]
In sharp contrast, women are often targeted and discharged as the
result of mass investigations,[8] which military women, their advocates, and the media refer to as *witchhunts*. As a standard interro-
gation technique in such investigations, women are forced to name
others who are or who might be lesbians in order to avoid prosecution or dishonorable discharge.

Women in the military who are most likely to be lesbian baited
are those who serve in nontraditional jobs, regardless of their actual sexual orientation.[9] Current examples of women holding nontraditional jobs include mechanics, system maintenance special-
ists, heavy equipment operators, pilots, and drill instructors.
Nontraditional job sites include Navy ships, Army field units, Air
Force flight lines, and the Marines. By contrast, traditional positions include clerk-typist, supply, personnel, and medical specialties. Women in nontraditional jobs are targeted in part because the
traits necessary for success in those jobs often coincide with stereotypical ideas about lesbians as aggressive, tough women.[10] For example, women in units that train outdoors for long periods of time

without basic comforts such as running water or those who operate dangerous machinery often wear their hair short for convenience and safety. Women in leadership positions depend on an assertive style to maintain authority. The strength to perform heavy manual labor is often a requirement for nontraditional jobs. Women who were targeted in the Parris Island investigation clearly recognize and describe this phenomenon: "The qualities and traits that we demand and are supposed to be training [into] our recruits are the same traits that they're saying make us look homosexual; I think the big picture is that our femininity is in question here because we're doing the job we were brought down here to do. . . . They don't like the way some of us look."[11]

Lesbian baiting of servicewomen and the military's antihomosexual policy hurt all servicewomen, not just lesbians. The policy helps create and support an environment in which all women are at high risk for sexual and emotional harassment. In addition, servicewomen's daily behavior is confined and controlled through the internalization of coping mechanisms that they adopt to ward off hostility and reduce the danger of being called *lesbian*.

Lesbian baiting is tied to sexual harassment of military women in that it is often triggered by a servicewoman's refusal of sexual advances. For example, one officer told of sexual advances made by a male peer toward her and two women colleagues. All three made it clear that they were not interested in pursuing a sexual relationship. Soon after, they learned that the spurned officer was suggesting to other men in the unit that the three were lesbians and were engaging in sexual acts together.[12]

In some respects, situations of this sort follow the typical pattern of sexual harassment.[13] The difference in the military is the degree of pressure that can be brought to bear against a woman not only by her superiors but also by her peers and, in the case of a woman officer or noncommissioned officer, by her subordinates. The legitimation of lesbian baiting arms all men with a tool for sexual harassment. To avoid the harsh consequences of being labeled *lesbian*, many women who become the focus of unwanted attentions from male servicemembers "will either backtrack from their assertiveness or comply sexually."[14]

While not all servicemen seek to extort sexual compliance from their female peers through such methods, those who do are extremely dangerous to servicewomen. A common maxim in the military is that a woman must be three times as good as a man to be recognized and absolutely above reproach. Given the small size of the community in a particular specialty and branch, a single allegation can haunt a woman throughout her career.

Recourse for women faced with lesbian baiting or sexual harassment is limited. This is especially true when women serve under sexist leaders, a situation that is likely to occur in nontraditional jobs.[15] Women in the military are in a particularly vulnerable position with regard to sexual harassment by those within their "chain of command" or successive hierarchy of leaders. A woman's superiors have control over virtually every aspect of her life. They can give her extra duties, charge her with disciplinary infractions, and write poor evaluations into her file. Servicewomen cannot simply leave their jobs: only a woman's command has the power to release or reassign her. A woman who reports abuse is likely to be "labeled as . . . not being a team player,"[16] an extremely degrading pronouncement in the military.[17] One sailor recounts her experiences thus: "Those times when I did move to make official reports, I met hostility and reluctance to believe that incidents like these could happen aboard such a fine vessel."[18] In addition, because of the military's antihomosexual policy, a woman who reports lesbian-baiting harassment risks focusing increased scrutiny on herself, which may lead to full-blown investigation.[19] As a result, many women are reluctant to report incidents, and many accede to sexual demands.[20]

The practical consequences of lesbian baiting to women in the military are extreme. Servicewomen in nontraditional jobs expend an enormous amount of energy seeking to walk the fine line between effective competence and nonthreatening femininity; they must be feminine enough to reduce harassment but not too feminine; otherwise they risk being considered inferior or incompetent. Because of the threat of harassment against women who associate together in groups, servicewomen cannot even turn to each other for relief and support in the face of this daily challenge.

Women quickly learn the restrictions on their behavior. This education often takes place informally, for example, listening to their male peers speculating about other women:

> To put it delicately, the talk is directed to determining the answer to the question "does she or doesn't she?" At first those set on categorizing the woman have nothing to go on but their first impressions of her appearance; but that is enough. "Is she or isn't she too pretty to be queer." Does she wear makeup, have short hair, prefer flat shoes to heels? Has she gone to bed yet with anyone we know?[21]

In an attempt to counter such speculation, many women adjust their appearance and behavior. In a recent sociological study, one researcher noted a "hyperfemininity" among many women Marines that resulted from their efforts to counteract assumptions that they were all lesbians.[22]

This need to cultivate one's femininity directly conflicts with the need to avoid supervisors' perceptions that feminine women are incompetent or inferior to men.[23] Women in nontraditional jobs are newcomers to a system that was created by men for men. Thus, when women are evaluated by superiors, it is "on the men's terms rather than on their terms or even on 'human,' androgynous terms."[24] Women complain that evaluative categories such as *forcefulness* are often euphemisms for *masculinity*.[25] A supervisor who perceives any sign of femininity, or even femaleness, as signs of weakness or inferiority will not consider women "up to snuff."[26] The result is poor performance evaluations for the servicewomen under such leadership.

The balancing act in which servicewomen must engage is crucial not only to the reduction of the threat of harassment in their daily lives but also to their advancement within the military. When promotion boards are given servicemembers' files and evaluations, "the first thing they see when they open a file is a photograph."[27] To those who have served on such boards, and to those who observe patterns of promotion, it is clear that women must be attractive and feminine looking to succeed in the military. If a woman is too pretty, however, evaluators will not take her seriously. A woman must look athletic, but not too "jockish," to avoid the suspicion that she may be a lesbian.[28]

Women of color are especially hard hit by the underlying dynamics of the military system.[29] Promotion boards are likely to be composed of white men whose perceptions are often tainted by racism as well as sexism. Because of this, the records of women of color on their way up the ranks will tend to be scrutinized more closely and with greater skepticism than those of white women.[30] One former officer, an African-American male, who has prepared and observed many promotion boards went as far as to state, "If you're a black gal, you can hang it up" with regard to promotion decisions.[31] This may in part explain why women of color are underrepresented in the officers corps[32] and why women of color above the grade of 03 (analogous to mid-level management positions) are almost nonexistent.[33] When women of color seek each other out and spend time together, their smaller numbers may open them to special scrutiny and thus to greater danger of investigation.

Rather than turning to each other for support, solidarity, and assistance in learning successfully to negotiate a path through the stresses of their daily lives, servicewomen are forced to remain largely isolated from one another because of the tendency of women in groups to trigger lesbian-baiting harassment and investigations. Guilt by association makes women especially shun lesbians or women who fit the traditional stereotypes.[34] The damage resulting from "the consequent emotional isolation for military women, especially when they are in a small minority, as aboard a ship, can scarcely be overstated."[35]

NOTES

I would like to acknowledge the military leaders who treat women in their units fairly. Despite many difficult times, I had the good fortune to serve under several exceptional men in a field where hostility toward women is still pervasive. M.M.B.

1. 32 C.F.R. pt. 41, app. A, pt. 1.H (1989). A recent Department of Defense (DOD) study questions the need for the policy (see Theodore R. Sarbin and Kenneth E. Karols, "Nonconforming Sexual Ori-

entations and Military Suitability," Defense Personnel Security Research and Education Center, PERS-TR-89–002 [December 1988]). For more information about the performance and suitability of gay and lesbian servicemembers, see Michael A. McDaniel, "Preservice Adjustment of Homosexual and Heterosexual Military Accessions: Implications for Security Clearance Suitability," Defense Personnel Security Research and Education Center, PERS-TR-89–004 (January 1989). (Copies of these two reports may be obtained through the office of U.S. Representative Gerry E. Studds [D-Mass.]).

2. 10 U.S.C. 925, Art. 125 (1988) (sodomy); 10 U.S.C. 933 (1988) (conduct unbecoming an officer and gentleman); 10 U.S.C. 934, Art. 134 90 (1988) (indecent acts with another) (Uniform Code of Military Justice).

3. Jim Lynch, "Witch Hunt at Parris Island," *The Progressive* (March 1989), 26.

4. *ACLU News*, ACLU press release, 29 December 1989 (on file with the authors); Lisa M. Keen, "Board Advises Discharge for Woman with Lesbian Friend," *Washington Blade* (3 March 1989), 9. See also Testimony of Mary Beth Harrison, Defense Advisory Committee on Women in the Services (DACOWITS) 1988 Spring Conference, 16–20 April 1988 (on file with the authors) (hereafter cited as Harrison Testimony).

5. Telephone interview with Captain Kozloski, public affairs officer, Marine Corps Recruit Training Depot at Parris Island, 5 February 1990.

6. "Court Overturns Conviction of Female Marine in Sex Case," *New York Times* (19 February 1990); "Gay Groups Suggest Marines Selectively Prosecute Women," *New York Times*, (4 December 1988).

7. See, e.g., Bob Baker, "Marine Told to Prove He's Gay to Get Discharge," *Los Angeles Times* (9 October 1985).

8. Telephone interview with Sue Hyde, National Gay and Lesbian Task Force, 16 October 1989.

9. Kathy Gilberd, "Both Lesbians and Straight Women Face 'Witch-hunts,'" *The Objector* (October 1987), 10.

10. For a more thorough explanation of the causes of lesbian baiting and its prevalence in nontraditional jobs, see Michelle M. Benecke and Kirstin S. Dodge, "Military Women in Nontraditional Job Fields: Casualties of the Armed Forces' War on Homosexuals," *Harvard Women's Law Journal* 13 (1990): 215.

11. "Marines Are Said to Suspend Alleged Lesbians," *New York Times* (23 February 1988).

12. Interview with military officer, December 1989. Throughout the remainder of this piece, we cite two interviews with military officers who, for their own safety and the sake of their careers, felt the need

to remain anonymous and requested omission of the details of their locations, branches, and specialties.

13. See generally Catharine A. MacKinnon, *Sexual Harassment of Working Women* (New Haven, Conn.: Yale University Press, 1979); Barbara A. Gutek, *Sex and the Workplace* (San Francisco: Jossey-Bass, 1985).

14. Lisa M. Keen, "Women Are Separated from Military at a Higher Rate," *Washington Blade* (3 March 1989) (quoting Vicki Almquist, Women's Equity Action League).

15. Anonymous interview.

16. Linda Grant De Pauw, "Gender as Stigma: Probing Some Sensitive Issues," *Minerva* (Spring 1988): 34 (quoting from a letter written to her by an Air Force Equal Employment Opportunity officer with twenty years' experience).

17. Anonymous interview.

18. Harrison Testimony, 4.

19. Keen, "Women Are Separated from Military."

20. Interview with Vicki Almquist, Women's Equity Action League in Washington, D.C., 10 November 1989; anonymous interviews.

21. De Pauw, "Gender as Stigma," 33.

22. Christine L. Williams, *Gender Differences at Work: Women and Men in Nontraditional Occupations* (Berkeley and Los Angeles: University of California Press, 1989), 6.

23. Ibid., 64, 67.

24. Mary Ann Tetreault, "Gender Belief Systems and the Integration of Women in the U.S. Military," *Minerva* (Spring 1988): 57 (citing Jeanne Holm, *Women in the Military: An Unfinished Revolution* [1982]); Judith Stiehm, "Women and the Combat Exception," *Parameters* 10 (1980): 156–57.

25. Williams, *Gender Differences at Work*, 68.

26. See ibid., 79.

27. Anonymous interview.

28. Anonymous interview.

29. We rely on personal experience, interviews, and anecdotes to piece together our assertions in this paragraph. It is extremely difficult to find statistical evidence for the disparate effect of military policies of women of color.

30. It is a risky proposition to seek to describe with any certainty the selection for and timing of promotions. It is a plausible assumption (based partly on our anonymous interviews) that factors such as appearance and military bearing that are based on a white male stan-

dard are even more difficult for many women of color to meet than for white women.

31. Anonymous interview.

32. As of September 1989, women of color (African-American, Latina, and "other/unknown" groups of women) constituted 37.9 percent of all women in the services but only 19.1 percent of women officers. Representation of African-Americans among women in various branches of the military ranged from a high of 43.3 percent in the Army to a low of 23.5 percent in the Air Force. In comparison, the representation of women of color among women officers ranged from a high of 19.19 percent in the Army to 11.3 percent in the Air Force. Overall, people of color constitute 28.7 percent of all military personnel but only 11 percent of all officers. (Telephone interview with Lt. Col. John Dyeski, Office of Assistant Secretary of Defense for Force Management and Personnel, Military Manpower and Personnel Policy, Officer and Enlisted Personnel Management, 23 February 1990.)

33. Almquist interview.

34. Gilberd, "Both Lesbians and Straight Women," 10.

35. De Pauw, "Gender as Stigma," 43.

11

Loving What Is Real: Toward an Inclusive Jewish Family

MARGARET HOLUB

What I remember most clearly about the synagogue of my youth is a running commentary—from whom I cannot recall—about what color Mrs. So-and-so's hair was that year. I also remember as a very young girl jumping out of the car at a stop sign and running down the street to avoid religious school. I cannot remember exactly what had me so upset that day, but my memories are full of the pretty girls, the popular girls, and of being absolutely miserable in the same classroom with them. Pervading the culture of that synagogue was a ruthless focus on externals—hair, clothes, makes and models of cars—and of course a sanctimonious veneration of the Jewish family as the reason Judaism had survived and the hope for Judaism's future. Real families mattered little. My mother, single and struggling, turned to that synagogue for spiritual and social support and was utterly shunned. As a young teenager full of questions and rebellion, I turned there too. I found nothing there that spoke to my heart, no truth, no justice, and no community that I could imagine being a part of.

The synagogue of my childhood did not invent this empty world. I am sure my neighbors found more or less the same thing when they went to the Episcopal or Methodist or Catholic churches of our neighborhood. And all of us certainly experienced this passion for surface conformity in our schools, businesses, and, above all, on television. Even the Jewish veneration of the idealized family was not specifically Jewish—heaven forbid we should actually do anything culturally specific, anything that would differentiate us from our non-Jewish neighbors. Our synagogue just gave in to the culture all around us. Folks there had the same infatuation with the glossy image of the attractive, white, upwardly mobile nuclear family and the same fear and revulsion of anything that did not conform to that American dream that was trumpeted by every instrument of American culture during those decades. Everyone was doing it, and just about everybody still is. But that does not make it right.

None of this has anything to do explicitly with gayness. I assure you I never heard the word until I was well into high school. In fact, I seem to be quite heterosexual, so being a lesbian has not been the issue for me personally. But it seems to me that hardly anybody fits into that view of the normative Jewish family that my childhood synagogue so unthinkingly and unfeelingly perpetuated. Very few of us came from married, monogamous parents, fewer still from families where there was not some alcoholism, some physical or sexual abuse, some other dark secret. Fewer still of us went to college, took up respectable professions (after all, there are only two—even the rabbinate is looked at as a little questionable), married other Jews, did not perpetuate the dysfunctions of our childhoods, stayed married, and sent our kids to Jewish camp. Yet who are our synagogue members these days? And who are our rabbis?

This fantasy of the normal Jewish family excludes practically everybody. This might be acceptable if the Jewish community were just some club you would not want to be a member of even if it did take the likes of you. But the rest of us Jews still get ill and die, still fall in love and want our unions honored, still have spiritual questions and struggles and need as much as the normal folks to make meaning of our lives. So it is not acceptable to cut us all out of Jewish life, even if the institutions could survive without us, which they can only in the most stunted form.

I am writing this essay just a few days after the Central Conference of American Rabbis, the professional union of Reform rabbis to which I belong, took the nominally historical step of voting to ordain and admit to the conference rabbis who are openly lesbian or gay. I am thrilled that it happened. In fact, with Rabbi Margaret Wenig, I drafted the original resolution that, years later, came out quite altered in the form of this decision. But the current decision to admit gay and lesbian rabbis is a footnote in a longer document. The same document, in its final incarnation, goes on to say, "In Jewish tradition heterosexual, monogamous, procreative marriage is the ideal human relationship for the perpetuation of the species, covenantal fulfillment and the preservation of the Jewish people."[1]

Ideal for whom? Apparently not for the large majority of us who are not in heterosexual, monogamous, procreative marriages—those of us who left such marriages when they were strangling us, who have chosen another life work than having children, who are concerned about the resources that those covenantal children consume over an American lifetime, who are lesbian or gay, or who simply see that there are a lot of ways to support the human species and the Jewish people besides getting married and having babies.

We All Need Models of Different Ways to Be

This would all be easier if every one of us who did not fit the fantasy were absolutely sure of ourselves and our paths. But it hardly ever happens that way. Being a child of my generation meant trying to measure up to Beaver Cleaver and the local cheerleaders, the youth arm of heterosexual, procreative monogamy. Heterosexual procreative monogamy is not just about who you sleep with. It is a whole vision of who we should be and never are.

Few children are inherently comfortable with their particulars. It takes a lot of support from our role models, both up close and in the larger culture, to help us love our ethnicity, our religion, our bodies, our minds. I realize now that my wonderful fourth-grade math and music teacher was probably a lesbian. But, as I have said, I never heard the word. How nice it would have been if she could have felt free to mention it now and then, to say to us, "Here I am, a healthy, happy, creative woman who loves other women. I'm a lesbian. Some of you probably are too. Enjoy it." We all needed lesbian models, bisexual models, gay male models, twice-married models, unmarried models, models in wheelchairs and models with epilepsy, models of different physical statures, races, experiences, and life-styles, to say to us, "There are many possibilities in life. Be yourself and be glad you are who you are."

Thank heavens the women's and the gay, lesbian, and bisexual movements have exposed some of the damage that this heterosexual, procreative, monogamous fantasy wreaks on every woman and man. There is at least a minority opinion heard these days that it is all right for a man to express a tender feeling, for a woman to get paid a decent wage and not get felt up by her boss. These new ideas represent a radical departure from the culture of my relatively recent youth. What stands out to me looking back to that time is that practically everyone around me was in some kind of closet. Thank heavens there is now some level of freedom to tell these secrets, if not in public, at least in your support group. It is a strange and painful world in which practically everybody feels like a deviant.

When I think about how homophobia harms heterosexuals— how it has harmed me—I think primarily of this blanket of silence thrown over everything that does not appear in "Father Knows Best." Homophobia is a part, a significant and pernicious part, of a larger conspiracy of silence that leaves us no tools for understanding, much less embracing, what is happening in our own lives. It is not just gayness but everything interesting, unique, and real that is hidden, making everyone who does not conform to some fantastic ideal feel like a freak.

These days I hear about programs that attempt to reach out to single Jews, usually to marry them off, and to intermarried couples, usually to persuade the non-Jewish member to raise Jewish children. With the increasing number of gay and lesbian synagogues around the country as a striking exception, there is remarkably little effort to open the organized Jewish community to anyone who does not fit the parameters of the fantasy. Jewish institutions continue to foist this fantasy of monogamous, procreative normality onto the whole rainbow of people who should be welcome within their walls but certainly are not.

Nice People and Hidden Homophobia

A couple of weeks ago I experienced some homophobia in a place where I would not have expected it. I am the rabbi of a small and, I dare say, very special Jewish community on the far northern coast of California. Many of the Jews here moved "back to the land" in the early 1970s and have been living lives very consciously informed by values of community, respect for the earth, and spirituality. Among the homesteaders of our community are many lesbians, and there is a prominent and impressive women's community here. A number of local lesbians are Jewish, including a few who participate actively and regularly in Jewish community activities. I have always appreciated the presence of these few lesbians at our gatherings and shared an unexamined sense of pride that our community is clearly inclusive and welcoming, judging from the participation of these two or three women over the years.

A few weeks ago I was invited to dinner with several local Jewish lesbians. We got to talking about whether our Jewish community is truly as inclusive as I had assumed it to be. I was startled to hear each of these women describe ways in which they drop their lesbianness at the door, the ways in which they attempt to "pass" in the Jewish community, which they perceive as straight. "I'm always glad to see the Jewish community at holidays and things," said one woman, "but I can't imagine being more social with any of those people. I never talk about being a lesbian to anyone in the Jewish community."

It happened that I had invited a speaker from out of town to come talk with our community about a completely unrelated topic. The speaker, an old friend of mine, is a lesbian and was planning to come here with her lover. The idea arose in another conversation with local Jewish lesbians that we should use the occasion of this speaker coming to have a gathering in the women's community. We would invite lesbian Jews and have the meeting in the home of a lesbian. Such a meeting would be a gesture of invitation, given what I had been hearing from Jewish members of the lesbian community, a sign that the Jewish community welcomes and honors its lesbian members or is at least aware of their presence. My hope was that, if it could be shown that the Jewish community can say the word *lesbian* as easily as it can say *children* or *wedding*, the beginnings of a bridge would be built.

Word spread in the lesbian community that this plan was afoot, and the responses were warm. Not imagining it to be controversial, I went back to my Board to let them know the details of our speaker's visit. I looked around the table and noticed for the first time that, while diverse in many other ways, every Board member is heterosexual and a parent (excepting one woman who is, with her husband, now trying to adopt a child). As I described the plan for a gathering in the lesbian community, a chill went around the table. Several Board members were seething. An explosion followed: 'What's with those women that they need special outreach? We've never done anything homophobic. Why do we need to go to them? Let them come to us and tell us if they are so unhappy!"

I tried to recount my conversation that led to the outreach plan in the first place. I explained that, even though we perceive ourselves as being "not homophobic," we are perceived by Jewish lesbians as "heterocentric." I explained that people we had thought were comfortable members of the Jewish community in fact felt that they needed to "pass" and not mention significant aspects of their lives. Anger boiled in several Board members and, for different reasons, in me. That night and the next I had nightmares and tossed and turned with knots in my stomach.

I have been trying to understand why I felt so personally endangered by this experience. I realize now that, for a moment, looking through the eyes of Jewish lesbians, I saw our Jewish community very differently than I usually do. Our Community Covenant says, "We aspire to be a community which is welcoming to everyone who wants to participate . . . [which] makes a special effort to be accessible to people who are often excluded (e.g. elderly people, gay men and lesbians, people with disabilities)." Inclusiveness is a canon of our community, or so I thought. Suddenly, I caught a glimpse of the synagogue of my youth within our charmingly marginal, hippie, rural congregation—a congregation that says, "What's wrong with these people? We don't exclude them. Let them check their differentness at the door, and they are wel-

come to join us." I felt the betrayal in my gut as well as in my head.
A community that does not want to hear about lesbians may not
want to hear about me at some point either. I am happy to say now
that this small incident provoked a great deal of soul searching on
the part of all involved, and we are now involved in organizing
some community-wide dialogue between gay, lesbian, and heterosexual members of our Jewish community. I think that in the long
run this is even more hopeful than not having the issue arise explicitly in the first place.

Texts Are No Excuse

The members of my Board did not feel uneasy because Leviti-
cus 18:22 says, "A man may not lie with a man in the way that he
lies with a woman; it is an abomination before God." Neither did
the rabbis of the Central Conference of American Rabbis cite that
biblical text directly when they said that heterosexual, monogamous, procreative marriage is the ideal of our tradition. They did
not have the nerve to. For the role of texts in Jewish tradition is
somewhat different than in the Christian tradition.

A few people choose to be Jewish, but for the most part it is a
religion you are born into. There is a reality factor here—whatever
the traditional texts may say, the tradition has to cope with there
being all kinds of Jews. It is not particularly free to write out whole
categories of people. We who are outside the world of Jewish or-
thodoxy tend to look at Jewish law as a monolith, as a unilateral
pronouncement of thou shalts and thou shalt nots. In fact, Jewish
law, even in its orthodox manifestation, is far from unilateral on
most points. It must always accommodate the reality of Jewish
people who deviate from a theoretical mainstream.

While it is true that there are scorchingly homophobic passages
in the Bible and in some later Jewish texts, actually surprisingly
little is said throughout a tradition that is notable for its vast attention to legal detail. What is stated in the legal literature is far from
unanimous. For example, the Mishnah, an early rabbinic text, says
that two bachelors should not sleep under the same blanket lest
they be sexually tempted.[2] But, rather than being elaborated by

later decisions, this ruling is largely abandoned by Jewish law. Rabbi Norman Lamm, a contemporary Orthodox spokesman for heterosexual, procreative monogamy, proposes that this abandonment of the prohibition is due to the rarity of homosexual behavior in Jewish communities.[3] I suspect just the opposite, that there have always been a good number of people in any Jewish community who have significant same-sex attractions and experiences and that our tradition, for demographic if not ethical reasons, could hardly afford to cut so many people out of the fold. The two men under a blanket ruling crops up now and then throughout Jewish legal history but is mostly negated or ignored. Jewish law tends to be unilateral on very few points, and it certainly is not on this one.

But even if it were, Jews who are not orthodox have no business becoming textual literalists when the texts suit them. I am a Reform Jew, and Reform Judaism is characterized by a proud critique of those aspects of our tradition that may be unethical. The Board of my Jewish community was angry not because of the Bible but because of their own pain and fear. So too was the Central Conference of American Rabbis, which courageously offered ordination to lesbian and gay rabbis but turned around in the same document and refused to offer support to rabbis who lose their jobs by coming out of the closet. It was their own fears, and certainly not the Bible, that kept these Reform rabbis from fully allying themselves with their gay and lesbian colleagues.

If anything, Jews share with lesbians and gay men a history of persecution that ought to strengthen our sense of alliance. The same Nazis who forced the yellow star on Jews forced the pink triangle on gay men, and Jews and gay men died side by side in many of the same concentration camps during the Holocaust. In our own time, the New Right in this country is both anti-Semitic and homophobic. The specter of Jews marginalizing and oppressing gay men, lesbians, and bisexuals is especially odious in this light.

Why not welcome lesbians, gay men, and bisexuals? Why not enjoy their presence, their different experiences and expressions? Why the attachment to a vision of normality that enhances no one and disenfranchises almost everyone? In the case of Judaism, the tradition by its very multifaceted nature does not support it; the Reform critique of the repressive aspects of tradition supports it even less; and our shared history of victimization makes Jewish homophobia a *shanda*, a scandal.

I long with all my heart to be part of a community that fully enjoys difference, that bonds not on the basis of sameness but rather out of true affection for what is sparklingly unique about every person. I wish for this not only because to continue otherwise is to perpetuate injustice and hurtfulness but for a more personal reason as well. As an individual, I long to be welcomed in all my specific dimensions and not because, or because of the extent to which, I conform to an externally imposed stereotype. That superimposed stereotype cuts the arms and legs off of each of us, not just lesbians, gay men, and bisexuals. Each of us "passes" in the "normal" world by cutting off parts of ourselves. The more restrictive the keyhole through which each of us must fit, the more we each bleed.

Much better to see bisexuals, lesbians, and gay men as gifts from God, as are we all. We are very lucky, very blessed, to have gayness among us and particularly to live in a day when, at least more than before, gayness is out where we can enjoy it and be moved by it. Gayness is good for the Jews—it is good for everyone. Lucky is the Jewish family that has a lesbian daughter or mother, the Torah school faculty that has a gay teacher, the synagogue rich with lesbian, gay, and bisexual members active in its every facet. Difference is what is real. Enjoying the difference between gay, lesbian, bisexual, and straight people is just one step toward making space for each one of us to be the wonderful unique beings that we are.[4]

NOTES

1. Report of the Ad Hoc Committee on Homosexuality and the Rabbinate, presented to the Central Conference of American Rabbis, June 1990, 4.
2. Mishnah Kiddushin 4:14.
3. Norman Lamm, "Judaism and the Modern Attitude to Homosexuality,"

Contemporary Jewish Ethics, ed. Menachen Keller (New York: Sanhedrin, 1978), 381.

4. For further reading, see Christie Balka and Andy Rose, eds., *Twice Blessed: On Being Lesbian or Gay and Jewish* (Boston: Beacon, 1989); and Evelyn Torton Beck, ed., *Nice Jewish Girls: A Lesbian Anthology* (Boston: Beacon, 1989).

12

True to Our Tradition

GARY E. DOUPE

If what we think is right and wrong divides still further the human family, there must be something wrong with what we think is right.

—*WILLIAM SLOAN COFFIN*, The Courage to Love

A Personal Word

When the former Jesuit priest and psychotherapist John McNeill began to address a United Methodist convocation on the topic of "homosexuality and the church," he noticed in the back of the large auditorium the denomination's bicentennial banner, which reads, "For 200 years proclaiming grace and freedom." Referring to speeches earlier in the day that described homosexuality as "sin" (separation from God's will), McNeill said, "Let's have some *grace* and *freedom* as we think about the church's ministry with gay men and lesbians!"

Grace and *freedom* are the heart of Christian faith. These words describe my life and experience in a church that has lifted up my strengths and played down my weaknesses. I am a divorced and remarried heterosexual clergyman. In my failings and struggles, related to the dissolution of my former marriage, not once has any church member or ecclesiastical leader chastised or belittled me. There was a time when people in my situation would not have been able to continue their pastoral work. But my church has shown me love, not judgment.

My hope for my denomination is that, one day soon, people

187

who are gay, lesbian, or bisexual will experience love and acceptance, grace and freedom, in no less measure than I.

I have greatly needed the church's ministry of unconditional love. I believe all of us need that. But I have been, at times, a particularly challenging candidate for grace. In my family, feelings were expressed openly—often forcefully—and without much reserve. As an adult I have carried on that tradition and sometimes suffered from "hoof in mouth" disease. I will relate a brief example.

A colleague in ministry once began to tell me about his living situation: there was evidently some uneasiness surfacing between him and his male housemate, and my friend believed that one of them would have to relocate. Flippantly, I asked, "Why? Is he gay?" "No," my friend said. "*I* am."

I had always thought of myself as open and accepting of others, no matter what their race, religion, or sexual orientation. But sensitivity and genuine acceptance, I have learned, require more. They mean listening more deeply and patiently than I have often been willing to listen. They mean going beyond the assumptions of a "liberal attitude," to hear the reality of another's experience, whether that be merely a "different reality" than our own or some private pain we had never before realized.

Rare and wonderful individuals have come into my life, to penetrate my shallow liberalism with their trust and honesty. By the quality of their lives, their patience and integrity, they have invited me to be a better person. Some of these wonderful people have been gay, lesbian, and bisexual.

When I hear people without genuine understanding in my "Christian" denomination suggest that gay men, lesbians, and bisexuals are implicitly deficient—either morally or psychologically—I feel angry. My irritation has nothing whatever to do with my "charitable" nature—which is mostly on the surface. It has everything to do with the honesty and insight, compassion, and sensitivity that gay, lesbian, and bisexual people have extended to me and embodied in other personal and social relationships. Such people have helped many of us understand God's gift of sexuality as more deeply a part of our spirituality than we had ever realized.

In her book *Touching Our Strength,* Carter Heyward speaks of the perverse legacy of dualism "between flesh and spirit, between sex and God," that keeps us from the grace of knowing our erotic power as "the love and power of God." Many who fear or reject the "homoerotic" are still wrestling, one may presume, with the place of the erotic in their own lives. We have been well taught to fear the power of our sexual desires and to associate our strong desire for sexual pleasure with "selfishness, sin, sickness, or perversion." The idea that "erotic feelings pull us away from God," says the Reverend Heyward, is part of a pornographic religious culture, in which sexual pleasure has been treated as shameful.[1]

The grace of a holy power of affirmation pulls us out of our closets of self-rejection. We may never leave all our fears behind, but courage operates in spite of them: "Courage is the opening of our minds, and hearts, and our bodies to the unknown and to one another. Becoming friends, we learn to stretch the boundaries of what we have believed to be safe. In so doing, we step together into realms of stronger confidence in ourselves and one another."[2] Gay, lesbian, and bisexual Christians have helped make our tradition believable again, by the personal risk entailed in trusting before others have "earned" such trust. Such people, even while objectively oppressed by those who identify religion with judgment, have become liberators. Gay, lesbian, and bisexual Christians have taught us again what *grace* can mean. The reader is invited to share a journey that, with its many risks, takes grace (love that makes whole/holy) as its all-sufficient guide.

Reflections: Theological and Pastoral

The Creator's "Word" has gone out—not merely in theory, but in caring human flesh—to embrace and welcome those whom society has marginalized. The presence of the "Holy One" brings healing. When Christians reflect theologically, almost always they see the *diversity* of life within its created unity not as "sin" but rather as the signature of gracious divinity. Yet when asked to accept a holy diversity in matters sexual, many within the Christian family still struggle. The purpose of this essay is to affirm that, by accepting the grace of our existence, we are reconciled to one another across all humanly created chasms of diversity and restored to wholeness. When heterosexuals feel alienated from the homosexual minority and refuse to see homosexuality as honorable, they negate the diversity of a holy Creation, a Creation that includes the unitive impulses of our sexuality and that is divinely blessed.

According to the *Gospel of Matthew*, the joining of divine holiness and human flesh not only took place in Jesus, called *Christ*, but continually takes place in Christ's mystical identification with all who bear unjust burdens (Matt. 25:40). One's caring response to a sister or brother thus becomes an occasion of reunion and communion within the holy presence of the Christ. A contemporary theologian, James B. Nelson, suggests that Jesus "did not aim to control and hoard the Christic possibility, but rather to release and share it among and with everyone." To love God in another human being is therefore the holiest of deeds. When such an opportunity expands the boundaries of our capacity to accept human diversity, this "human" love becomes simultaneously a divine revelation.[3]

Is a Christian bound, therefore, to accept as sisters or brothers all people, including those whose sexual orientation is different from his or her own? The answer is simply yes, without qualification. For those who have been taught to fear homosexuality, learning to show hospitality and care for gays, lesbians, and bisexuals may take time. (In most cases, as I will suggest later, the issue may be intertwined with self-acceptance.) But the mandate to show love and acceptance cannot be avoided.

What is "acceptance"? Is it endorsement of another's behavior? I think not. A part of Christian freedom is the freedom not to make judgments about the conduct of others. It is not part of the act of "acceptance" to decide whether some behavior on another's part is either right or wrong. To "accept" a gay, lesbian, or bisexual person is, therefore, an act of positive regard rather than a recommendation of a life-style. Christians must make judgments only when someone's behavior threatens to injure or destroy the community (of the church or the larger community). If one truly believes that the community's life is threatened, the burden of proof necessarily falls on the person so convinced. Numerous times, homophobes have asserted that gay men, lesbians, and bisexuals constitute a "threat," just as racists, sexists, and nationalists have asserted their feelings. But where is the evidence supporting such claims?

More often, such claims are advanced abstractly, on the basis of highly debatable and selective "scriptural authority." On this professed basis, some feel obliged to exclude gay men, lesbians, and bisexuals from either their personal friendship or from positions of church leadership. This decision *against* another, unsubstantiated by rational evidence, must be recognized and identified as a prejudice. Responsible Christians do not legislate discrimination against others on the basis of scriptural proof texts, as some churches are now doing with respect to determining eligibility for ordination. Such exclusionary, prejudicial practices not only ignore the question of the integrity of a particular candidate but represent the polar opposite of what the Christian tradition is all about. And *polar* may be the correct word: the warmth of divine affirmation has too often been swept away by the biting chill of arctic winds that would freeze forever the demand for conformity. The church's real work, I contend, is to thaw hardened hearts with the mutual recognition of our humanness: to participate in the whole/holy community of the One.

Many Christian conservatives have said, regarding homosexuals: "I can accept the sinner, but not the sin; for God gives homosexuals the power to be 'healed,' "—that is, the power to be changed into heterosexuals. "And if they cannot accept that, they have the option to remain celibate." This position hardly rests on firm ground. Not only is its basis in Scripture highly questionable, but its connection to the love of Christ is difficult to fathom. What is demanded in the guise of "healing" is nothing less than a massive denial of the structures of feeling and identity that are most integral to the personalities of gays, lesbians, and bisexuals. Because of the prejudice and discrimination they have experienced, most gay, lesbian, and bisexual people clearly would not have chosen that identity had there been a real choice open to them.

As one gay psychologist put it, speaking of the numerous young gay men whom he had counseled, the common theme of their struggle with their self-identity was a prayer: "Please, God, take this away from me!" A question posed by the speaker is worth our reflection: "Who would ask to become a pariah and the object of scorn among his peers?"[4] Yet this is daily reality for self-affirming, openly gay people. If "healing" required a change of identity on their part, what would be the evidence for that need? Are these people less well adjusted than heterosexuals? Are they less productive and less creative? One might argue in precisely the opposite direction. Martin Rochlin's "heterosexual questionnaire"—reprinted in the appendix to this essay—makes the point with good humor as well as insight. Is it because gays, lesbians, and bisexuals need to correct their "condition" that some church leaders speak as they do, or is there an illness in the body of faith that results in trauma, hopelessness, self-hatred, and even death for sexual minorities.

There are biblical issues that scholars have discussed at length, but none so important as how the Word of grace is related to human need. William Sloan Coffin summarizes accurately what cannot be detailed within the scope of this work, regarding the seven possible references to homosexuality in Hebrew and Christian Scriptures:

> Most of all, what we need to remember is that nowhere does Scripture address a specifically homosexual orientation. Biblical writers assume that homosexual acts are being committed by people whose basic orientation is heterosexual. . . . The Bible says nothing directly one way or another about . . . the loving, lasting relationships that patently exist today between so many gay people in this country, in every city, and in so many churches. . . .
>
> Clearly, it is not Scripture that creates hostility to homosexuality, but rather hostility to homosexuality that prompts certain Christians to retain a few passages from an otherwise discarded law code. The problem is not how to reconcile homosexuality with scriptural passages that appear to condemn it, but rather how to reconcile the rejection and punishment of homosexuals with the love of Christ. I do not think it can be done. I do not see how Christians can define and then exclude people on the basis of sexual orientation alone— not if the law of love is more important than the laws of biology.[5]

The conservative reply, especially in the past few years, has been in fact biological: "What, then, of diseases transmitted sexually through large segments of the gay community, most prominently the deadly AIDS virus?" The answer is not self-evident to everyone; therefore, the question must be taken seriously. If homosexuality were, in some abstract sense, a "moral cause" of the AIDS crisis, one would expect to find all homosexuals threatened in some way. In fact, exclusively lesbian women are less likely to contract AIDS than heterosexual women. (Also, in many countries around the world, straight men and women are hardest hit by the virus.)

Gays bear responsibility for communicating sexually transmitted diseases, just as heterosexuals do. The essential problem is high-risk unprotected sexual activity rather than the form of sexual expression. Sexual activity does not cause AIDS: a virus does.

If stable relationships between partners tend to favor sexual and emotional health, should not persons of conscience do all they can to affirm such relationships? Yet heterosexist (homophobic) prejudice has made it extremely difficult for gays, lesbians, and bisexuals to live in socially recognized and supported relationships. The entire community therefore bears responsibility for the special burdens placed on these relationships.

In a similar way, the healing of human relationships is the ongoing task of all maturing persons, both gay and straight. Homophobic attitudes, even when justified by religious belief (and I believe justification is problematic), can be only harmful. There is undeniable wisdom in the words of the Reverend William Sloan Coffin: "If what we think is right and wrong divides still further the human family, there must be something wrong with what we think is right."[6]

I have asserted that the "holy" is the power to heal. Some persons appear to believe that holiness and "healing" depend on others' conversion to their point of view. Jesus told a parable about such attitudes, in which he suggested that people of faith should not presume to claim divine prerogatives (Matt. 13:24–30). What looks like a weed may not be a weed! And when we try to judge (uproot) what we take to be weeds, all we accomplish is the destruction of the garden. Some interpreters, by the way, suggest that God's people are not the "good seed" mentioned in the parable but rather the field. The good seed is planted in us, and in the course of our human "night" the weeds also take root. Through excessive weeding (judgmentalism), we destroy the vital wheat of our personalities, along with useless weeds. Often, it is better to concentrate on enhancing the vitality of the good than to worry about eradicating deviations. Excessive scrupulousness regarding ourselves and/or others, as Luther discovered, leads not to salvation but to despair. The divine mercy will bring to purity all that we offer out of the richness of our nurturing ground.

Throughout Christian history, gracious openings to new understanding have brought healing where many had been victims of ideological blindness and blockage. It must never be forgotten that within the overt power structures of "Christendom" have been harbored incredibly destructive attitudes toward people of other faiths (witness the Crusades and the Holocaust), toward dissenters within the "family" (inquisition and the silencing of heretical others), toward science (Galileo, Darwin), and toward minority groups and women. As the sadder moments of that history show, conviction does not equal competence. Institutional forms of the church have eclipsed the barrier-breaking spirit of its founder. Yet one must remember as well that people possessed of the uniting, reconciling spirit (toward which the early Christian community struggled) have broken hardened ground to prepare the soil of a more just, more inclusive human community.

Today a somewhat strained debate is taking place within the churches of North America as to whether gay, lesbian, and bisexual people will be treated as people of equal worth, with the same opportunities to exercise leadership in the church as heterosexuals. To many the answer is obvious and the fearful reactions of some in the church hierarchy inexcusable: "Of course one treats all people equally—that is the Gospel!" How could one consider homophobia to be different than racism or sexism when it comes to judging an individual's fitness to serve in the pulpit? Yet many progressive church leaders seem less than forthright when confronted with sexual diversity. In the past, there was always the risk that contributions might be withheld if church officials "did the right thing." We can be thankful that, in many cases, they were unafraid to set a standard of truth and justice. Not always, but often! Yet some of those once-courageous souls seem less eager to claim the "high ground" of acceptance and inclusivity with regard to gay, lesbian, and bisexual Christians. And we must ask why.

For some who are generally liberal in spirit, the concept of homosexual identity seems unclear. The taint of sickness or moral compromise still clings to the gay, lesbian, and bisexual community in the minds of many. As we struggle to comprehend what is taking place, beneath the surface of supposedly scientific or biblical debates, we come face to face with a deeper issue: our anxieties about our own sexuality. There has been, throughout Christian history, a recurrent tendency toward suspicion of the power of sexuality. For the apostle Paul, whose letters have so greatly shaped the Christian vision, *flesh* (*sarx*) was the term chosen to indicate "moral corruption." We too quickly forget the noble connotations that Paul brought to the word *body* (*soma*), including the holy relation of complementary "members" in the *body* of Christ. Paul's delicate balance between a natural affirmation of Creation (from his Hebrew roots) and his distrust of human motivations (echoing Persian/Greek dualism) was not always maintained by his successors. Suspicion about the body's goodness was perhaps natural for Paul's readers in the light of his suggestion not to marry—unless one could not resist the flames of sexual desire. Yet the reason was not primarily sexual: Paul felt strongly the pressure of time to proclaim the message entrusted to him—he simply could not afford the distraction of marriage.

There is also little doubt that Paul was appalled by rampant sexual abuse in contemporary religious cults. Many biblical scholars read *pederasty*—the sexual use of young boys by older men in pagan temples—as the context of Paul's apparent condemnation of homosexuality (Rom. 1:26ff.). For Paul, such exploitive "worship" represented the refusal to acknowledge a true God of righteousness.

It bears repeating that the reality of a homosexual orientation as such was unknown to Paul. In fact, as far as anyone knows, the concept was not advanced until the nineteenth century. Paul can hardly be blamed for his limited understanding of the matter and therefore can hardly be credited with advocating a true and complete answer to the church's present inquiry into the meaning of nonexploitive homosexual relationships.

Aside from Paul's assertions (often read out of context), why do so many contemporary church leaders—even some of those usually sophisticated, antiliteralist, prointellectual "liberals"—allow an unrighteous bigotry against homosexuals to flourish, with few if any of the strong admonishments against prejudice that were heard during the 1960s civil rights movement? A part of the answer may lie in rather deep conflicts that stem from widespread uncertainties about what human sexuality—and, in particular, masculinity—means.

A rich, compassionate reflection on the nature of these conflicts is provided by the distinguished ethicist James B. Nelson, the author of several insightful books on sexual meaning and relating:

> The gay male is resented because he symbolizes the intimacy of men with men, which all men desire but few seem to have. So I punish in others both what I desire and what I also fear in myself. Thus, homophobia strikes most men because we feel in the depth of our own beings our desire for closeness to other men, emotionally and physically even if not genitally. So the resentment against gay males builds. And it builds in all of us regardless of our sexual orientation, for gays inevitably internalize homophobia in a homophobic society, and it becomes self-rejection.[7]

If homophobia reflects uncertainty about our own sexuality, does it not also suggest uneasiness about the structure of our relationships with both women and men? The often positive, nonaggressive relationships gay men enjoy with women frequently make heterosexual men conscious of the less than full mutuality expressed in many heterosexual unions. Unwanted guilt is aroused in straight men, which may be twisted and deflected onto gay men, who become objects of resentment. Women who have internalized and accepted the traditional demands of patriarchy may oppose the women's movement because of the fear of insecurity (what might happen in their marriages should they suddenly become assertive) or simply because of misplaced anger toward themselves for having accepted an unequal role. For some women, it is no small task to reconstruct their worldview after many years of indoctrination about their place in the divine plan. Faced with the painful and confusing need to reexamine the adequacy of past convictions and attitudes, some women have initially lashed out at messengers of change, including spokespeople for the rights of sexual minorities. For homosexual identity implicitly threatens the idealized tradition of (American) gender relations. Gay men, lesbians, and bisexuals thereby incur disdain from all who assume a divine imprimatur for their threatened traditions.

Gains and Losses

In the face of our inherited cultural attitudes, personal pressures, fears, and self-doubts, it would seem that heterosexuals might gain greater insight by opening new doors. Perhaps our dawning awareness of sexual diversity, as a part of the "whole" reality in which people express their sexual selfhood, is a gracious (and holy) invitation to self and mutual acceptance by all people— gay, lesbian, bisexual, and straight. When we stop to realize how much the fear, fascination, and unconscious envy of homosexuals controls and limits others (who may not have accepted their own sexuality fully, as a good gift), not to mention the continuing abuse suffered by members of the gay community, we have no other choice but to work and pray for healing.

Obviously, our children need healing. (Because they absorb very quickly the prejudices of their parents—and, through their peers, the prejudice of other parents—children need healthy adult role models.) Among our youths, we should be aware that "distancing" behavior (from homosexuals) is commonplace: "In a survey of 2,823 students from 8th to 12th grade, three-quarters of boys and half the girls said it would be bad to have a homosexual neighbor."[8]

A University of Manitoba psychologist, Bob Altemeyer, developed a scale measuring attitudes toward homosexuals. Those with the greatest hostility tend to be very fearful "that the world is an unsafe place and that society is at risk; [they also tend] to judge those who hold different values as morally inferior. . . . Their self-righteousness makes them feel they are acting morally when they attack homosexuals. It overcomes the normal inhibitions against aggression."[9] The tragedy in such misstructured "morality" is that people undermine the growth of their own self-understanding by becoming hardened against accepting emotions in themselves and others that they have been conditioned to regard as dangerous. Such categorical thinking does not just supplement feeling—it utterly usurps its place. Friendships that could be greatly enriching are rejected out of hand. Even the slightest association with or acceptance of a homosexual might undermine one's standards of character and good reputation.

An illustration comes from a pastor in a medium-sized city in Pennsylvania. A businessman was active in his church, serving on program and property committees and teaching a Sunday School class. As a businessman, he was effective in community outreach groups that served the neglected and disenfranchised. He called for everyone's help in making the community safer and healthier. As a member of the church, he brought children and youths into his congregation's fold, where they were loved and nurtured.

After retirement, he was elected to represent his congregation at the annual regional meeting of his denomination. At this meeting, resolutions were presented favoring action by the state legislature to legitimize gay, lesbian, and bisexual marriages and recommending that the denomination ordain openly gay, lesbian, and bisexual people as pastors. When the businessman told his pastor that he could not support such resolutions, the pastor simply advised him to vote his conscience, as others would do. The businessman voted in opposition, the pastor (without speaking publicly on the issues) in favor. The resolutions were soundly defeated.

On the drive home, the retired man was visibly upset. He described how he had seen "the things homosexuals did," hanging out in parks and preying on children. His pastor agreed that there were homosexuals who behaved in this manner, just as there were heterosexuals who engaged in predatory behaviors. He pointed out that there were also many homosexuals who were unknown to others because of their discreet, responsible life-styles. Perhaps, the pastor suggested, the issue was not homosexuality per se but rather sexual responsibility.

After returning home, the retired man left his church. He said nothing to his pastor, nothing to church members, nothing to the young people in the congregation who respected and revered him. He resigned from committees, turned in his keys, and attended church nowhere.

Even though "his side" prevailed in the voting, the threat represented by the fact that ordained clergy and elected lay delegates could even *discuss* accepting homosexual unions or homosexuals as pastors was apparently so upsetting to him that he abandoned the church to which he had pledged loyalty. No one in his congregation ever discovered what inner fear fueled this reaction. The only explanation was his act of complete withdrawal: he no longer contributed in any way to a group which had appreciated and affirmed his involvement. He abandoned the children and youth he had brought into that community of faith. Most of all, he abandoned himself. In apparent frustration and emotional turmoil, he cut himself off from his professed source of meaning.

Each of us could speculate on the power of a deeply held feeling in this man's life. Of his actual experience we know almost nothing. We do know, from much wider experience, that prejudice *is* a matter of deep feeling, which makes rational discourse seem pointless. One of the best reasons to resist prejudice is to create a social climate in which indoctrination by fear becomes less and less commonplace.

In this instance, it was not sexual minorities who were harmed by a man's inability to come to terms with his own prejudices and fears. It was he who experienced loss, along with those of his community and congregation who had looked to him as a source of guidance, support, and direction. After initial confusion, a youth delegate to a similar regional meeting wrestled with the issue of homosexuality for herself. After continued study, discussion, and prayer, she prepared a report for her rural congregation. She shared it first with her family, only to have her father react, "Why don't you hang out with more 'guys'?" After giving her report in church, a supportive lay member of her church was worried that she might be labeled a lesbian and thereafter pushed away. Her pastor observed, "Homophobia discourages openness about human sexuality among our youths and inhibits rational inquiry. Anyone who appears overly supportive of gay and lesbian rights is suspected of being gay or lesbian. And in the church, where suspicion can be . . . grounds for discrimination, it is a sufficient restraint."

One hopes that his fears are exaggerated. I suspect that, in some locales, they are not. Where homophobia takes root, heterosexuals lose touch with their humanity, with compassion, and with perspective. There is neither wisdom nor love when fear dominates. Love must be liberated that fear may decrease.

A second casualty to homophobia is the needless loss of sensitive and significant leadership. The list of gay men, lesbians, and bisexuals whose poetry, music, painting, choreography, dramatic gifts, preaching, educational leadership, and pastoral acumen have enriched the life of church and society is very long indeed. How fortunate we are to enjoy the gifts of such messengers of the spirit as Benjamin Britten, Dag Hammarskjold, W. H. Auden, Walt Whitman, Leonardo da Vinci, Michelangelo, Albrecht Durer, and Malcolm Boyd. Arthur S. Sullivan's tune "St. Gertrude" ("Onward, Christian Soldiers") is sung (I suspect) by many unsuspecting homophobes! These gay musicians and artists are only a tiny sampling of the vast company whose gifts have touched the church's life with beauty.

Yet when they are discovered within the ranks of the clergy, gay men, lesbians, and bisexuals have often been humiliated or pressured into resigning. The lack of self-esteem on the part of one pastor so confronted, together with the powerlessness of his closest pastoral colleagues, resulted in a tragic, hushed-up expulsion. Local news reports of the pastor's arrest for a supposed public indiscretion (a legal charge that was later dismissed) may have accentuated the fears of church leadership that their failure to act decisively would have lasting repercussions. But the net effect for the church has been the loss of a valued, intelligent, competent, and caring pastor. This account is not intended to condemn the church for its embarrassment and fear but rather to encourage honest self-examination and thoughtful pastoral care. The church's

Gospel is the affirmation of holy gifts and the reconciliation of people needlessly alienated by lack of understanding and self-esteem.

A third area of concern, in which antigay feelings hurt us all, is the loss of the complementarity of human life. Just as when we discriminate on the basis of race, gender, age, ability, or economic class, we begin to lose sight of the humanity of those who are perceived to be different. And in such moments we lose a large part of our own humanity. This is not only a violation of long-standing religious tradition but also a violation of our hearts. As with all forms of prejudice, the fear of homosexuality makes one more parochial, more isolated, less developed, and less fulfilled.

Prejudice is always violent, harming both active and passive victims. Stories of queer bashing—physical as well as emotional—could fill volumes. Yet the person filled with prejudice is also hurt: one who feels fear or rejects others for some isolated characteristic (behavioral or physical) loses both rationality and the capacity to respond to those who are different with appropriate affect and understanding. Such people needlessly limit themselves by succumbing to stereotypical assessments of others. The ability to be perceptive, to learn from the other, and to appreciate differences begins to disappear, as a prescribed and arbitrary belief system rides roughshod over reason and specificity.

Fourth, the fear of homosexuality depresses our sensitivity to the best interests of society as a whole. The AIDS crisis is but the most obvious example. Revulsion felt toward sexual minorities has made the heterosexual community less concerned and compassionate in the face of the AIDS crisis, a hard-heartedness that is coming to haunt us as increasing numbers of heterosexuals become infected with the AIDS virus.

But there is more to our prejudice than the temptation to judge people with AIDS as guilty victims. By cutting off gays, lesbians, and bisexuals from our friendship, we betray our continuing captivity to moralism, which undermines the operation of grace in our own lives and in our social relations.

Fifth, homophobia causes men, in particular, to distance themselves from an important part of their own being and the vital need for relationship. Out of homophobic fear, men have been socialized to reject traits associated with "female" patterns of nurturing. Male role models, both parents and peers, therefore tend to emphasize independence rather than mutuality. Boys are often encouraged to be tough and unyielding, traits that may undermine their future marriages. The large number of women who are battered by their husbands may be the result of a pattern of male socialization that fails to appreciate and cultivate gentleness and affection beyond the bedroom. An overemphasis on male and female differences keeps men from experiencing and expressing emotion.

Whereas women and men relate best when gender stereotyping is not exaggerated—when both men and women enjoy a wide range of activities and allow themselves a broad repertory of physical and emotional responses—homophobia tends to narrow rather than enlarge our human possibilities. Thus, homophobia becomes a subtle form of masochism.

In summary, persons who fear lesbians, gays, and bisexuals tend to fear their own sexuality and thus distance themselves from a connective and integrative grace. Our sexuality is integral to our being and self-expression. When we fear the sexuality of ourselves or of others, we tend to amputate a vital part of our humanity, thereby limiting the life of our spirits. To the degree that we remain prejudiced, we sentence ourselves to a circumscribed life. But to the degree that we open ourselves, trusting in the God who has created life in its fullest diversity—to that degree we participate in life's rich tapestry.

The ministry of Jesus was an affirmation of common people, who had become in effect "aliens" in the eyes of those preoccupied by religion. To some rabbis, the "people of the land" were religious illiterates, unconcerned with ritual cleanliness, immoral, ignorant of the law. Jesus refers to these people as "sheep without a shepherd," urging the religious sages of his day to greater pastoral concern and much less judgment. To Jesus, judging men and women was far less helpful than reaching out in compassion.

The churches of America will do well to reflect on Jesus' attitude, which is at the heart of the biblical tradition, rather than on peripheral (and poorly interpreted) proof texts as they consider their response to sexual minorities. When people of faith become overly judgmental, their vocation—to invite all receptive hearers into wider community—is destroyed.

For many years, gays, lesbians, and bisexuals have been the invisible minority. Heterosexuals, by and large, have thought little about the damage these people have been asked to inflict on themselves: "If you are really good at hiding who you are, we won't bother you." That attitude can no longer be defended. Gays, lesbians, and bisexuals will not go away; were that to happen, the human community would be incredibly diminished. With the church's protagonist of rock-like faith we can affirm, "I truly understand that God shows no partiality, but in every nation anyone who fears him and does what is right is acceptable to him" (Acts 10:34–35).

NOTES

1. Carter Heyward, *Touching Our Strength* (San Francisco: Harper & Row, 1989), 134.
2. Ibid., 139.
3. James B. Nelson, *The Intimate Connection: Male Sexuality, Masculine Spirituality* (Philadelphia: Westminster, 1988), 110; see also p. 66.
4. D. Bruce Carter, address to the Wyoming Annual (United Methodist) Conference, 9 April 1988, Scranton, Pa.
5. William Sloane Coffin, *The Courage to Love* (San Francisco: Harper & Row, 1982), 42–43.
6. Ibid., 46.
7. *The Intimate Connection*, 64.
8. *New York Times* (10 July 1990), sec. C, p. 11.
9. Ibid.

APPENDIX

Heterosexual Questionnaire
MARTIN ROCHLIN, PH.D.

1. What do you think caused your heterosexuality?

2. When and how did you first decide you were a heterosexual?

3. Is it possible that your heterosexuality is just a phase you may grow out of?

4. Is it possible that your heterosexuality stems from a neurotic fear of members of the same sex?

5. Isn't it possible that all you need is a good gay lover?

6. If heterosexuality is normal, why are a disproportionate number of mental patients heterosexual?

7. To whom have you disclosed your heterosexuality? How did they react?

8. The great majority of child molesters are heterosexuals (95 percent). Do you really consider it safe to expose your children to heterosexual teachers?

9. Heterosexuals are noted for assigning themselves and each other to narrowly restricted, stereotyped sex roles. Why do you cling to such an unhealthy form of role playing?

10. Why do heterosexuals place so much emphasis on sex?

11. There seem to be very few happy heterosexuals. Techniques have been developed that you might be able to use to change your sexual orientation. Have you considered aversion therapy to treat your sexual orientation?

12. Why are heterosexuals so promiscuous?

13. Why do you make a point of attributing heterosexuality to famous people? Is it to justify your own heterosexuality?

14. If you've never slept with a person of the same sex, how do you know you wouldn't prefer that?

15. Why do you insist on being so obvious and making a public spectacle of your heterosexuality? Can't you just be what you are and keep it quiet?

13

Homophobia, Censorship, and the Arts

DAVID EBERLY

During the last several years, our country has faced a wide-ranging, well-financed, and protracted campaign by conservative groups to curb certain kinds of expression, particularly those that celebrate and defend homosexuality or that criticize our society's entrenched attitudes of racism and sexism. By deliberately choosing gays and lesbians as the focus of most of these attacks, the political Right has sought to exploit the public's antipathy toward them to achieve its own goals. The success or failure of this campaign, however, has consequences that extend far beyond the issue of gay rights to the rights of all citizens to speak, create, and publish as they choose without government interference.

One of the most visible and controversial examples of his homophobic campaign has been the attempt to weaken or abolish the National Endowment for the Arts (NEA). From its beginning, gay and lesbian artists have been singled out for vilification. Perhaps its most conspicuous target has been Robert Mapplethorpe. A posthumous exhibition of his work at the Corcoran Gallery in Washington, D.C., was canceled under intense pressure, and the gallery where the exhibition was subsequently shown in Cincinnati was charged with and tried for (and acquitted of) obscenity, primarily for including in the exhibit photographs depicting acts of sadomasochism. But other artists have been targeted during the past two years as well. Money to support "Witnesses: Against Our Vanishing," a show of artists' responses to the AIDS epidemic, was withdrawn after NEA chair John Frohnmayer reviewed the exhibition catalog. Frohnmayer also overturned the recommendations of the NEA's own peer panel and refused funding to four artists, three of whom—John Fleck of Los Angeles and Holly Hughes and Tim Miller of New York—are gay or lesbian and all whom have examined the oppression of women and sexual minorities in our society. (Later, Hughes and Karen Finley would receive new grants, Frohnmayer admitting his "mistake.")

Controversial from its inception, the NEA had seen its budget grow from $8.4 million in 1970 to over $173 million twenty years later. Initially criticized for funding the more traditional work of white male heterosexuals, by the late 1970s the NEA had begun to support a more representative range of American art through its community-based arts program and increased grants to minority artists, including lesbians and gays. As a result of this growth in size and scope, the NEA was targeted early by the Reagan administration, which sought to cut its funding drastically. Through the 1980s, however, the NEA successfully fought these cuts with the support of Congress.

All this quickly changed when the Reverend Donald W. Wildmon, founder of the American Family Association and antipornography zealot, began a campaign against "anti-Christian and obscene art," designed to win control of the NEA for his conservative allies and change the cultural climate of the nation. Soon joined by Senator Jesse Helms of North Carolina, Wildmon began to pressure both Congress and the NEA, which responded by instituting a series of compromises whose aim was to eliminate funding of "objectionable" work.

It became immediately evident that homosexuals, particularly those who explicitly extol or examine their gender and sexuality, would be the first to be eliminated. This intent was made even clearer when the NEA promulgated its notorious "loyalty oath" to be signed by all grant recipients, indicating their understanding that the NEA is prohibited from funding "obscene materials including but not limited to depictions of sadomasochism, homoeroticism, the exploitation of children, or individuals engaged in sex acts" and acknowledging their liability. Artists found violating this regulation could be forced to return their grants.

The language of this regulation was taken almost directly from an amendment introduced into the Senate by Helms and reflects the Right's virulent antipathy toward homosexuals. By locating homoeroticism on a continuum between sadomasochism and the sexual abuse of children, the regulation strengthens the homophobic argument that all homosexuals are potential child molesters who seek to recruit others at an early age, "infecting" them with the "disease" of homosexuality. The sexual abuse of children by homosexuals is an unquestioned tenet of the homophobic Right, despite the overwhelming evidence that most of the abuse is perpetrated by heterosexual men within the family setting. The continued and calculated repetition of this lie, so similar to the forged *Protocols of the Elders of Zion* used by the Nazis to defame Jews, plays on the deepest fears of the American public for the safety and well-being of their children. It has become an even more dangerous weapon against gays as the fear of AIDS has escalated, reinforcing the perception that homosexuality is a disease that can be spread, only now with fatal consequences. This link between art and disease was succinctly drawn by the president of the Massachusetts chapter of Morality in Media, who was reported to have said, "People looking at these kinds of pictures become addicts and spread AIDS."[1]

But if the initial goal of Wildmon and his allies was the suppression of overtly gay writing and art, the results of this campaign have been far reaching and have affected many other segments of our society. As the poet Audre Lorde, joined by a number of other lesbian writers, noted, "The current attempts to censor sexually explicit lesbian/gay art are tied to attempts to control information about sexuality in general, including safe sex and AIDS, about contraception and abortion, about lesbian and gay sexuality. This censorship is being imposed not just in the art world, but in radio programming, reproductive rights counseling, and classroom teaching."[2] The present situation, then, resembles other such "moral panics" that have been periodically fanned in the United States to further the agenda of those opposed to the empowerment of groups deemed "foreign" to our society—racial, ethnic, sexual, or political. Anthony Comstock's campaign against "smut," waged

first in New York City in the 1870s and then throughout the country when he was appointed a special postal inspector, linked the
fight against pornography with attacks against abortion and contraception that were tinged with strong anti-Irish sentiment. The result was a legacy of laws restricting speech and sexual rights that
took almost a century to overturn.[3]

Similarly, fifty years later Will Hays, a former postmaster general, responding to Christian and right-wing elements in our country alarmed by the increasing freedom displayed by the rapidly
growing motion picture industry, helped create the Motion Picture
Production Code. For over a generation, the code, whose rem-
nants remain today, regulated what Americans could see on the
screen, stereotyping and marginalizing women, blacks, and gays—
those few who could be recognized—and forcing all films to portray a sexually sanitized view of relationships.

The current situation is strikingly similar, with lesbians and
gays, feminists, and African-Americans bearing the brunt of the
onslaught. While the prosecutions of both the rap group 2 Live
Crew and the director of the Cincinnati Arts Center for obscenity
have been the most visible examples, other attempts to silence
artists have continued unabated. Local authorities entered and
vandalized the studio of West Coast photographer Jock Sturgis,
seizing prints of nude children and accusing him of pornography.
In New York City, the Franklin Furnace, a basement space dedicated to experimental work that had staged a performance by
Karen Finley, one of the four artists refused NEA funding, was
shut for fire-code violations, and the W.O.W. Cafe, a club that also
stages lesbian work, has been served an eviction notice. West
Coast radio station KPFK-FM is currently engaged in a legal dispute with the FCC over its broadcast of the sexually explicit play
Jerker. Essex Hemphill, a gay African-American poet, has reported
that his poems have been censored by a radio station and rejected
by a magazine whose editor feared the loss of NEA money. In San
Diego, the Sushi Gallery, which announced that it would present
the work of the four artists rejected by the NEA, has faced harassment by the Christian right. Even an artist as renowned as Judy
Chicago, whose artwork *The Dinner Party* is one of the monu-

ments of feminist art, has not been exempt from censorship, as the House of Representatives voted to cut funding to the University of the District of Columbia, which had planned to house her piece.

As troubling as these attacks are, their real aim has been to generate an atmosphere of self-censorship among artists and institutions. "From the censor's viewpoint," one critic has argued, "self-censorship is an ideologue's dream, since it is cheap, self-enforcing and doesn't require a large bureaucracy to administer. It is more effective than legal regulation, since fearful individuals, trying to stay out of trouble, anxiously elaborate the category of what is likely to be prohibited. Best of all, self-censorship occurs privately, without contentious and public struggles."[4] Certainly, the NEA statement that every grant recipient must sign creates such a climate. It forces individual artists, whatever their race, sexual preference, or political beliefs, to acquiesce personally and silently to the language and beliefs of the regulation. The regulation itself has been backed by sporadic, but highly visible, prosecutions that label their victims *perverts* and *pornographers*.

Marilyn Arsem, codirector of Mobius, an artist-run center for experimental work in all media located in Boston, has discussed the effects of these homophobic attacks on the gallery, now struggling with the decision to accept NEA money. She, too, noted the closing of the Franklin Furnace and the vulnerability of similar spaces that must struggle to fit the needs of galleries to codes that were not written with them in mind. The members of the group have suddenly seen how "frightening it is to think about what might happen if someone who is hostile to your viewpoint tried to prevent you from making your work, or have the authorities arrest you, or try to have your funding withdrawn. For the first time, all of us have been looking back at the work that we've done in the past that has been criticized for various things. There is paranoia in retrospect."

The paranoia is personal for Arsem, whose own work with raw meat in a piece once provoked an audience member to ask if she were a Satanist: "You start thinking back on your work, and you think that someone could really flip over it." The women artists in Mobius, some of whom have used nudity in their pieces, feel especially at risk and subject to arrest. Yet, despite these fears, Arsem believes that Mobius remains committed to presenting work as it has done in the past, including work that is explicitly homoerotic. Such work would be treated like all other work, subject to the same criteria and the decision of the group.

Institutional criteria and review were also on the mind of Trevor Fairbrother, curator of the Contemporary Arts Department of Boston's Museum of Fine Arts, who, along with Kathy Halbreich, now director of the Walker Art Center in Minneapolis, organized "Figuring the Body," a show mounted during the same period that the Mapplethorpe exhibit ran at the city's Institute of Contemporary Arts. As the curators noted, "Recent Congressional calls for censorship in the arts dramatically demonstrate our deep-seated ambivalence about the human body." The museum had to confront its own ambivalence as well, as it sought to accommodate the sometimes explicit and challenging pieces chosen by the curators of the show with the perceived resistance of the museum-going public, a perception proved wrong by the large numbers of people who crowded the gallery.

"Figuring the Body" did have the support of Alan Shestack, the museum's director, who suggested the inclusion of what might have been, along with Andres Serrano's "Untitled VII (Ejaculation in Trajectory)," the show's most controversial work, Elsa Dorfman's life-size frontal nude photograph of Allen Ginsberg. Yet Shestack nevertheless requested that a notice be posted warning of the explicit nature of the work displayed, a decision prompted by Dorfman's photograph. Ironically, on entering the gallery after being so warned, visitors were confronted either by a series of drawings by Vesalius taken from a medical text or by a Picasso etching. (No such warning was thought necessary for an earlier exhibition of Edward Weston's photographs, which included many female nudes, an apt comment on the entrenched homophobia of the art establishment.)

As a result of the lengthy process of curating the "Body" show, Fairbrother learned how "easy and dangerous it is to make a statement to the public, and how hard it is to be clear. You are subject to misrepresentation by a whole range of people, even the ones you think that you are supporting. It becomes an issue of self-censorship." The entire process of curating contemporary art in a major institution is subject to those concerns. Kathryn Potts, an NEA fellow responsible for many of the extensive labels used in the show, also noted how much negotiation was involved in anticipating what would be acceptable: "So much is cut out and not said because someone will find it offensive."[5]

If one result of the current homophobic hysteria has been the intimidation of artists and institutions to prevent them from making or displaying homoerotic or sexually explicit work by creating a politicized environment of threat and personal liability leading to self-censorship, another has been the outright attempt to censor work legally. In this, the Right has sometimes been abetted by artists who have argued that they prefer the standards set by the Supreme Court's *Miller* decision—which ruled a work obscene if it lacked serious value and was judged prurient by "an average person applying contemporary community standards"—to the broader and more confusing terms of the NEA regulation.

Just how flimsy the protection of the *Miller* decision can be was demonstrated by the trial of 2 Live Crew for obscenity and the conviction of Miami store owner Charles Freeman for selling their album "As Nasty as They Wanna Be." Rap music has always been a convenient target for those seeking to limit free speech. Its sometimes violent and graphically misogynistic lyrics offend many who would otherwise be drawn to its sexual energy, anger, raunch, exuberance, and political savvy. When confronted by "Nasty," Judge Jose Gonzalez ruled it obscene.

Judge Gonzalez's ruling demonstrates all that is wrong with the attempt to apply the *Miller* test to a work made by a minority artist. While arguing that "the message covered by obscene speech is of such slight value that it is always outweighed by the compelling interests of society," Gonzalez goes on to state that sex, the "great and mysterious motive force in human life," is so powerful that federal and state governments have chosen to regulate it. (Why is sex always "mysterious?" Why is its expression not in the "compelling interest" of society?) Although the judge found that "the Nasty recording did not actually physically excite anyone who heard it and indeed, caused boredom after repeated play," he nevertheless

ruled that the album was prurient.[6] He could do so, a commentator
has written, by subdividing the community and finding the work
of one group offensive to another: "Not surprisingly, this is the escape hatch used by the Supreme Court to permit suppression of
homoerotic, sadomasochistic, or other 'deviant' pornography—
deem it someone else's turn-on, but offensive to the community at
large. And this may be the truest account of what is really going on
in the 2 Live Crew case: the dominant culture is reining in a black
male youth subculture whose portrait of its own sexuality offends
those outside it."[7] This tactic differs little from those used by the
government in their decades-long attempt to suppress any overt
expression of homosexuality by ruling it a priori obscene.

The strategy of dividing one minority community from another
or, more truthfully, of pitting each against the dominant white,
male, heterosexist, Christian culture that continues to define
"community standards" is central to the censorship of those
groups. It could be seen most clearly in the prosecutor's success in
empaneling a jury in Cincinnati whose members had never entered a museum and who were unfamiliar with contemporary art
and one in Miami whose white, middle-aged members convicted
Charles Freeman for selling 2 Live Crew's album. The exclusion of
anyone perceived as "different" from juries selected to decide
questions of community standards mirrors exactly the exclusion of
minorities from other positions of political and cultural power. As
Marilyn Arsem pointed out, "If you talk about community standards, you should get the whole range of the community. You
should get people who go see art, and you should get people who
look at pornography." In fact, the legal system is designed to ensure
that the opposite occurs, making the process of defining obscenity
extremely sensitive to pressure by organized groups and government prosecutors, who portray themselves as representing the values of a "moral majority."

David Leavitt has noted that the attack on the NEA and on the
arts in general "has little to do with the arts at all, and everything
to do with the extreme right wing's determination to terrorize an
already ambivalent American population by manipulating its entrenched fears of anything foreign, unfamiliar or explicitly sexual."[8]

It can only succeed when it has excluded these "foreign" groups from American society. Thus, today gays and lesbians have been defined out of the community, as have African-Americans, Jews, feminists, and artists. This same demonization of the "other" similarly characterized the thought of Adolph Hitler, who quickly and ruthlessly sought to control all forms of public expression with the support of powerful segments of the German establishment.

Reaction to the Right's homophobic attack on the arts has been often confused. The most disappointing response has been that of the NEA itself, whose Bush-appointed chair, John Frohnmayer, proposed a series of "reforms" that legitimize and strengthen the right's primary goal of silencing gays, lesbians, and other minorities. After having suggested the divisive obscenity statement, one of whose principal effects was to pit artists against the NEA instead of the real perpetrators of the assault on their rights, Frohnmayer agreed to a number of other changes to the NEA's structure. These included the reduction of applications by "prescreening" and limiting the number submitted by an artist to one per year, the addition of nonartists to peer-review committees, the curtailment of the number of small grants to be awarded, and the establishment of a "watchdog" committee to respond to allegations of obscenity.

The result of these changes could be the censorship of all those whose work is judged to be provocative or offensive. Small grants, for example, have been important to the publishers, magazines, galleries, and theaters of minority communities and to the artists within those communities. What would be an insignificant amount of money to a major cultural institution is crucial to a small periodical publishing the writing of people of color; that "insignificant amount" often means the difference between survival and failure. "Now with reforms," it has been noted, " 'risky' grants will be weeded out by intimidating guidelines, procedural oversight, and cautious panelists, as well as by vigilant Council members with their own agendas and a veto-happy chairperson."[9]

Perhaps the most chilling "reform" is the establishment of an oversight committee to investigate any charge of obscenity made against artists supported by the NEA. This committee can only have a disastrous effect on all artists, but it will affect lesbian and gay artists especially since they are already highly vulnerable to anonymous smear campaigns charging them with child molestation, criminal sexual activity, and spreading AIDS. While heterosexual artists have noted the similarity between this committee and those of the McCarthy era (during which, it should be said, thousands of gay men and lesbians were harassed, fired, and imprisoned), few share the threat of blackmail that can still ruin a career or a life and that is the common memory and experience of all homosexuals.

Major cultural institutions, too, while often leading the fight against censorship in general, have been conspicuously silent in identifying the explicitly antihomosexual nature of the attack or linking it to the increase in violent attacks against lesbians and gays. Because the targets of the Right's attacks remain unnamed, they also remain undefended and unprotected. This shortsighted strategy, which generalizes the problem as "only" one of censorship and ignores the homophobia directed against specific individuals and their work, seriously weakens any response by tacitly agreeing with the Right that such work is "unspeakable" and best left unseen.

This problem has been recognized by Trevor Fairbrother, who, as a museum curator, has sought to show and discuss controversial images through exhibitions like the "Body" show as well as to explore them in smaller discussion groups. His attempts to present difficult issues in the supportive environment of the smaller groups have proved surprisingly effective. He had anticipated resistance but found that "people learn a lot when it's coming directly from another person." But he also sees the need for this process to be continued at a higher level as well and hopes that the museum's director will make a similar effort to educate the Board of Trustees.

Mobius, too, has sought to create more interaction between the group and the public, although with a smaller and more art-aware audience. Exploiting its intimate spaces—where, Marilyn Arsem has said, "you're likely to run into the artist in the bathroom"—the gallery has instituted more programs in an informal setting where work can be shown and also discussed and is planning to focus on those areas where art and social issues interact. Its "works-in-progress" series allows artists to interact with their audiences, whose reactions help shape the final work. This process of education, this naming, makes the artists more visible, more accessible, and more human.

More important, Mobius is one of the founding members of the Boston Coalition for Freedom of Expression, which is housed at the gallery. Created in response to the prosecution of the Mapplethorpe show in Cincinnati, the coalition initially sought to preempt any right-wing attack when the exhibition traveled to Boston. The coalition has also sought to address larger issues of homophobia and censorship in a proactive way, shaping the issue through discussion, the media, street theater, demonstrations, and the legislative process. Along with the Cambridge Research Associates, a watchdog group that monitors extremist activity, the coalition was instrumental in countering both the Right and the Roman Catholic church when the exhibit opened in Boston and in establishing the framework for community response.

For years, the Right and its allies in Congress have sought to exploit the homophobia of many in this country to further their own goals. By choosing a politically marginal organization—the National Endowment for the Arts—and by attacking its weakest constituency—lesbian and gay artists—the Right has calculatedly attempted to increase its influence and power at a time when it is generally perceived to be waning. In doing so, it has endangered the communication and culture of a minority already devastated by disease. Gay and lesbian artists "face the imminent evisceration of our right to read, our right to write, our right to earn a living, and our right to free expression as Americans." The same rights are being threatened in other minority groups, most notably the inner-city black community. Both groups are particularly vulnerable and lack meaningful access to power. But "we are Americans too," the Publishing Triangle Steering Committee has forcefully stated, and "because we are Americans too we have a right to free expression. Because we are Americans too we have a right to talk about our homosexuality and not be punished for being queer. Because we are Americans too, the moment you censor us, you censor every American."[10] Not to recognize this simple truth will lead not only to the silencing of a generation of lesbian and gay artists but to the destruction of our precarious and increasingly endangered democracy."

NOTES

1. Paul Mattick, Jr., "Arts and the State," *The Nation* (1 October 1990), 365.
2. Elly Burkin et al., *Bay Windows* (26 July–1 August 1990), 7.
3. Bruce Shapiro, "From Comstockery to Helmsmanship," *The Nation* (1 October 1990), 335.
4. Carole S. Vance, "Misunderstanding Obscenity," *Art in America* (May 1990), 53.
5. I want to thank Marilyn Arsem, codirector of Mobius; Trevor Fairbrother, curator of the Department of Contemporary Arts of Boston's Museum of Fine Arts; and Kathryn Potts, NEA fellow and now curatorial assistant of contemporary art, also at the Museum of Fine Art. Their comments and help were essential to this essay.
6. Skyywalker Records, Inc. v. Nicholas Navarro (Sheriff, Broward County, Florida), U.S. District Court, S.D. Florida, 6 June 1990.
7. Kathleen M. Sullivan, "2 Live Crew and the Cultural Contradictions of *Miller*," *Reconstruction* 1, no. 2 (1990) 20.
8. David Leavitt, "Fears that Haunt a Scrubbed America," *New York Times*, (19 August 1990).
9. Brian Wallace, "Bush's Compromise: A Newer Form of Censorship," *Art in America* (November 1990), 63.
10. Publishing Triangle Steering Committee, *Outweek* (8 August 1990), 52, 53.
11. Since this essay was written, John Frohnmayer was forced by the Bush administration to resign as chair of the NEA. This move leaves open the door to increased conservative influence in that organization.

14

Homophobia and AIDS Public Policy

JEFFREY LEVI

This essay examines the effect that homophobia has had on the development of AIDS public policy and, on the response of heterosexual society to AIDS. I argue that homophobia resulted in delayed and often inappropriate responses to the epidemic. To do so I pursue two seemingly contradictory points.

First, homophobia, along with sexism and racism, contributed to the delayed response to the AIDS epidemic. This delayed response placed gay men at increased risk because federal programs of prevention and research were instituted only slowly. Heterosexuals, however, were placed at equally great risk because the programs that were developed focused on gay men, obscuring the links, sexual and otherwise, that exist between gays and heterosexuals.

Second, homophobia was not introduced into the health-care system only with the AIDS epidemic. Rather, its long-standing legacy of discrimination and exclusion had resulted in the creation of a separate health-care system within the gay community, a health-care system that responded to this new crisis immediately, saving countless gay lives—and heterosexual lives as well—while the government-sponsored system floundered, unable to find the will or the funds to respond.

It should be noted from the start that more factors than homophobia contributed to the U.S. response to AIDS. The AIDS epidemic first struck in the early years of the Reagan administration, an administration that not only was unsympathetic to the interests

217

and concerns of sexual minorities but also, beginning in 1981, imposed massive cutbacks in two of the agencies critical to the initial response to AIDS: the National Institutes of Health and the Centers for Disease Control. This essay, while detailing one specific aspect of the nation's inadequate response to AIDS, should be placed in the context of a larger disabling of our nation's public health care system—a situation from which it is still recovering.

It should also be noted that this is an essay, not a comprehensive history. It reflects impressions received from and analyses based on personal experience as an advocate for the gay community in the AIDS policy debate. Even within that context it is selective. Many aspects of the gay community's response and the establishment's response—and nonresponse—are not discussed.

Gays in U.S. Society

The status of gays in U.S. society has had profound implications for the AIDS epidemic—for the gay community's response to it and for society's response to those in the gay community affected by AIDS. That legal, political, and social context must be understood before the AIDS experience can be discussed.

Gays, lesbians, and bisexuals are among the most invisible of minorities. The social, cultural, legal, and moral stigma of identifying oneself publicly as gay, lesbian, or bisexual keeps most gay people in the closet. But the many gay people who have come out of the closet also remain invisible—rendered silent by media unwilling to cover our community or report on our lives for fear of alienating their audience or because of internal biases. With the advent of AIDS, gay and bisexual men have become somewhat more visible, but ironically lesbians and bisexual women have become even more marginalized. Also on the down side, too much of the early coverage if AIDS reinforced dangerous negative stereotypes and fears about sexual minorities.

While the most visible people with AIDS are gay and bisexual men, lesbians have also been affected—as people with AIDS, as advocates for political reform in the context of AIDS, as caregivers and service providers, and as the victims of discrimination based on the irrational association of HIV infection with all homosexuals. Lesbians have borne the political liabilities of the AIDS epidemic as they have affected the lesbian and gay community generally; they have at the same time been forced to put many political objectives on hold as the community confronts this epidemic.

The notion of a gay community—one formed on the basis of sexual orientation—is often difficult for many heterosexuals to understand. But we are indeed members of a community, despite our incredible diversity. We come from every segment of U.S. society, whether those divisions are based on class, race, gender, religion, or politics. We have essentially one thing in common: we share oppression as a minority discriminated against, looked down on, attacked, and rejected because of what is perceived as a "deviant" sexual orientation.

It is discrimination and oppression that unite us. In that regard we are like many other minorities for whom shared oppression can be a defining characteristic. But we are also different. Black children, for example, learn from parents, family, the church, and the community the history of the black struggle for freedom; they share with their parents similar experiences of oppression. As gay males, lesbians, and bisexuals, however, we must form our sense of our gay identity on our own. Only then can we learn to relate to a new community. We must learn this from our peers—often late in life. Each generation must build its own sense of community and history. As our community institutions grow and our visibility in society increases, that job becomes easier. But every day another child or adult, learning and accepting his or her sexual orientation as different from the norm, must discover a community that for many other minorities comes with birth.

And just what is the oppression that gay males, lesbians, and bisexuals face? The most explicit form is the criminalization of our sexuality by the government. Twenty-five states and the District of Columbia still have laws—so-called sodomy laws—that make certain forms of consensual adult sexual behavior illegal. Six states single out homosexual activity only. These laws are often selectively enforced against gays, deliberately used to frighten and intimidate a minority.

Sodomy laws are also used to rationalize other forms of discrimination. How can a gay person be a good parent if he or she engages in criminal acts? How can a police department hire someone gay in a state that has sodomy laws on the books? Similar questions are never asked about the sexual practices of heterosexual parents or police officers, even in the nineteen states that criminalize heterosexual sodomy. Of course, for the state to criminalize behavior that, for reasons of public health, it seeks to influence sends at best a mixed message to gays in the United States. Indeed, because of this contradiction, many health officials have joined the call for the repeal of sodomy laws as a means of promoting AIDS-prevention efforts and establishing their credibility with affected communities. Lesbian and gay Americans do not have the same privacy rights that the U.S. Constitution affords most other citizens. In June 1986, in *Bowers v. Hardwick,* which involved a gay man's private consensual activity in his own home, the Supreme Court essentially wrote gays out of the Constitution by upholding a Georgia sodomy law dating back to 1816. Without constitutional protections, we are left to the whims of the states. By 1992, in all but five states (Connecticut, Hawaii, Wisconsin, New Jersey, and Massachusetts), it is legal to discriminate against gays in employment, housing, and public accommodations—in all those areas in which we as a society have come to accept it is improper and illegal to discriminate on the basis of race, religion, nationality, sex, age, or physical or mental ability. Around eighty cities and counties have passed legislation outlawing such discrimination, a first step toward building broad-based support for and experience with such protections. Some of these communities are in states with sodomy laws, creating the irony that being homosexual is legal but that engaging in homosexual acts is not. Again, in the context of an epidemic so closely identified with a single group—gay men—this lack of protection has had profound implications.

Not only is the federal government unwilling to protect us; its policies affirmatively seek to discriminate against us—the only affirmative action gays have ever received from the federal government. The military considers (known) homosexuality to be incompatible with military service even though gay and lesbian servicepeople have performed countless acts of bravery in action. It is feared that mixing gays and straights in the military will undermine morale. These arguments are not at all dissimilar to those made in the 1940s against racial integration in the armed forces. The fight against AIDS in the military has been, at a minimum, confused by the denial that there could be a significant amount of homosexual activity because that activity is forbidden. Statistics do not lie, however; all branches of the armed forces have reported significant numbers of AIDS cases. (Interestingly, but not surprisingly, the fear of disclosing homosexual behavior has made epidemiology among the military AIDS cases fairly unreliable; some notions of heterosexual transmission rates are therefore probably exaggerated.) The willful denial of the existence of homosexual behavior makes education about the prevention of HIV transmission difficult. Military policy also makes servicepeople afraid to seek counseling or treatment, thus compounding the problem and the danger of further transmission.

The national security agencies either automatically deny security clearances to lesbians and gays or subject them to a higher level of scrutiny—on the basis of the (false) notion that homosexuals are more susceptible to blackmail than are heterosexuals. (Most, if not all, sex scandals in which national security has been compromised have, however, involved heterosexuals.) Rather than singling out one group, a single standard ought to be applied to all.

Another form of government-supported discrimination was the prohibition against immigration by gays and lesbians, repealed in late 1990 as part of a larger immigration reform package. Until then, the Immigration and Nationality Act classified homosexuals as psychopathic personalities. Gays and lesbians could therefore be excluded on medical grounds even though both the American Psychiatric Association and the American Psychological Association had removed homosexuality from their list of disorders. Ironically, the very Public Health Service that asked the gay community to trust it during the AIDS crisis was the government agency assigned the job of enforcing this provision of the Immigration and Nationality Act banning homosexuals. In defense of the Public Health Service, however, it must be said that it did not want this job, arguing that homosexuality cannot be diagnosed during a medical exam. Indeed, for a number of years it had not enforced this provision, only to be compelled to do so by the Reagan administration Justice Department.

Congress has also imposed a ban on immigration by those infected with HIV—at the behest of Senator Jesse Helms. This is counter to international public health standards, including the policies of the World Health Organization. It is even opposed by the Public Health Service. HIV is communicable through unprotected sexual activity; the mere presence of foreigners with HIV poses no public health threat. The ban incensed representatives to the International AIDS Conference in San Francisco in June 1990, and many mainstream international and U.S. organizations boycotted the event. This is but one example of the fear and hysteria surrounding AIDS resulting in congressional involvement in public health policy-making. (As part of the 1990 immigration reform law Congress restored to Secretary of Health and Human Services Louis Sullivan the power to remove HIV from the list of excludable conditions. By 1991, President Bush refused to take Sullivan's suggestion to remove HIV from this list. Because of Bush's blatantly discriminatory policy, the Harvard AIDS Institute [the sponsor of the 1992 International AIDS Conference] carried through on its threat to transfer the conference outside the United States from Boston to Amsterdam.)

The federal government's official policies have reflected society's irrational hatred and fear of homosexuality. It is not surprising that so many people in the United States misunderstand and are intolerant of gay people when they live in a culture where many mainstream religions condemn homosexuality and Far Right fundamentalists make their living promoting antigay bigotry. The toll of this type of oppression is documented by the startling increase in violence against gays, lesbians, and bisexuals over the last several years. That toll has increased during the AIDS epidemic, as people play out their own fears about AIDS against the one group that is so visibly identified with the epidemic.

A final aspect of the discrimination under which gay people live is rejection by our parents and families—from whom most of us seek comfort, support, and love. While many families are support-ive—witness the growing number of Parents and Friends of Les-bians and Gays (PFLAG) chapters around the country—far too many reject their gay children. The spiraling rate of suicide among gay youths attests to that. Even acknowledging that spiraling sui-cide rate as a serious problem is, however, controversial in the current political climate. When a National Institute of Mental Health study suggested that antigay attitudes might be the cause of the high suicide rates among young gays and lesbians, pressure from California Congressman William Dannemeyer, one of the leading congressional homophobes, caused Louis Sullivan to call for a review of the study. Sullivan issued a statement distancing himself from any definition of family that included homosexuality. Sullivan, of course, heads the agency charged with the fight against AIDS. And he wonders why the gay community is angry and frus-trated.

I have detailed the status of gay men and lesbians in U.S. so-ciety at such length because of the profound effect that status has on the public health problems posed by AIDS. I have also meant to show why the traditional approach taken by the public health community has both faced resistance and required adjustment when applied to the AIDS epidemic.

Delayed Response: Homophobia or Reaganism?

While the delayed response to the AIDS epidemic by the fed-eral government has been well documented, the causes of that de-layed response are various. Was it a result of overt homophobia? Or can it simply be attributed to a public health system crippled by Reagan administration budget cuts?

I think the problem must be assessed at different levels. There is no doubt that key policymakers at the White House, most no-tably domestic policy advisor Gary Bauer, introduced elements of overt hostility toward gays into the debate. But such overt hostility was not a factor at the Public Health Service. Indeed, many PHS employees turned out to be sympathetic toward and supportive of gays. Since much of the initial response to AIDS was channeled through existing PHS programs, why then the delay? I think the answer is ignorance. While the responsible officials were not necessarily homophobic, they knew nothing about the gay community. The gay community did not even exist in the minds of all too many public health officials until the epidemic forced recognition. Only minimal lines of communication linked the gay community and the public health system—lines certainly not strong enough to recognize the growing problem or to activate the system. And because there were few established ties—and in their place a legacy of distrust—it was hard to establish stronger ties quickly. Without such ties, the government developed no sense of urgency—all budgetary constraints aside. Inertia prevailed in a system already unable to keep up with current public health demands. As a result, thousands of lives were lost.

Saving the Government from Itself

Without an appropriate government response, the gay community had to turn to itself to provide the initial, and continuing, response to the AIDS epidemic. Oppression has served us well in one regard, however—probably saving tens of thousands of lives in the process. Because of the suspicion with which society, government, and the medical establishment viewed the gay community and we them, a gay health movement took hold in the mid- to late 1970s, inspired in large part by the women's health-care empowerment movement beginning in the 1960s.

In many of the larger cities across the nation, gay men had formed gay health clinics as early as the late 1960s, not trusting the medical establishment to treat them for sexually transmitted diseases. In the early 1980s, the gay community turned to these groups to generate the original AIDS service organizations. Providing care and AIDS education, these organizations saved the government from its own inaction, and they continue to form the basis for the local response to AIDS. They are a model of Reagan Republican voluntarism or George Bush's "thousand points of light." But they are also being asked to carry a burden far in excess of what would ordinarily be asked of the private, voluntary sector.

Normally, volunteer organizations receive substantial government assistance when confronting a new problem as overwhelming
as the AIDS epidemic. Yet no federal funding for AIDS prevention
was available until 1984, when Congress created a program of minimal assistance to community-based organizations funded by the
U.S. Conference of Mayors. Several years into the epidemic, even
sympathetic members of the Public Health Service recognized that
the federal government was providing inadequate assistance to gay
organizations fighting AIDS. Through some imaginative financ-
ing—conceived by a Reagan appointee but carried in Congress by
California Democrat Ed Roybal—funds were funneled to these organizations through the Conference of Mayors ($150,000 the first
year, a sum that grew over time). Ultimately, community-based
prevention programs were funded directly. Because of homophobia, such funding came only after a delay and probably at a lower
level than would have been granted to a more politically acceptable
cause.

The funding of AIDS-related service and prevention programs
by local governments has followed a similar pattern. Community-
based organizations were at first allowed to struggle on alone. But
several years into the epidemic, as voters began to demand the
government do *something* about the epidemic, local politicians began to fund AIDS service organizations. Enjoying the best of both
worlds, these politicians could provide the mandated AIDS-
related services while sidestepping the social and political controversy necessarily involved had those services been introduced in
existing public health programs.

There is a certain logic to this: the gay community itself had
argued that prevention efforts should be targeted and that those
affected would deliver the message more effectively, that gays
would accept suggestions about changes in sexual practices more
readily from other gays than from an employee of a government
that still endorsed sodomy laws. But these gay organizations were
being asked to take on the entire preventative effort, not just that
focused on the gay community, and were given limited funds to do
so. As a result, the needs of many in the heterosexual community—those at risk because of sexual activity and those at risk be-

cause of intravenous drug use—were neglected. So were the needs of many segments of the gay community itself. Many of the gay-based AIDS organizations drew their volunteers from the white middle class, volunteers either unwilling or unable to speak to the diverse gay population.

What is the result? Across the nation, AIDS services and prevention programs have not been adequately incorporated into the public health system. The spread of HIV beyond the gay community has been barely slowed, and the government, once again relying on existing service organizations, has failed to meet the needs of those new groups affected. Only now are some of those communities being reached. Once again, the response to AIDS has been a case of too little too late.

Who Placed Politics over Public Health?

Throughout the AIDS epidemic, the Far Right has argued that the gay community has used the attention and access to the political system generated by the crisis to further its civil rights agenda, placing politics above public health. I would argue that it is the other way around, that throughout the epidemic the Far Right has imposed its own political agenda on the nation by fighting funding for gay community-based organizations or in trying to restrict the content of AIDS education efforts.

The gay community has never opposed measures that it thought might stop the spread of AIDS, for it is our own lives that are at risk. Our position has been and is much more complex. No attempt to control the spread of disease can be successful without the cooperation of those affected. That cooperation can be based only on trust, but there can be no trust without understanding. Health-care policies cannot be devised without taking into account the social factors governing the lives of the people they affect. In other words, good public health requires a healthy respect for civil liberties.

The gay community has managed to convince the overwhelming majority of the public health community that the issues of confidentiality and nondiscrimination had to be addressed before an effective public health strategy to fight the spread of AIDS could be implemented. In the historical context of officially sanctioned discrimination, it is particularly impressive that the gay community was so willing to cooperate with the public health community. We often asked our challengers to put themselves in our shoes, asking them, Would you come forward to be tested for HIV or participate in a prevention program if by so doing you would publicly proclaim yourself as gay and at risk—thereby leaving yourself open to losing your job, custody of your children, or your home? Would you speak frankly to government epidemiologists if the manner in which you contracted AIDS is a felony? Would you cooperate with a Public Health Service that worked with the government to deny your fellow gay men the right to travel and emigrate? Would you be responsive to public health education campaigns that condemn who you are, telling you to change your sexuality in the name of the public good—as so many of the governments' early publicity efforts did?

Looking at it from this perspective, it is amazing that, despite the risks, gays have indeed answered yes to these questions, but such a response was necessary to halt the spread of HIV. Nevertheless, the battle against AIDS would have been easier and more effective had it not been necessary first to fight homophobia and the discrimination that has resulted. This is where the civil rights agenda and the public health agenda merge: the society that now so fears AIDS is paying the price of generations of discrimination against gays by having created conditions that do not encourage those most affected to participate in public health measures.

Despite the clear link between antigay discrimination and HIV-related discrimination, despite the link between anti-gay policies and attitudes and the fact that many homosexually active men at risk are still driven underground by the fear of discrimination, there has been little progress in the fight for greater civil rights protections for lesbians and gay men as a result of the AIDS crisis. This runs counter to the image that the Far Right puts out, but it is true. By 1992, ten years into the AIDS epidemic, only four states, Massachusetts, Connecticut, New Jersey, and Hawaii, have been added to the list of those outlawing discrimination based on sexual orientation. Few states have repealed their sodomy laws—though many in the public health community argue that they impede frank discussion of risk in prevention and epidemiology programs. While many local jurisdictions and the U.S. Congress *have* approved protections against discrimination based on HIV status and, in some cases, perceived risk for HIV, the situation remains that gay and bisexual men are protected from discrimination only if they are infected with HIV. Noninfected gay and bisexual men are afforded no such protection.

Some public health measures meant to combat the spread of AIDS could not be implemented until nondiscrimination and confidentiality were guaranteed. Confronting the issues, however, meant diverting attention from preventative efforts. Those efforts were delayed, and that delay killed. And it increased the risk faced by all people in this country who might be exposed to HIV.

Homophobia or Sexphobia?

HIV is transmitted primarily though unprotected sexual activity. Even as more and more cases of HIV infection can be attributed to intravenous drug use, sexual transmission—between drug users and their partners—continues to play a major role in the spread of AIDS. U.S. society has never dealt well with sexuality in general, let alone homosexuality. The history of sexually transmitted disease control in the United States is one of repression rather than one of confronting the realities of sexual expression.

Repressive attitudes obviously hinder efforts to prevent an infection that is sexually transmitted, especially when the only truly effective preventative measure is education about behavior change. But at the outset of the epidemic, AIDS struck gay men almost exclusively. Is it therefore sexphobia or homophobia that has prevented an appropriate response? Put differently, could we have expected any better had HIV affected heterosexuals almost exclusively?

Certainly, efforts at education within the gay community have prompted some of the most virulent homophobic attacks to date. Nevertheless, the gay community has developed model programs aimed at effecting behavior change. There is almost universal agreement in the public health community that the results among gay men have been dramatic—often gauged by dramatically declining rates of sexually transmitted diseases (rates that have recently skyrocketed among certain segments of the heterosexual population). Safer sex is now de rigueur in many gay circles, a fundamental change in behavior that few experts would have believed possible.

The programs that have accomplished so much have been frank, gay positive, and sex positive—and they have usually not had government funding. Those programs that are most effective are feared by government officials—because they might be seen as promoting homosexuality. Perhaps the most infamous expression of that point of view came in 1987 from Senator Jesse Helms of North Carolina, who proposed an amendment to an AIDS appropriations bill that would prohibit federal funding of materials that "promote or encourage . . . homosexual sexual activities."

Helms's amendment passed by a vote of ninety-six to two. The amendment has since been rewritten, more neutral language now linking any discussion of sexuality to the promotion of risk reduction, but its chilling impact is still felt today. The overwhelming initial vote, and the great struggle necessary to overcome opposition, stems from Helms's uncanny ability to turn AIDS discussion into a condemnation of homosexuality, tapping the greatest personal and political fears of many members of Congress. In this instance, he used a relatively explicit campaign launched by the New York-based Gay Men's Health Crisis (GMHC), including their publication of "safe sex comics," in his attack on gay-positive safer-sex education. Indeed, Helms and several other right-wing members of Congress seem to derive a particularly strange pleasure from detailing allegedly common sexual practices among gay men. Helms, however, omitted two facts in the debate: the GMHC materials were not published with federal dollars, and such material has been demonstrated to be the most effective means of inducing changes in behavior.

The effects of the Helms amendment went well beyond the gay community. All explicit safer-sex education is threatened when only the promotion of abstinence is politically safe. More broadly, however, and more dangerous, the approach Helms takes—that HIV is spread by homosexuals pursuing pleasure with abandon and without considering of the risk posed to the rest of society—makes heterosexuals feel safe, feel that they are not at risk. So much of the debate about HIV that is homophobic creates a sense of "otherness" about those infected, allowing people to rationalize not dealing with their own risk of exposure to HIV.

The homophobia expressed in all AIDS-related issues covers up an even more deeply rooted sexphobia. Both are hard to challenge in public policy debates, especially when those debates are overtly homophobic. At least our elected officials think so, and the price they pay is having placed at greater risk the very people they are seeking to protect.

Is There a Lesson to Be Learned?

If there is an overriding lesson to be learned from this sketch of the gay community's experience with the AIDS epidemic—and how society's attitudes toward gays have driven so much that is wrong with the national response to the epidemic—it is that discrimination kills both those who are discriminated against and those discrimination is meant to protect. Delaying or hampering a response to what was perceived as simply a problem of the homosexuals in fact harmed many heterosexuals. The extent of the problem was underplayed, the likelihood of heterosexual spread was minimized. And while the rate of infection has not risen as rapidly among heterosexuals in the United States as among gay men, it is rising steadily.

Most people in the United States have not overcome their sense of otherness in coping with this crisis. First only gay and bisexual men were affected—and the majority of society could breathe a sigh of relief. Now injection drug users and their partners are affected, most of whom are poor and black or Hispanic—and the majority can still breathe easily. But this false sense of security cannot continue. Never before has a sexually transmitted disease remained confined to one group; there is no reason to believe HIV will be the exception. Many heterosexuals—forewarned as gay men were not—have squandered the extra time given them.

Public health officials have learned some important lessons working with the gay community. They have come to respect the gay community's work combatting the AIDS crisis, and they now understand that cooperative efforts can be quite successful. Mistakes continue to be made, however. The gay community was assumed to be monolithic, and minority gays were therefore neglected. No account was taken of the fact that intravenous drug users might be just as mistrustful of and alienated from the public health system as gay men once were. No one remembers that community-run programs are the most effective.

The conclusion to be drawn is that discrimination and prejudice are legacies that hamper public health efforts and place the entire population at great risk. Society is paying for its legacy of homophobia—not only in gay lives lost but also in heterosexual lives placed at risk and social institutions overwhelmed, their existence jeopardized. There is still time to turn this sad experience around—if in the future we recognize that feelings of otherness do not protect us from disease and possibly place us at greater risk.

FURTHER READINGS

ACT UP/NY Women and AIDS Book Group. *Women, AIDS, and Activism.* Boston: South End, 1990.

Blumenfeld, Warren J. *AIDS and Your Religious Community.* Boston: Unitarian Universalist Press, 1991.

Crimp, Douglas, and Adam Rolston. *AIDSDEMOGRAPHICS.* Seattle: Bay Press, 1990.

Dossier, Panos. *AIDS and the Third World.* Philadelphia: New Society, 1989.

Kramer, Larry. *Reports from the Holocaust: The Making of an AIDS Activist.* New York: St. Martin's, 1989.

Monette, Paul, *Borrowed Time: An AIDS Memoir.* New York: Avon, 1988.

Nussbaum, Bruce. *Good Intentions.* New York: Penguin, 1990.

O'Malley, Padraig, ed. *The AIDS Epidemic: Private Rights and the Public Interest.* Boston: Beacon, 1989.

Patton, Cindy. *Sex and Germs: The Politics of AIDS.* Boston: South End, 1985.

Shilts, Randy. *And the Band Played On: Politics, People, and the AIDS Epidemic.* New York: St. Martin's, 1987.

PART FOUR

BREAKING FREE

15

On Being Heterosexual in a Homophobic World

COOPER THOMPSON

If you were to meet me, before I had the chance to tell you anything about me, you would know that I am white and male. If I told you about my work—teaching about racism, sexism, and homophobia and the coordinator of the Campaign to End Homophobia—you might assume that I am gay. In fact, I am heterosexual. I am also homophobic; in my experience, being homophobic is the predictable result of growing up and living in a homophobic world. My life has been affected at every turn by these conditions.

In the following pages, I want to talk about being heterosexual in a homophobic world. I want to explain some of the ways I came to know about homophobia and, in the process, some of the ways I noticed that I was homophobic. I want to describe some of the ways homophobia has hurt me as a heterosexual and how I believe that ending homophobia is in my own interest as a heterosexual. I want to make some comments about heterosexual privilege. And, finally, I want to share some of my optimism about the potential for a less homophobic future.

Learning about Homophobia

In the summer of 1972, during a phone call in which she sounded far away but very sure of herself, K. told me that she was a lesbian. She and I had flirted with being lovers, and I also knew that she cared deeply about a woman with whom she lived. Earlier that spring, I had wondered about her sexual orientation, but I

235

believe that this was the first time I *knew* that I knew a lesbian. Despite my desire for her, and some feelings of jealousy about her relationship with a woman, I felt satisfied knowing that she was claiming a lost part of herself. I was OK, and so was she.

I have no specific memories of contact with openly lesbian or gay people prior to that summer, although I clearly knew that there were lesbians and gay men in the world. Having grown up with a healthy dose of traditional masculinity in a traditional family, and having been a successful football player in high school, I must have known the stereotypes, and I was certainly acquainted with homophobia. Yet I was somehow prepared to accept K. for who she was. I did not try to talk her out of it; I did not assume that I could change her.

Over the next four years, in graduate school, I met other lesbians and other women whom I assumed were lesbian. I recall being curious about them—perhaps we talked about what it meant to be a lesbian—and my general sense is that I liked these women and admired who they were and what they did in the world.

On the other hand, my consciousness of homophobia in my relationships with men began much earlier and was a very different experience. I recall a sixth-grade classmate who was accused of being a "homo" because my friends and I thought he was weird and somewhat effeminate; we teased him, sometimes shoved him, and certainly excluded him from our social group. Then there was a man at the local soda shop who allegedly liked boys and about whom my parents warned me; I believe that we liked the attention he gave us, yet we would make "jokes" about his being a "homo." Then there was the routine way in which we sneaked looks at other boys in the locker room shower, trying to satisfy our curiosity about other guys' genitals, and the fear I felt when I sensed someone looking at me.

In contrast to the little I knew about lesbians, by college I had acquired substantial (mis)information about male homosexuality. It was not until 1977—after graduate school, when I was teaching high school—that I first met an openly gay man. B. was a student of mine. Over time, he told me about his social life outside school, his experiences with classmates, and his relationship with his parents. I knew about the concerned yet accepting attitude of his parents, the rejection from classmates and the feelings of loneliness at school, and the excitement and fear he felt in dating men and looking for love. B. challenged my stereotypes about homosexuality.

I now know just how courageous B. was. He was the only male student who was out; his only real friend at school was a young woman who had been ostracized for having been sexually involved with several guys. I believe that they understood, at some level, how the oppressions they experienced were related.

The relationship I had with B. seems, in retrospect, comfortable. I enjoyed our conversations and had a good rapport with his parents, with whom I discussed his work at school as well as their feelings about his sexual orientation. I suspect I was nervous about saying or doing the right thing around him, yet I generally recall that I was a good adviser and that B. appreciated my support.

At about the same time, I began to meet adult gay men. Instead of feeling confident, I was afraid. Homophobia had set me up to fear gay men's sexuality; male conditioning had set me up to fear men in general. A friend introduced me to L. and implied that he was gay. The first time we met, I had enjoyed the conversation and told him so, but in a second get-together, I told him that I did not want to spend time with him, giving the excuse that I was too busy. I was scared that he was coming on to me, and rather than confirming my suspicions, I ran from him. I felt guilty.

I had a similar experience with a man in an exercise class at the YMCA, and he was angry that I ran away. What I now understand is that underneath my terror was confusion; I wanted closer relationships with men, but I was not interested in sexual intimacy. Having known intimacy only in sexual relationships with women, which usually began with flirtation, my interest in men must have had sexual overtones, to which, not surprisingly, gay men responded in kind. I was not prepared for that, so I cut off contact as soon as it was made.

Through participation at Men and Masculinity conferences in 1981 and 1982, I began to explore my relationships with other men and the nature of my own manhood. I knew that there were gay men at these conferences, and I heard about sexual contacts between some of the men, but I was somehow untouched by this. I was preoccupied, and excited, by all the talk of feminism and a "new masculinity"; I was thrilled that I had found a community where I could be myself and not have to compete, at least in the old ways, with other men.

At the 1982 conference I met D., who was quite openly gay. We became friends. During a visit to Los Angeles I stayed at his house. He came on to me and I responded simply by telling him that I was not interested in a sexual relationship. He respected that. It was a brief but profound exchange: I learned that the cultural mythology suggesting an unbridled gay male sexuality might be inaccurate. In the years since that evening, I have rarely been afraid of a gay man's sexual interest in me; in fact, most of the gay men with whom I have had contact have never demonstrated *any* sexual interest in me.

At the same time, I have come to believe that gay men, like heterosexual men, are socialized as men before any consciousness of sexual orientation. Part of male socialization is learning to be sexually aggressive. Therefore, I believe that trusting any man with sexual limit setting is a risky business. Nonetheless, I have continued to trust not only D. but most of my gay male friends. Not only do I generally feel safe around gay men, but I have often discovered in these friendships a sense of intimacy that is usually missing in my friendships with heterosexual men. In fact, I am more likely to be afraid in the presence of heterosexual men, or those men whom I presume to be heterosexual; I am more alarmed by the ways in which men threaten one another in everyday acts of male aggression that are not explicitly sexual.

The Effect of Homophobia

Over the past five years, my friendships with both lesbians and gay men have grown deeper, and at some points I have noticed that most of my friends and acquaintances are lesbian or gay. There is a freedom I feel with these friends. Not only is the potential for intimacy greater with gay male friends, but I can also cross sex-role boundaries more easily with them than I can with heterosexual male friends. With lesbian friends, there is an opportunity for intimacy that is different from the intimacy I experience with heterosexual women: from the start I assume that we will be friends, not lovers, so I focus my attention on our friendship instead of becoming sidetracked by the possibility of a sexual relationship. Our different sexual orientations act to limit my sexual aggression, and, in the end, I feel less confused about the sexual nature of our relationship.

At the same time, in predominantly heterosexual social settings and with some heterosexual friends, I feel a certain pressure—sometimes self-imposed, but sometimes coming from others—to be a more traditional, or at least predictable, man. I have to decide if I want to talk about my work on homophobia or about the fact that I play in a lesbian and gay jazz band; I have to decide if I have the energy to deal with the reaction. If I hide this information, I feel as if I have left part of myself at the door. The feeling is one of distrust; I do not know if it is safe for me to be myself in the presence of other heterosexuals. I also feel confused by the sexual energy I experience in heterosexual social settings: the sexual attractions between myself and other women and the sexual fears separating me from other men.

There is no question about the effect of homophobia on lesbian, gay, and bisexual people in this society. As a group, they have been, and continue to be, oppressed because of their sexuality. The oppression takes many forms: invisibility, harassment, assault, damnation, denial of police and judicial protection, discrimination, etc.

While heterosexuals, as a group, are not actually oppressed by homophobia, I believe that we are profoundly hurt by it. The fear of being thought homosexual keeps us from being intimate with same-sex friends; this same fear can lock us into rigid definitions of masculinity and femininity. Homophobia can destroy our families when we discover, and cannot accept, a family member who is lesbian, gay, or bisexual. In a society where the achievements of lesbian, gay, and bisexual people are hidden, we get a distorted view of reality; we learn only about the lives of other heterosexuals. The denial of equal civil rights to sexual minorities inevitably leads to limitations on the rights of all: if one group can be targeted for discrimination, any group can be targeted. In the end, homophobia prevents us from being fully ourselves.

My Self-Interest in Ending Homophobia

In my work on racism, I have often noticed how I have more energy for my work when I can articulate what I am moving toward rather than what I am trying to avoid. As a result, I have begun to focus on the ways in which it is to my benefit to live in a multicultural world in addition to the ways in which I am hurt by racism. In the case of homophobia, the benefits of living in a less homophobic world include expanding my options as a man, expanding the types of relationships I have with women and men, a greater appreciation of my own sexuality, an increased sense of safety as I interact with other men, learning from the experiences of lesbian and gay people, continuing my friendships with lesbians and gay men, learning about other forms of oppression in a way that is facilitated by my understanding of homophobia, and the possibility for greater justice and love in the world.

Expanding My Options as a Man

I learned the male role well. To expand that role beyond the limits defined by traditional masculinity means overcoming my internal sense of what is appropriate as well as the culture's judgment of what is appropriate behavior for me. The primary way in which our culture enforces sex roles for men (and women) is through homophobia; same-sex attraction and sexuality are linked with "inappropriate" sex roles. The feminine man is labeled *gay, faggot*. The masculine woman is labeled *lesbian, dyke*. A reduction in cultural homophobia will, therefore, mean an expansion of sex-role opportunities for me. I will be able to do the things traditionally assigned to women without being stigmatized as less of a man.

Expanding Types of Relationships

For many heterosexual men, their friendships with women often carry a sexual tension—will we have sex? At the same time, their

friendships with men are competitive and emotionally distant—
how can I keep from being vulnerable around him? In my friendships with lesbians and gay men, I have the opportunity to move
beyond these limitations. With lesbians, it is a given that our relationship will not be sexual, so I find that there is the possibility of
a solid friendship developing, free from the tension of sexual feelings. (I believe that this is what heterosexual women often mean
when they say that gay men are more "sensitive"; it is not that gay
men are less sexist per se but that the fear of sexual assault is not
present, thus allowing for better communication and greater intimacy.) With gay men, there is a possibility of emotional intimacy
beyond what I often find with heterosexual men. From my experience, gay men are generally less afraid of being close to other
men and thus more available for intimate friendship.

A Greater Appreciation of My Own Sexuality

In the time that I have spent trying to understand homophobia and
come to terms with my own prejudices, I have learned to ask questions about my own sexuality and the assumptions that accompany
traditional heterosexuality. I have discovered new patterns of loving; I feel freer in my sexual relationship with my partner, knowing
that there really are no "right" ways to love.

An Increased Sense of Safety

After a young gay man was murdered in Bangor, Maine, several
years ago, I was asked to come and work with public school teachers on issues of homophobia. As I walked through the town, I
sensed that *every* man in Bangor must adjust his behavior; *any*
man was vulnerable to attack if the attackers thought he were gay.
About a year later, I was walking in Harvard Square in Cambridge
(a place with a reputation for personal freedom) and was verbally
assaulted for having my arm around another man (I was helping
him through a difficult period in his life).

Although I may not be as vulnerable to physical or verbal attack as many gay men, an end to homophobia would mean an increase in my personal safety. I believe that homophobia is a stim-
ulus for male violence: men who are insecure about their

masculinity or who fear peer rejection for not being sufficiently masculine may use violence as a way to prove their manliness. I would love to feel safer from all forms of male violence, from street crime and fistfights in sports to economic exploitation and war.

Learning from the Experience of Lesbians and Gays

I have learned a lot from my friends. For example, lesbians and gay men have shown me ways to challenge traditional assumptions about sexual relationships. Listening to gay men's stories of the bathhouses in the 1970s or knowing that sexual contact between friends is more common in the lesbian and gay community has helped me understand that consensual sexual activity is primarily an experience in giving pleasure to oneself and one's partner. Too often, heterosexuals are taught—and believe—that sexual activity can take place only in the context of marriage or a love relationship. AIDS, or course, has changed the landscape, bringing fear where there was liberation. I feel sad that our society missed an opportunity to expand its appreciation of sexuality as a way to build self-esteem and to come to know oneself.

I have also learned about commitment. Although my partner and I have discussed marriage, I have resisted participating in a state and church-sanctioned ceremony upholding heterosexual privilege. Recently, however, I attended the wedding of two gay men and saw an option for us. During the ceremony, the friends and family who attended the wedding were granted the power to pronounce the two men "lifelong partners." In this act, I saw the process of empowerment at work; I felt the excitement of naming something for ourselves rather than having it named for us. One of the partners pointed out that heterosexuals often fall into legal, church-sanctioned marriage without considering creative alternatives; for these men, being gay meant the opportunity to think through their commitment to one another carefully and then create a ceremony that would fulfill their needs, not just satisfy legal or religious requirements.

Continuing My Friendships

Many of my closest friends are lesbians and gay men. Homophobia threatens their existence and makes it difficult for them to be fully themselves. Those friendships are important to me. I want us to be able to know one another fully.

Learning about Other Forms of Oppression

Although each type of oppression is unique, there are also similarities between, say, racism and homophobia. Knowing about the dynamics of homophobia helps me understand how racism operates, and vice versa. As a white male, I can use all the help I can get.

Greater Justice and Love in the World

I want to live in a world of freedom and justice for all people. Whenever I witness acts of homophobic injustice and recognize the contradictions inherent in a society that professes equality for all, I feel pain. If I am told by a fundamentalist that homosexuality is evil, I feel a deep hurt that good people who live their lives with at least the same levels of commitment and integrity as heterosexuals are so judged.

I also want there to be more love in the world; if it comes in the form of same-sex sexuality, that is fine with me. I feel the loss of that love whenever I realize that same-sex couples cannot safely show their affection in public places in the many ways that heterosexuals can: hugging, kissing, holding hands. I believe that this will be a better world when all people are free to express their love for one another.

Self-Interest and Heterosexual Privilege

Focusing on heterosexual self-interest is controversial. For those who are acutely aware of the oppression of lesbian, gay, and bisexual people—and the relative freedom of heterosexual people—such talk can lead to feelings of resentment that heterosexuals are interested only in getting more privileges than we already have. For others, talk of self-interest flies in the face of the liberal position that ending oppression is for the benefit of the oppressed, never the oppressor—to have it otherwise would be selfish. (Of course, underneath this position one often finds an assumption of superiority and a feeling of pity for the oppressed.)

When a colleague first suggested to me several years ago that I might want to look at my own self-interest in doing this work, I resisted her; it seemed like a contradiction to me. I experienced the question itself as an invitation to selfishness. How could I worry about increasing my lot when there was so much oppression to be fought? But like most people—and perhaps all people—my energy for a task is strongest and most resilient when my self-interest is at stake, when what I am doing directly benefits me. Furthermore, if I am doing something for someone else's benefit and not my own, I run the very real risk of deciding what they need rather than listening to them articulate their needs. I also run the risk of doing their work for them, thus depriving them of the opportunity to learn new skills to defeat their oppression. Thus, I have come to believe that I will have the most energy to challenge oppression when I define the benefits that I will receive in a less oppressive society, knowing full well that others will benefit from the work I do for myself.

While I am focusing on the long-term goal of a nonhomophobic society—where the benefits I have described will accrue to *all* people, regardless of sexual orientation—there are questions I have about managing my heterosexual privilege in the present. Will I confront those who would give me benefits for being heterosexual while denying the same benefits to lesbian, gay, and bisexual people? Will I confront the omnipresent cultural homophobia that renders anyone who is not heterosexual invisible, abnormal, immoral, or sick? Will I give up the privilege in those settings where I have the power to exercise it?

The privilege is certainly real: it includes the many ways in which I automatically reap the benefits of living in a society that believes that heterosexuality is normal, moral, and healthy. I am free to talk about my sexual partner—in fact, if I were to run for political office or seek certain jobs, having a wife would be a clear asset in terms of public image. If I marry, or at least have a woman as a partner, my decision will be celebrated in my family, and it will be assumed that I have become more responsible as a man. As an employee, I will not have to worry about discrimination because of my sexual orientation; as a citizen, I will have other heterosexuals representing me in political offices and see my heterosexuality reflected positively in the culture. I certainly benefit by being free from physical and verbal assault—this freedom allows me to focus my energy on what I want to do with my life without having to worry about other people stopping me. (I am also privileged by my status as a white male; it may be difficult to separate those privileges that accrue only to my heterosexuality.)

It seems easiest to confront others who would grant me privilege, provided that I am aware that I am being favored. One of the dynamics of being a member of an oppressor/dominant group is a relative unconsciousness about the oppression, so I assume that I will not always know about the privilege being given or denied. It may be easiest to see the privilege in context, for example, in a case where a gay coworker is being questioned about his ability to work objectively with young males. I might realize that my ability would never be questioned simply because of my sexual orientation. I would then have the option of challenging our supervisor about homophobic stereotypes.

It seems nearly impossible to challenge cultural homophobia, given its depth and breadth in our society, yet I believe that I can challenge it in specific cases: by calling attention to homophobic advertising practices, writing a letter to the editor concerning a homophobic news story, or challenging the homophobic behavior of a prominent public official. In addition, I can acknowledge and appreciate individuals and institutions when actions are taken to reduce homophobia. I believe that my work on homophobia, by its very nature, challenges cultural homophobia; it stands as a statement that homophobia is not in all our best interests.

As for those situations in which I can choose to exercise heterosexual privileges, some privileges seem insignificant and are easy to give up, while others are difficult and exact a price in the casting aside. Although I have the privilege of casually sharing information about my sexual orientation, I do not always feel a need to tell others about my heterosexuality. I can easily give up that privilege in some social and work settings.

The price goes up, however, if it is a privilege that I really want or one that I believe everyone ought to have. For example, whenever I am with my partner in a public place, I am acutely aware of how we can hold hands or kiss without any threat to our physical safety. The reality for same-sex couples is quite different. Consequently, I have chosen to touch her far less than I would like. At the same time, I believe that we need more expressions of love in this world, not fewer, so this decision is unsettling. In general, is giving up a privilege that I believe to be fundamentally good a strategy for countering oppression?

Perhaps in the Next Generation

In the last few years, I have become a father to two teenaged children. Technically, they are my unofficial stepchildren, as I have no legal relationship with my partner. But we are a family. Homophobia—as well as racism, sexism, ableism, classism, and a host of other oppressions—is a regular topic at the dinner table. My home is yet another place where I can challenge heterosexual privilege.

My daughter, who is fifteen years old, is learning far more than I ever did about people who are different from her. When she began to be conscious of the sexual orientation of some of my friends, she was curious but nervous and so kept her distance. She was reluctant to baby-sit for a lesbian couple, asked me in a cursory fashion if her piano teacher were gay, and was impatient with me when I suggested that her friends might not all be heterosexual. But she is now great friends with her piano teacher, comfortable with baby-sitting in a lesbian home, and very outspoken at school about the fact that she has lesbian and gay friends. She challenges peers who are openly homophobic. Recently, I invited her to attend a gay wedding with me; she changed her plans for the weekend and made a special trip from where she was vacationing with a relative. She told me, "I wouldn't miss this for anything." We both cried at the wedding.

My son has gone through his own changes. At fifteen, he and his friends used words like *faggot* as put-downs. At nineteen, he is saddened by the homophobic comments made about a dormmate presumed to be gay; as a residence hall president, he is meeting with the lesbian and gay support group to develop educational programs to reduce homophobia on the campus. He is still a little nervous being around lesbians and gay men, but he realizes that it is his homophobia getting in his way.

I am proud of them. I think they are both extraordinary young people. I am also proud of my decision to encourage their contact with lesbians and gay men. I have asked each of them about their sexual orientation—I want them to be conscious of the question. In their own ways they have each laughed and mentioned their obsession with the other sex, as if to say, "It's hopeless."

My daughter and son frequently tell me about the harassment of friends and peers who are presumed to be lesbian or gay. They are concerned, often angry about the mistreatment. At the same time, I notice how easily they are accepted, supported, and encouraged in their heterosexual relationships. Friends and extended family simply assume that they are heterosexual and therefore "normal." To some extent, they realize that they are the beneficiaries of heterosexual privilege.

I am excited and hopeful about their future and the effect they are having and will have on other people in their lives. At the end of their lifetimes, I expect that this world will still be a homophobic place to live—cultural change is a long and difficult process. But at a personal level I see profound change. In contrast to what I knew when I was young, they know that the world contains proud and healthy lesbian, gay, and bisexual people; they know that oppression is to blame, not the victims of oppression. Although I have never heard them articulate this, I believe that they realize that homophobia hurts them.

Although I have a vision of a world free of homophobia, I do not consider myself free of homophobia; in fact, I assume that I always will be homophobic. It is not necessarily pleasant to come to terms with this; I sometimes feel guilty, or shameful, or sad, that my homophobia affects my life and those around me the way it does. But in coming to terms with my homophobia, I feel more whole. I am integrating parts of myself that our society has tried to keep separate. Perhaps this is the strongest reason for me to continue doing this work.

NOTE

Although much of this essay is based on my recollections of experiences I have had over the past forty years, I want to acknowledge the many people who have in one way or another influenced and shaped my thinking about homophobia and provided me with support and inspiration to continue my work. They include Pat Griffin, Molly Gierasch, Jeff Beane, Peggy McIntosh, Angela Giudice, Zoe Perry, Althea Smith, Barbara Zoloth, Hilda-Gutierrez Baldoquin, Jamie Pierce, Robert Stein, my daughter, my son, John Stoltenberg, the lesbian and gay people in this essay referred to here (their names have been changed), and the women and men in the profeminist and gay-affirmative men's movement. There are undoubtedly others, and I regret not being able to list them all.

16

Homophobia and the Healing of Society

AMANDA UDIS-KESSLER

As we learn that perhaps one-third of all Americans do not have health insurance, as we watch a peace dividend that could have reduced hunger and hopelessness go up in flames in the Persian Gulf, as we wonder why American children are so poorly educated compared to those in other modernized societies, we are not likely to think that homophobia plays a role in these problems. What could homophobia have to do with the threat of a nuclear holocaust? Or with the crumbling of America's infrastructure, such as highways and bridges? Or with the growing "purchase" of scientists and their research by defense contractors? Or with environmental destruction, unemployment, inflation, recession, workplace hazards, the feminization of poverty, the redesigning of jobs so that workers can be paid less, the soaring rate of violence, the use to excess of alcohol, tobacco, and other drugs?[1] These are some of the basic structural problems that plague our country and diminish the richness of our lives when not actually killing us outright; what part could homophobia play in them?

The reason that we so rarely consider links between homophobia and large-scale socioeconomic and "quality of life" problems is that homophobia is often seen as a matter of individual prejudice, something that can be cured by education and thoughtful self-examination, while the other problems mentioned here seem to take place on a grand scale, outside our control as individuals, even behind our backs as citizens. What I want to suggest in this essay is that homophobia functions systematically to keep us from understanding the nature and depth of large-scale social problems as well as the ways in which we need to address these problems collectively if we are to bring about change.

Sociologist C. Wright Mills distinguishes between "personal troubles" and "public issues"[2] when considering how we understand problems with which we are faced.[3] He notes that, because of the individualistic temperament of our society, we tend to define the problems we encounter as personal troubles, results of personality quirks and individual biography, when in fact many of them are public issues. He gives the example of unemployment: if one person in a city is unemployed , she (as are we) is likely to consider the situation her fault (or at least her problem). In contrast, if 30 percent of the country's population is unemployed, we ought to consider this a public issue: a matter not just of personal biography but of large-scale socioeconomic trends that affect the country on many levels. A public issue is a problem whose effects are felt both by individuals and by institutions ranging from the government to the family, a problem for which some sort of collective or governmental action (rather than just individual action) will be needed to provide a solution.

The distinction between personal trouble and public issues does not seem to be so difficult to make, but it is important to realize that, unless a public issue is *defined as such,* it will remain a problem without solutions. To use Mills's example, individualistic solutions to a personal trouble ("Work harder!" or, "Get an education!") will not be very helpful if the public issue is that the economy as a whole cannot support full employment. Therefore, how we understand a problem will make all the difference in whether and how it gets solved. There are a number of questions that we will need answered in order to address public issues most effectively. Who gets to define a certain situation as a public issue rather than a personal problem? Who benefits from this situation? Who is hurt by it?Who or what is the cause of the problem? How did it come into existence? What factors contribute to its continuation? Who is responsible for proposing and implementing solutions?

These are all questions that can be asked about any of the large-scale problems with which I began the essay. However, they are not regularly asked by most individuals, and those who do ask them (such as antinuclear activists, worker's rights advocates, and proponents of socialized medicine) are presented to us (by the media, e.g.) as a small, strange faction, holdovers from the 1960s, out of touch with America today. Thus, while questions about these problems are being raised that could lead to solutions, they are not being taken up by large numbers of people. They are not leading to massive political action of any sort, and the problems do not seem to be getting solved. Certainly, there are some people who are "beating the system," but the bulk of those most affected by the loss of the peace dividend, environmental damage, increases in violence, and the various traps of poverty are not finding their situations improving. While these problems are arguably public issues, they are not being taken up in a large-scale, systematic way by the public.

What part does homophobia play in the silence about these problems? We can begin to answer this question by considering how homophobic people understand homosexuality. Some familiar sentiments speak of "a threat to the family," "moral decay," and "corrupting innocent children." This "threat to the American way of life" has been linked to Communist infiltration (as well as "leftism" in general), the liberal cosmopolitan aura of major cities,[4] and feminism—perspectives that are seen as challenging traditional religious and patriotic values, thereby weakening America.[5]

The language used here is quite revealing: *threat, decay, corruption, loss of innocence, weakening, infiltration.* It indicates a great fear, anger, and sense of loss somewhere in the collective American psyche, the presence of unease and discomfort and a certain kind of powerlessness. Because lesbian, gay, and bisexual rights activists have been so busy countering the stereotypes about homosexuality, including the ones focusing on moral decay and the threat to the family, we have not always taken the time to ponder whether these cries of anguish could be something *other than* homosexuality. We are so used to seeing homophobia as a matter of irrational prejudice with its roots in religious intolerance and sexphobia that we may be missing the ways in which completely different sets of fears[6] are being projected onto sexual minorities.[7]

What if the notions of corruption, loss of innocence, and weakness that appear in homophobic thought and speech are displaced responses to *actual* corruption, loss of innocence, and weakness elsewhere?

If homophobia is actually a matter (in part) of displacement, we need to discover the target at which this sense of fear, anger, and loss would be more appropriately aimed. Correctly identifying this target will allow us to work much more effectively against both homophobia and whatever actual ills are at work that are too scary to encounter directly. I propose that the source of anguish is none other than those large-scale problems that I have defined as public issues. There is, indeed, a loss of innocence in America, but it has more to do with political and economic corruption in high places and low than with sexuality. There is, indeed, a threat to the family, but it appears in contaminated water supplies and toxic dumps, hangs overhead in pollution, and waits silently in the possibility of hunger and homelessness. Workplace policies that force both parents to hold two jobs in order to keep up with the bills or that exhaust and embitter workers pose more danger to families than lesbian or gay child rearing ever has. Our educational and medical systems, the radioactive isotopes used to make atomic weapons, and the very roads we drive on are decaying faster than anybody's morals. Moreover, the very lack of resistance to these threats suggests that despair is infiltrating our souls far more effectively than so-called perversion.

This argument may be able to make sense of how homophobia hurts, not just heterosexuals, but Americans in general. But there is an important piece still missing: the process by which the fear, anger, and grief gets transferred from these problems to sexual minorities in the first place. How is it that clear and present dangers that threaten our very survival are the subject of dejected and cynical talk rather than collective action while some forms of love and erotic connection are able to mobilize thousands of people overnight in protest?

The perception of homosexuality as a threat seems to be a matter of moral rather than socioeconomic or structural language; its dangers are always couched in ethical, if not outright religious, terms. If in fact the public issues that I have identified are in some way behind the gut responses (fear of decay, sense of inefficacy, grief and anger about what has been lost) that are rerouted toward homosexuality, we may find that public discussion of these issues will take a moral tone. This way of framing the problems hides their structural aspects and also provides us with scapegoats. Thus, problems will be individualized and made to seem a matter of personal will rather than of social forces, and there will be particular people or sets of people who can be blamed for them. It is this sort of process that may be responsible for the "homosexualizing" of American decline.

Ironically, one of the best examples of this process does not concern sexuality at all; rather, it focuses on crime. If I am concerned about crime only because I am afraid of getting shot on the street at night, the obvious answer will appear to be more police and jails rather than delving into the complex roots of crime, especially when such an examination may involve an indictment of our current economic system. It is easier to attribute laziness, rebelliousness, lack of will to succeed, and outright evil to those individuals or groups whom we define as causing the problem than it is to examine the environment to which these people are responding, in which the deck is consistently stacked against them.[8] Sociologist Robert Merton contends that crime is one of a number of possible responses to a situation in which one is systematically blocked from attaining cultural goals (money, consumer goods, status) through socially acceptable means (advancing through a career).[9] If Merton is right, focusing on the evil of those who commit crimes will not help us change the society enough to eliminate this social root of crime.

It will, however, provide us with scapegoats (in this case, the poor and people of color) against whom we can vent our anger, sense of loss, and fear. We thus are able to discharge enough emotion to keep from asking certain questions (Why is the government cutting educational funds? Why do we expect the poor to take an "honest" job for five dollars an hour that we ourselves would not take rather than scoring big by selling drugs?) that might point us toward more institutional sources of violence and thus more structural and long-lasting solutions.

Such analyses of crime are not new, but the "blaming the victim" that they pinpoint is rarely compared to the scapegoating of sexual minorities.[10] Yet such a comparison may provide us with an interesting perspective about how manipulation works in our society. The poor and people of color are symbolically linked with crime, thus letting those in power (who tend to be rich and white) off the hook. In a similar way, sexual minorities are symbolically linked with danger, death, corruption, and decay, letting those in power (in this case, those who are in charge of institutions such as the government, the media, and the educational and medical systems) off the hook. This representational work has differently damaging effects on the poor and people of color, on the one hand, and sexual minorities, on the other (with, of course, a particular double whammy for those who fall under both designations), but the difference in effects should not blind us to the fact that the processes, and the functions they serve, are quite similar.

Central to the moralizing and scapegoating process are comparisons of current decay with the "good old days." Harking back to a golden age is neither new nor unique to our society; the Chinese philosopher Confucius, who lived in the sixth century B.C., offered his moral prescriptions as a way to return China to its golden age. Yet our society is particularly prone to focus its discomfort on time-honored institutions that seem to be changing; we link such changes with the decay that we experience.[11] Thus, "homos," "women's libbers," blacks and Latinos, and the poor come under assault for destroying communities, contributing to the decline of the family, and corrupting innocent youths.

I do not mean to suggest that sexual minorities have been favored throughout history until our time or that homophobia is in any way new. What I do mean to suggest is that scapegoating sexual minorities serves the function of helping us displace the sense of rage, helplessness, disgust, and grief that might otherwise force us to examine the structures within which we live for sources of our discontent. Perhaps such scapegoating has always served this function. But our era is one in which the stakes of social disintegration and corruption are particularly high *and* in which there are visible and organized sexual minority communities to attack. This combination could be part of a process in which the misdirections of our discomfort could prove lethal to large numbers of people. Certainly, it is proving lethal now to those with AIDS, regardless of how they contracted it. However, there may also be a multitude of deaths from toxic waste, drunk driving, nuclear accidents, hunger, exposure due to homelessness, lack of medical care, assault against women, and workplace hazards that would not occur if the energy that goes into homophobia went instead into organizing for consumer safety, environmental cleanup, a just economic system, alternative energy sources, socialized medicine, and the like.[12]

It is ironic that *homophobia* translated literally means "fear of sameness," given the extent to which homophobia is a fear of difference: wanting things to be the same as they were in the (reputedly heterosexual) past and wanting all people to be (heterosexually) the same. However, there is a greater irony here. Homophobia as I have described it deeply impedes an understanding of a much larger sameness that transcends sexuality: the sameness of being citizens in a nuclear age under a government that regularly lies to us; the sameness of trying to maintain human dignity while scrambling for good jobs in a society that provides too few of them; the sameness of breathing polluted air and drinking polluted water; the sameness of worrying about the future and wondering what, if anything, we can do about it.

The public issues described in this essay do not just happen like earthquakes, hurricanes, or floods. There are people responsible for them, people with enough resources and institutional authority to have their decisions count more than the decisions that most of us get to make.[13] In the same way, unjust structures cannot exist independently of the people who put them into practice. Certainly, such structures are controlled by people who are in some ways beyond our reach, but all of us cooperate in living with them. While it can be disheartening to think that each of us plays a role in the public issues considered here, there is an important corollary to our part in the problem, and that is our potential part in the solution. These structures can be changed when enough people do whatever is necessary to refuse to participate in the "business as usual" that damages and destroys so many lives. Homophobia is part of this business as usual. It deflects our responses to injustice, and it scapegoats certain people in exchange for offering a false and dangerous peace of mind to the rest. It hurts everyone. Overcoming homophobia is part of building a just and humane society.

NOTES

Let me make some of my biases clear. I am a white middle-class college-educated bisexual woman. I make use of a sociological perspective and advocate feminism and democratic socialism as ways to approach social problems. I mention these aspects of myself in hopes that this essay will spark responses from others located at different places in our society and will be part of a much larger collaborative effort to rethink these concerns. Let me also here take a moment to warmly thank Warren Blumenfeld for his support and Jaki Ortiz for her comments.

1. The phrase *the feminization of poverty* refers to the growing trend that the poorest Americans are women and their children.

2. C. Wright Mills, *The Sociological Imagination* (New York: Oxford, 1959), 8–9.

3. In most places where I use *we* in this paper, I mean individual Americans. I especially have in mind those Americans who are in a position to vote, protest, lobby, mobilize mass movements, and in other ways affect public policy. In the few cases where *we* designates a smaller group, I will try to make the special usage clear.

4. New York City has been called "Sodom-on-the-Hudson," while there are regular predictions that San Francisco will fall into the Pacific as punishment for its sins.

5. These perspectives do in fact identify certain public issues and propose solutions for them; this is, in large part, why they are so threatening.

6. There is a set of arguments linking homophobia to the fear of embodiment and especially the fear of death. While this essay does not focus on these arguments, they are interesting and compelling and may be most useful in conjunction with ideas such as those presented in this essay (see James Nelson, *Embodiment: An Approach to Sexuality and Christian Theology* [Minneapolis: Augsburg, 1978]; see also my "Present Tense: Biphobia as a Crisis of Meaning," in *Bi Any Other Name: Bisexual People Speak Out*, ed. Lani Kaahumanu and Loraine Hutch-

ins [Boston: Alyson, 1991], 350–58; the essay has also been published in *Empathy* [2, no. 2 (1990–91): 23–28]).

7. Transgender people, as well as lesbians, gay men, and bisexuals, are included here.

8. The social definition of whose crime gets to count as crime is crucial. White-collar crime and crime committed by the rich rarely make the papers. We are willing to define only the poor as dangerous, not the rich. Yet studies of class stratification, such as G. William Domhoff's *Who Rules America Now?* (New York: Simon & Shuster, 1983) and Lillian Rubin's *Worlds of Pain* (New York: Basic, 1976), indicate that the kind of control that the very rich exercise can indeed be hazardous to our health.

9. Robert Merton, "Social Structure and Anomie," *American Sociological Review* 3 (October 1938): 672–82.

10. See William Ryan's *Blaming the Victim* (New York: Vintage, 1972).

11. An important example here is the family, which comes to stand for security and a sense of community potency. The movement against reproductive rights has been successful to the extent that it has by using the fetus in a similar way, playing on insecurities about safety and well-being to blame "baby killers" for the ills of society. However, as Howard Zinn (*A People's History of the U.S.*, [New York: Harper & Row, 1980]) argues, there have been a lot of people for whom the good old days were not so good.

12. It has also not helped us that we have entrusted so many of our problems to "experts" to solve. Problems that are defined (by the government, the media, the educational system) as too distant, technical, or overwhelming for individuals to tackle have simply been handed over to people who have been granted authority to respond to them. Some particularly clear examples include global climate change, air pollution, economic recession, and foreign policy. However, most large-scale problems ultimately wind up in the hands of experts simply because they are understood to be out of our control. I am not suggesting that every individual ought to be a political scientist, economist, and environmental analyst rolled up into one, but it is interesting to note the seductiveness of coming to regard major social concerns as "not my problem."

13. People are generally said to be agents insofar as they can play an active role in shaping their environments and thus in shaping their lives. In comparison, sociologist Paul Schervish (personal communication) speaks of the "hyperagency" of the ultrarich.

17

Benefits for Nonhomophobic Societies: An Anthropological Perspective

WALTER L. WILLIAMS

In a recent publication of the Coalition for Traditional Values, the Reverend Lou Sheldon commits himself to "open warfare with the gay and lesbian community. . . . [This is] a battle with one of the most pernicious evils in our society: homosexuality."[1] What does the Christian Right think is so bad about homosexuality? We are all familiar with the litany: homosexuals are seen as evil because they are said to be a threat to children, the family, religion, and society in general.

In sharp contrast to the heterosexist views of some people in Western society, the majority of other cultures that have been studied by anthropologists condone at least some forms of same-sex eroticism as socially acceptable behavior.[2] Beyond that, quite a number of societies provide honored and respected places for people who are roughly comparable to what we in Western culture would call gay men and lesbians. One example is the Navajo people of Arizona and New Mexico, the largest American Indian group in North America. *Nadle*, a Navajo word meaning "one who is transformed," is applied to androgynous male or female individuals who combine elements of both masculinity and feminity in their personalities. The rare case of a person who is born hermaphroditic, with ambiguous genitalia or with the sexual organs of both the male and the female, is also considered to be a *nadle*, but most *nadle* are individuals whom Western society would characterize as effeminate men or masculine women. While each society of course constructs its own categories of sexuality in different ways, Navajo people traditionally accepted the fact that such androgynous people almost always have inclinations to be sexually active with people of the same biological sex.

Today's Navajos, like other Native Americans, have been significantly affected by Christian attitudes condemning homosexuality, but among those who value their traditions, there still continues a strong respect for *nadle*. We can see traditional Navajo attitudes more clearly by reading the testimony of an anthropologist who lived among the Navajos in the 1930s, before they had been so affected by Western values. This anthropologist documented the extremely reverential attitudes toward *nadle*. He wrote that traditional Navajo families who had a child who behaved androgynously were "considered by themselves and everyone else as very fortunate. The success and wealth of such a family was believed to be assured. Special care was taken in the raising of such children and they were afforded favoritism not shown to other children of the family. As they grew older and assumed the character of nadle, this solicitude and respect increased. . . . This respect verges almost on reverence in many cases."[3]

To illustrate these attitudes, this anthropologist quoted what the Navajo people told him about *nadle:*

They know everything. They can do both the work of a man and a woman. I think when all the nadle are gone, that will be the end of the Navajo.

If there were no nadle, the country would change. They are responsible for all the wealth in the country. If there were no more left, the horses, the sheep, and Navajo would all go. They are leaders, just like President Roosevelt. A nadle around the hogan will bring good luck and riches. They have charge of all the riches. It does a great deal for the country if you have a nadle around.

You must respect a nadle. They are, somehow, sacred and holy.[4]

On reading such quotations, the insight that immediately springs to mind is how attitudes toward similar phenomenon may differ widely from one culture to another. Presented above are opposing views of homosexually oriented people, condemned by Christian fundamentalist as "one of the most pernicious evils in society," but seem by the Navajo as something "sacred and holy." Why the difference?

My research in societies that do not discriminate against homosexuals suggests that the main reason for nonprejudicial attitudes is that those societies have figured out specific ways that homosexuality can contribute positively to the good of society as a whole. In other words, acceptance of sexual diversity is due not so much to "toleration" on the part of the heterosexual majority as it is to distinct advantages perceived by the general populace in having a certain proportion of the population homosexually inclined.

In Western culture, where only heterosexuality is valued, it occurs to few people that homosexuality might enrich society. From over a decade of research on this topic, I have come to have a different perspective than most Americans. The knowledge that I have gained has come primarily from fieldwork with native people of North American, Pacific, and Southeast Asian cultures. After three years of documentary research in many libraries, I lived among the American Indians of the Great Plains and the Southwest (1982), the Mayas of Yucatan (1983), and Native Alaskans (1989). I also did field research among the peoples of Hawaii (1984, 1985, 1990), Thailand (1987), and Indonesia (1987–88).[5] This essay will refer to the results of my fieldwork among these indigenous peoples. Much more ethnographic fieldwork certainly needs to be conducted in these and other societies before we can draw firm conclusions, but I have formulated some tentative points that I outline below.

Benefits to Religion

In Western writings about homosexuality, the emphasis has usually been on its "cause," with the implication that homosexuality is an "abnormality" that must be prevented. In contrast, among American Indians the reaction is usually acceptance, based on the notion that all things are "caused" by the spirits and therefore have some spiritual purpose. It is left to them only to discover each individual's spiritual purpose.

Traditional American Indians seem more interested in finding a useful social role for those who are different than in trying to force people to change character. One's basic character is a reflection of one's spirit, and to interfere with that is dangerously to disrupt the instructions from the spirit world. Many native North American religions are of a type called "animistic"; they emphasize not one creator god but a multiplicity of spirits in the universe. Everything that exists has a spirit; all things that exist are due equal respect because they are part of the spiritual order of the universe. The world cannot be complete without them.

In this religious view, there is no hierarchy among the beings— the humans, animals, and plants—that populate the earth. Humans are not considered to be any more spiritual or any more important than the other beings. Neither is the spirit of man more important than the spirit of woman. Each spirit may be different, but all are of equal value. However, American Indian religions see an androgynous individual as evidence that that person has been blessed by being bestowed with *two* spirits. Because both women and men are respected for their equal but distinct qualities, a person who combines attributes of both is considered as higher, as above the regular person—who only has one spirit.

In contrast to Western sexist views, where a male who acts like a woman is considered to be "lowering himself" to the subordinate female status, in the egalitarian American Indian religions feminine roles are accorded equal respect with men's roles. Therefore, a male who acts like a woman is not "lowering himself"; rather, he is indicating that he has been favored with an extra gift of spirituality. He is respected as a "double person." Such an individual is considered to be not entirely man and not entirely woman but a mixture of both masculine and feminine elements with additional unique characteristics. Such a distinctive personality is respected as a different gender, distinct from either man or woman.

This concept of respect for gender nonconformity is quite foreign to mainstream American society today. Despite the gains made in recent decades by the women's movement, our culture still does not respect the social contributions of anyone other than masculine men. Perhaps the best way to see this is to look at attitudes toward androgynous males. On American schoolyards today, the worst insult that can be thrown at a boy is to call him a *sissy*. What does it say about a society's gender values when the worst insult that can be directed toward a man is to say that he is like a woman?

While androgyny among males is seldom defended in mainstream American culture, it can be argued that many men need social permission to express those aspects of their personalities that in our society are more commonly associated with women. American men in particular are under constant pressure to conform, to maximize their masculine side—to "be tough," not to show emotion. Seldom verbalized are the dangers to society of excessive masculinity, even though the evidence appears daily in newspaper headlines. Violence is preponderantly a characteristic of masculine personalities: physical and sexual violence by men against women, children, and other men is a major social problem. Not only are men's tempers not conducive to cooperation in the workplace, but they also lead to stress-related health problems for hot-headed men themselves.

In contrast, American Indian cultures that are not prejudiced against androgynous persons allow more flexibility among personality types. A major reason for this flexibility is the basic respect that their religions accord human diversity. According to these religions, since everything that exists comes from the spirit world, people who are different have been made that way by the spirits and therefore maintain an especially close connection to the spirit world. Accordingly, androgynous people are often seen as sacred, as spiritually gifted individuals who can minister to the spiritual needs of others. In many tribes, such androgynous men—called *berdache* by the early explorers and by modern anthropologists— were often shamans or sacred people who work closely with shamans. Females who were inclined to take the traditional masculine role of hunter and warrior were called *amazons* by the early explorers, after the ancient Greek legend of warrior women.

Nonprejudiced Native American societies recognized that the berdache and the amazon were almost always homosexual, but an androgynous personality, not sexual behavior, was the defining characteristic. Many tribes had special career roles for berdache and amazons. Many Indian tribes, believing that sickness can be cured by the intervention of the spirits, will turn to the spiritually powerful as healers. While conducting my fieldwork on a Lakota reservation in South Dakota, I often observed people who were ill calling on *winkte* (the word in the Lakota language meaning "half man/half woman") to perform healing ceremonies for them. *Winktes* spend much of their time helping others, visiting the ill and infirm, comforting those in distress, and drawing on their spiritual connections to help people get well.

With a spiritual justification provided by the culture, berdache and amazons are not seen as a threat to religion. Instead, they are often considered sacred. Sexuality—indeed bodily pleasure—is seen not as sinful but as a gift from the spirit world. Both the spirit and the flesh are sacred. The homosexual inclinations of such berdache and amazons are accepted as a reflection of their spiritual nature. The American Indian example shows that it is not enough for a religion to "tolerate" sexual diversity; it must also provide a specific religious explanation for such diversity.

Some worldviews see reality as pairs of opposites: everything is viewed as good versus evil, black versus white, the spiritual versus the physical. The latter derides the needs and desires of the physical body as "temptations of the flesh," in contrast to the devotions of the spirit. The American Indian religions take a different view, seeing both the body and the spirit as good, as reflections of each other. As a consequence, sexual behavior—the epitome of the physical body—may be seen as something positively good, as something spiritual in and of itself, at the same time as it is physical.

The conceptualization by Native American societies of the berdache and the amazons as sacred has its practical applications. Those male berdache whom I have met and read about are uniformly gentle, peaceful people who would simply not fill the traditional Indian man's role of hunter and warrior effectively. By recognizing that they are special and encouraging them to become religious leaders and healers, Indian cultures give such people a means by which to contribute constructively to society. Rather than wasting time and energy trying to suppress their true nature or assuming an unsuitable role, they are encouraged to see their uniqueness as a special spiritual gift and to maximize their capabilities to help others. A Crow elder told me, "We don't waste people, the way white society does. Every person has their gift, every person has their contributions to make."[6]

Benefits to the Family

This emphasis on the social usefulness of the person who is different can be seen especially clearly in the contributions of such people to their families. Because most pre-Columbian Native Americans lived in extended families, with wide networks of kin who depended on one other, it was not necessary for everyone to have children. In contrast to a society with only nuclear families (father-mother-children), where all must reproduce to have someone take care of them in old age, an extended family offers some adults the opportunity not to reproduce. Childless people have nephews and nieces care for them. It is actually economically advantageous to the extended family for one or two adults *not* to reproduce because then there is a higher ratio of food-producing adults to food-consuming children. Also, by assuming gender roles that mix both the masculine and the feminine, the berdache and the amazon can do both women's and men's work. Not being burdened with their own childcare responsibilities, they can care for others' children or for their aged parents and grandparents.

The same pattern occurs in Polynesian culture, where an androgynous role similar to that of the berdache exists. Called *mahu* in Hawaii and Tahiti and *fa'afafine* among Samoans, such alternatively gendered people were traditionally those who took care of elderly relatives while their heterosexual siblings were busy raising their own children. With this kind of gender flexibility, and with their families holding high expectations for them (since they are spiritual people), berdache and amazons are often renowned for being hard workers, productive, and intelligent.

Since they are not stigmatized or alienated, berdache and amazons are free to make positive contributions to family life. Today, they often allow adolescent nieces and nephews to move in with them when the parents' home gets overcrowded and also help them finance schooling. A Navajo woman whose cousin is a respected *nadle* healer told me,

> They are seen as very compassionate people, who care for their family a lot and help people. That's why they are healers. *Nadles* are also seen as being great with children, real Pied Pipers. Children love *nadles,* so parents are pleased if a *nadle* takes an interest in their child. One that I know is now a principal of a school on the reservation. . . . *Nadles* are not seen as an abstract group, like "gay people," but as a specific person, like "my relative so-and-so." People who help their family a lot are considered valuable members of the community.[7]

It is thus in the context of individual family relations that much of the high status of the berdache and amazon must be evaluated. When such people play a positive and valued role in their societies, and when no outside interference disrupts the normal workings of those societies, unprejudiced family love can exert itself.

In most Western cultures, such people are often considered misfits, an embarrassment to the family. They often leave the family in shame or are thrown out by homophobic relatives, the family thereby losing the benefit of their productive labor. In contrast, traditional Native American families will often make such people central to the family. Since other relatives do not feel threatened by them, family disunity and conflict are avoided. The male berdache is not pressured to suppress his feminine behavior, nor is the female amazon pressured to suppress her masculine inclinations. Neither are they expected to deny their same-sex erotic feelings. Berdache and amazons thereby avoid the tendency of those considered deviant in Western culture to harbor a low self-esteem and to engage in self-destructive behavior.. Because they are valued by their families, few become alcoholic or suicidal, even in tribes where such problems are common.

Male berdache are often highly productive at women's work. Unlike biological females, who must take time away from farming or foraging when they are menstruating, pregnant, or nursing children, the berdache is always available to gather or prepare food. Anthropologists have often commented on the way in which berdache willingly take on the hardest work. Many berdache are also renowned for the high quality of their craftswork, whether pottery, beadwork, weaving, or tanning. In many tribes, berdache are known as the best cooks in the community and are often called on to prepare feasts for ceremonies and funerals. Women in particular seem to appreciate the help provided by berdache. An elderly Papago woman for example, spoke fondly of a berdache she had known in her youth (referring to him as *she*): "The man-woman was very pleasant, always laughing and talking, and a good worker. She was so strong! She did not get tired grinding corn. . . . I found the man-woman very convenient."[8]

The female amazon is often appreciated for her prowess at hunting and fighting. In the Crow tribe of the Great Plains, one of the most famous warriors of the nineteenth century was an amazon called "Woman Chief." Edward Denig, a white frontier trader who lived with the Crows for over twelve years, wrote that Woman Chief "was equal if not superior to any of the men in hunting, both on horseback and foot." After single-handedly warding off an attack by an enemy tribe, she developed a reputation as a brave fighter. She easily attracted male warriors to follow her in battle, where she always distinguished herself by her bravery. According to Denig, the Crows believed that she had "a charmed life which, with her daring feats, elevated her to a point of honor and respect not often reached by male warriors." Crow singers composed special songs to commemorate her gallantry, and she eventually became the third highest ranked chief in the entire tribe. Her status was so high, in fact, that she easily attracted women to marry her. By 1850, she had four wives, which also gave her additional status in the tribe. Denig concluded his biography of Woman Chief by saying in amazement, "Strange country this, where [berdache] males assume the dress and perform the duties of females, while women turn [like] men and mate with their own sex!"[9]

Whether attaining status as a warrior, a hunter, a healer, or an artist or simply by being hard working and generous, most amazons and berdache share an urge for success and prestige. They might not be good at doing the kinds of things that are typically expected of their sex, but instead of feeling deviant, they merely redirect their efforts into other kinds of prestigious activities. Moreover, berdache and amazons can gain notable material prosperity by selling their craftwork. Since they are considered sacred, their work is highly valued for its magical power as well as for its beauty.

The economic opportunities open to berdache and amazons are especially evident among the Navajo. Whereas average men and women are restricted to certain economic activities, *nadle* know no such constraints. Goods produced by them are much in demand. Also, because they are believed to be lucky, they usually act as the head of the family and make decisions about family property. They supervise the family's farming, sheepherding, and selling or trading. With such opportunities, talented *nadle* are valued and respected for their contributions to the family's prosperity.

More than economic success is involved in such people's striving for excellence, however. Atypical children soon recognize their difference from other people. Psychological theory suggests that, if a family does not love and support such children, they will quickly internalize a negative self-image. Severe damage can result from feelings of deviance or inferiority. The way out of such self-hatred is either to deny any meaningful difference or to appreciate uniqueness. Difference is transformed—from *deviant* to *exceptional*—becoming a basis for respect rather than stigma. American Indian cultures deal with such atypical children by offering them prestige and rewards beyond what is available to the average person.

Masculine females and effeminate males in Western culture are often equally productive and successful, but they are so in the face of overwhelming odds. They may eventually come to appreciate their difference, but such self-acceptance comes more easily when one is considered "special" rather than "deviant." Few Western families show such youths more than grudging tolerance. If American families would adopt an appreciative attitude when faced with difference, much conflict and strife could be avoided when a family member turns out to be gay, lesbian, or bisexual. Such children could be nurtured and supported, and such nonprejudiced treatment would ultimately rebound to the family's great benefit.

Benefits for Children

From the Native American and Polynesian viewpoints, then, homosexuality and gender nonconformity do not threaten the family. An unusual phenomenon is instead incorporated into the kinship system in a productive and nondisruptive manner. Similarly, berdache and amazons are not seen as a threat to children. In fact, because they often have the reputation for intelligence, they are encouraged in some tribes to become teachers. In my fieldwork on Indian reservations and in the Yucatan, Alaska, Hawaii, and Thailand, I met a number of gender nonconformists who are highly respected teachers. Many of the venerated teachers of the sacred traditional hula ceremony among native Hawaiians are *mahus*.

Native American amazons also have the opportunity to become fathers. Among the Mohave, for example, the last person to have sex with the mother before she gives birth is considered to be the true father of the child. This allows an amazon to choose a male to impregnate her wife yet still claim paternity. The child is thus socially recognized as having an amazon father, who is thus able to fulfill all social roles that any other father would do.

Berdache have the opportunity to become parents through adoption. In fact, since they have a reputation for intelligence and generosity, they are often the first choice to become adoptive parents when there is a homeless child. For example, a Lakota berdache with whom I lived while conducting my 1982 fieldwork had adopted and raised four boys and three girls in his lifetime. The youngest boy was still living with him at the time, a typical teenager who was doing well in school. The household consisted of the berdache, his adopted son, the berdache's widowed mother, a number of nephews and nieces, and an elderly aunt.

Such an extended family contrasts sharply with contemporary American society, where gays, lesbians, and bisexuals are often alienated from their families, have trouble becoming adoptive or foster parents, and are often denied custody of their own children. Whereas American Indian communities can remedy the tragedy of a homeless child quickly and easily, foster and adoptive families are not so easy to come by in mainstream American society. As a result, the costs that Americans pay are high—in terms of both tax dollars and crimes committed by homeless youths.

Of course, the main reason for preventing gays and lesbians from becoming adoptive or foster parents—or even Big Brothers or Big Sisters—is the often expressed fear that the youths will be sexually molested. Since recent statistics show that well over 90 percent of child molesters are heterosexual men and their victims young girls, sexual orientation by itself is not a valid criterion on which to base adoption decisions. If it were, heterosexual men would not be allowed to adopt. The fact that homophobic leaders continue to oppose gay and lesbian adoptions when they know the statistics suggests that this issue is merely a rhetorical ploy. The real issue emerges most clearly in custody cases. Children are taken away from lesbian mothers or gay fathers, not because of molestation, but because they will provide "bad role models."

To consider an adult lesbian, gay man, or bisexual a bad role model is simple heterosexism. Children growing up in America today, no matter who their parents are, will see plenty of heterosexual role models—on television, at school, among neighbors and the parents of friends. Why not have a few gay and lesbian role models as an alternative? The answer is simple: American culture still regards it as a tragedy if a youth turns out to be lesbian, gay, or bisexual.

Nonheterosexist cultures, by contrast, emphasize an individual's freedom to decide his or her own fate. Paradoxically, those cultures often see sexual variance or gender nonconformity not as matters of choice but as inborn or as determined by the spirit world. Ironically, while the professed American ideal is "freedom of choice," in reality every child is subjected to extreme social pressures to conform. Despite the omnipresent American rhetoric of freedom, mainstream American culture continues to deny lesbian, gay, and bisexual youths the freedom to choose their own lifestyles. Ever since Freud, however, research has made it abundantly clear that many psychological problems arise when childhood sexual desires are repressed. In fact, a greater incidence and severity of mental illness has been documented among more repressive cultures.[10]

Benefits for Friendship

In America today, many men are prevented from expressing their feelings or developing close friendships with other men by the fear that others will think them homosexual. Men can be coworkers, sports buddies, even social companions, but nothing more personal. Consequently, many American men are left with only one legitimate, socially sanctioned intimate relationship in their lives—that with their wives. Is it therefore surprising that most men equate intimacy with sex or that, starved for intimacy, many elect to keep a mistress? To expect marriage to meet all a person's needs—to expect a spouse or significant other to be sexual playmate, economic partner, and best friend—places too heavy a burden on what today is an infirm institution.

During my fieldwork in Indonesia, by contrast, I was struck by the intensity of friendships between men (friendships that reminded me of the intense "blood brother" relationships between Native American men). In Indonesia, the highly structured mixed-sex marriage and kinship system is balanced and strengthened by unstructured same-sex friendship networks. The one complements the other, and both provide men with the support that they need to get through their lives.

Once gay men, lesbians, and bisexuals have transcended the fear of being thought homosexual, they open themselves to whole new possibilities for more satisfying same-sex friendships. In nonhomophobic societies, heterosexual men are free to develop same-sex friendships and nurture their same-sex friends. Because no stigma is attached to same-sex friendship, no pressure exists to choose between an exclusively homosexual or heterosexual orientation. In contemporary America, by contrast, where men are socialized to equate intimacy with a sexual relationship, some may feel forced to abandon an exclusively heterosexual identity for an exclusively homosexual one. Homophobia creates two distinct classes of men, self-identified "heterosexuals" and self-identified "homosexuals." More flexible notions of same-sex friendship in nonhomophobic societies mean less of a need to compartmentalize people on the basis of sexual behavior and less social consternation should the relationship between same-sex friends become erotic.

Benefits for Society at Large

A culture that does not try to suppress the same-sex desires of its people can focus instead on the contributions that can be made by those who are different. We have already seen that American Indian berdache and amazons are honored for their spirituality, their artistic skills, and their hard work, all of which benefit the entire community. They are also often called on to mediate disputes between men and women. Married couples in particular turn to them since, as "half men/half women," they can see things from the perspective of both sexes. Their roles as go-betweens is integral to the smooth functioning of Native American communities.

Although there is not as much information on the social roles of amazons, the historical documents suggest that berdache performed their go-between function in traditional Indian cultures for males and females on joyous occasions as well. A number of tribes were noted to have employed berdache to facilitate budding romances between young women and men, a role that reached its highest development among the Cheyenne tribe of the Great Plains. One Cheyenne informant reported that berdache "were very popular and special favorites of young people, whether married or not, for they were noted matchmakers. They were fine love talkers. . . . When a young man wanted to send gifts for a young woman, one of these halfmen-halfwomen was sent to the girl's relatives to do the talking in making the marriage."[11] Because of their spiritual connection, berdache were believed to possess the most potent love medicines. A Cheyenne bachelor who gained the assistance of a berdache was believed to be fortunate indeed since the berdache could often persuade the young woman and her family to accept the gift-laden horses that a man offered when he made a marriage proposal.

Whereas American Indian societies recognize and incorporate sexual diversity, others simply ignore it. When I was in Southeast Asia in 1987 and 1988, I learned that it was commonly known in both Thailand and Indonesia that some major government figures were homosexual. Although those men did not publicly broadcast their homosexuality, neither did they make any attempt to hide their same-sex lovers from public view. Such tolerance benefits both the individuals, who are allowed to live their lives as they choose, and the nation, which utilized their leadership skills.

In my research, I have found that those societies with accepted homosexual roles ironically do not emphasize the sexual activities of homosexuals. Everyone knows their sexual preferences, but those preferences are considered matters for private, not public, concern. Homosexuality is therefore not politicized. In America, however, the homophobic Right has made such an issue of what it considers to be deviant sexuality that it has stimulated the development of a politically active gay community.

The suppression of sexual diversity *inevitably* results in social turmoil. Families and communities are divided by the issue. Suicides are occasioned by the discovery, or the fear of discovery, of secret sex lives. When the individuals whose secrets are uncovered are public figures, the ensuing media scandal can bring a community to the point of hysteria—witness Boise, Idaho, in the 1950s and schoolteacher firings in countless communities.

The persecution of gays, lesbians, and bisexuals also endangers the freedom of other groups—indeed, any group. For persecution rarely confines itself to one group. For example, Adolf Hitler tried to rid Germany of Jews, but also extended his campaign to include homosexuals. The Ayatollah Khomeini similarly exterminated infidels and beheaded homosexuals. The point here is that no one group is safe until all groups are safe.

By continuing to discriminate against lesbians, gay men, and bisexuals, the United States is losing the respect of many in the world community—the Dutch and other progressive governments have already made formal diplomatic protests against discriminatory U.S. policies. Sodomy laws remain on the books and are enforced in many states, homosexuals are excluded from the military, sexual minorities are denied equal protection under the law—all this in a nation devoted to "life, liberty, and the pursuit of happiness." The situation today is similar to that in the early 1960s, when progressive governments in Europe, Asia, and especially the newly independent African nations voiced their support for African-American civil rights protestors. Such diplomatic action helped pressure the Kennedy administration to take action against racial segregation. For how could America champion its ideals of freedom and expect to maintain its position as the leader of the "free" world when people of color were treated so unequally?

Acceptance of people's right to be different is the certain hallmark of democracy and freedom. This is why the New Right's attempt to suppress homosexuality is so dangerous for the larger society. The dominant message propounded by the New Right in the 1980s has been that everyone should be the same. That desire for sameness has a strong attraction for people living in a diverse and changing society. Instead, we should be thankful that we are *not* all the same. If we were, society would lose the creativity and vitality that comes from difference. Faced with the new global competitiveness of the 1990s, we as Americans are hardly in a position *not* to promote independent thinking and creativity. Mindless conformity is an economic and emotional and intellectual dead end.

An appreciation of diversity, not just a tolerance of minorities, is what will promote future American progress. As the American Indian example illustrates so well, far from being a threat to religion, to the family, to children, and to society in general, homosexuality can benefit both men and women as well as bring freedom to all.

NOTES

1. Quoted in *Project 10 Newsletter* (March 1989), 1.
2. Clellan Ford and Frank Beach, *Patterns of Sexual Behavior* (New York: Harper, 1951).
3. W. W. Hill, "The Status of the Hermaphrodite and Transvestite in Navaho Culture," *American Anthropologist* 37 (1935): 274.
4. Ibid.
5. The results of my 1979–84 fieldwork are reported in Walter L. Williams, *The Spirit and the Flesh: Sexual Diversity in American Indian Culture* (Boston: Beacon, 1986). Part of my Indonesian research is contained in Walter L. Williams, *Javanese Lives: Women and Men in Modern Indonesian Society* (New Brunswick, N.J.: Rutgers University Press, 1991). My research among Polynesians and Native Alaskans has not yet been written up. I express my gratitude to the Council for the International Exchange of Scholars, for a Fulbright research grant to Indonesia (with a side trip to Thailand and Malaysia), to the University of Southern California faculty research fund for trips to conduct research in Hawaii, and to the Institute for the Study of Women and Men for a travel grant to go to Alaska. My main work there was among Aleuts and Yupik Eskimos.
6. Quoted in Williams, *Spirit and Flesh*, 57.
7. Ibid., 54.
8. Ibid., 58–59.
9. Ibid., 245–46.
10. George Devereux, *Mohave Ethnopsychiatry* (Washington, D.C.: Smithsonian Institution, 1969), viii–ix, xii–xiii, and "Institutionalized Homosexuality of the Mohave Indians," *Human Biology* 9 (1937): 498–499, 518. For examples of other sexually free societies, see Williams, *Spirit and Flesh*, chap. 12.
11. Quoted in Williams, *Spirit and Flesh*, 70–71.

Conducting Antiheterosexism Workshops: A Sample

WARREN J. BLUMENFELD

As a longtime member of the Gay, Lesbian, and Bisexual Speakers of Boston, I have witnessed many changes taking place over the years in terms of strategies for conducting antioppression work, specifically around heterosexism. Speakers bureaus around the country continue to provide speakers to lead basic discussions on the topic of homosexuality and bisexuality in schools, businesses, and religious and community organizations. Requests are also increasing for antiheterosexism workshops as well as for prepared talks on such specific topics as gays and the Holocaust, parenting issues, movement history, political activism, and queer bashing. Some standard questions are asked at these engagements. "What causes homosexuality?" "How did your parents and friends react when you came out?" "What forms of discrimination do you face?" "Are you aware of what the Bible says about homosexuality?" "Do you ever want to raise children?" "Aren't you afraid of AIDS?" And so on.

Organizations around the country, including some of the speakers bureaus, have designed and lead antiheterosexism workshops to sensitize students, employees, and religious and community leaders. As in other forms of antioppression work, dominant group allies often cofacilitate these workshops as a way of modeling cooperation between members of the dominant and target groups and also as a way of testifying to the fact that prejudice does indeed affect everyone.

275

I began facilitating antiheterosexism workshops around 1982 in a variety of settings: high school and college classrooms, fraternities, legal aid agencies, union conferences, state police in-service seminars, leadership trainings, etc. Prior to that time, as an active member of the Gay, Lesbian, and Bisexual Speakers Bureau of Boston, I went out on the more "traditional" speaking engagements, beginning in 1971, where another speaker and I tell a little bit about what it is like growing up feeling different and what our lives are like today. We then field questions from audience members.

Although I still participate in this type of speaking engagement, I have come to believe that a workshop format, in which participants are guided through a variety of exercises, can bring people closer to their feelings *and* provide important information to contradict earlier misinformation, which has often led to prejudiced thinking. I conduct these workshop for a variety of reasons. Primarily, however, I am motivated by a desire to reduce heterosexism for young lesbian, gay, bisexual and transgender people today so that they will not have to face the harassment, the secrecy, the feelings of self-loathing, that many of us experienced growing up.

The U.S. Department of Health and Human Services (DHHS) Task Force on Youth Suicide issued a report in January 1989 concluding that lesbian and gay youths are at increased risk for suicide and calling for an end to discrimination.[1] The report found that lesbian and gay youths may constitute "up to thirty percent of completed suicides annually" and that "homosexuals of both sexes are two to six times more likely to attempt suicide than are heterosexuals." During a press conference following the release of this report, Kevin Berrill, director of the Anti-Violence Project of the National Gay and Lesbian Task Force, commented, "The increased risk of suicide facing these youth is linked to growing up in a society that teaches them to hide and to hate themselves. We welcome this report and hope it will lead to action that will save lives."

It is extremely important that young people not feel as though they are the only ones ever to have strong attractions for members of their own sex. Conducting workshops to sensitize youth workers and young people themselves can help end the silence and the isolation that imprisons so many.

In addition to conducting workshops in the schools, an important tool in the creation of a safe environment is the implementation of nondiscrimination policy guidelines. In 1987, the superintendent of schools for the Cambridge Public Schools in Massachusetts issued a set of antiharassment guidelines. Seven types of harassment were included, and discrimination was prohibited on the basis of race, color, sex, religion, physical ability, national origin, ancestry, *and* sexual orientation. The following wording can be used as a model for other school systems to protect school employees and students from harassment on the basis of sexual orientation: "Harassment on the basis of an individual's sexual preference or orientation is prohibited. Words, actions, or other verbal, written, or physical conduct which ridicules, scorns, mocks, intimidates, or otherwise threatens any individual because of his/her sexual orientation/preference constitutes homophobic harassment when it has the purpose or effect of unreasonably interfering with the work performance or creating an intimidating, hostile, or offensive environment." (For a full copy of the antiharassment guidelines, contact Superintendent of Public Schools, 159 Thorndike St., Cambridge, Mass. 02141.)

I also see antiheterosexism workshops as providing a space where heterosexuals can begin the process of purging early heterosexist conditioning, which has constrained them and compromised their humanity. As this anthology has pointed out, heterosexism oppresses lesbians, gay males, bisexuals, and transgender people while simultaneously hurting heterosexuals.

The third reason for my involvement in antiheterosexism work is more personal. Each time I end a workshop, I feel stronger, empowered, confident that I have replaced with affirmations yet another of those old destructive stereotypes I was taught. Although it is certainly hard work, I have found that few activities in my life give me as much joy and sense of accomplishment.

I include here a basic workshop structure that can be adapted to meet individual needs. Some of the activities I have originated, and some have come from individuals or organizations. I am indebted to Joan Lester, Jamie Washington, Carole Johnson, and all the other good people at the Equity Institute, Cooper Thompson and members of the Campaign to End Homophobia, Kathy Obear of *The Human Advantage*, and all my good friends at the Gay, Lesbian, and Bisexual Speakers Bureau of Boston for their encouragement and guidance in the formulation of this workshop outline.

Generic Workshop Structure

For best results, workshops should be limited to fifteen to twenty five participants. Every workshop, no matter the length of time allotted to it, should contain certain basic components (from the Equity Institute).

1. Needs Assessment

A needs assessment should be conducted prior to the preparation of the design, but under difficult circumstances it may be conducted at the beginning of the training through in-group assessment. Some questions to ask the sponsor could center around the makeup of the group, the group's prior knowledge of or experience with the topic, number of people in attendance, or the purpose of the workshop (in-service, conflict resolution, etc.).

2. Climate Setting

The introductory remarks and opening exercises should be carefully designed to build trust, encourage people to talk, and establish ground rules and a safe atmosphere for the workshop. It is here that you should also state your working assumptions about the topic and establish credibility as a trainer/facilitator by giving information about yourself that is relevant. Consider the physical setting of the room; opening, uplifting participatory activity; etc.

3. Informational (Cognitive) Component

This should include historical, political, economic, and/or sociological information about the topic and any related areas. Definitions of important words or terms should be given. Handouts and materials are important to back up your information.

4. Experiential Component

This component should be included throughout the workshop. Experiential activities come in various forms: role playing, small group discussions, working in pairs, fish bowls, speak outs (panels), and any other activities that involve people are included here.

5. Action Component

Develop something concrete that people can actually do when they leave the workshop. Preferably, the "action plan" should be developed by the participant near the end of the workshop. It may involve networking with others, or it may be any action the participant intends to take after the workshop is over. It is a good practice to ask the participant to write the plan down on paper or tell another person what he or she plans to do. You can develop a contract asking people what actions they will take following the workshop.

6. Closure Component

Design a short but precise and upbeat closing for the workshop. It is extremely important to send people away feeling "finished for the day" and hopeful.

7. Evaluation

It is crucial to get feedback (written—anonymously—or verbal) before participants leave the workshop. Be sure to explain that their feedback is important to you and that you learn from it. Also, ask group to evaluate itself: "How do you think you as a group did?"

Workshop Visuals

People learn in a variety of ways: visually, aurally, olfactorally, kinesthetically, etc. Placing information on large sheets of newsprint or on the board, which can remain visible throughout the workshop, can aid in providing clarity and retention of points included. The following material can be displayed.

1. Agenda (Climate Setting Component)

No matter what your agenda, it is a good idea to post it for participants to get a clear understanding of the parameters of the workshop. Following are points I included for a day-long training workshop for people interested in leading workshops:

> Facilitator Introduction
> Opening Exercise
> Participant Introductions: "Wants/Needs" Cards
> Read-Arounds
> Guided Visualization
> Concentric Circles
> Myths/Facts
> "Coming-Out" Role Play
> Diversity Panel
> Workshop Design: Small Groups
> Closing Exercise
> Evaluation

2. Workshop Title (Climate Setting Component)

Choose a workshop title according to the needs and composition of your group and post it at the beginning of the workshop. This can be written on the top of your agenda sheet.

Examples I have used include "Dismantling Heterosexism in the Classroom or in the Workplace," "Looking at Gay, Lesbian, and Bisexual Life," "Conducting Antiheterosexism Workshops," "Internalizing Prejudice," etc.

3. Goals (Climate Setting Component)

Each workshop should have a purpose or goals, which should be stated at the onset (some points listed below are drawn from the Equity Institute):

> Heighten Awareness
> Dispel Myths/Share Factual Information
> Share Personal Histories and Journeys

Support Individual Efforts to Interrupt Homophobia and
Heterosexism

Emphasize Value for Developing a Greater Sense of Community Where *All* People Are Treasured and Supported

Have Some Fun

3. Guidelines (Climate Setting Component)

Guidelines should be posted to establish parameters of safely
needed by participants to share with and engage each other.
Many of the headings listed below are taken from the Equity
Institute.

Confidentiality. People can share information with others
outside the workshop as long as workshop participants' names
are not used.

Respect for Ideas, No Attacks, No Blame. Heterosexism is
pervasive throughout our society; we did not cause it; therefore,
we are not to blame. We must, however, take responsibility for
working to overcome it within ourselves. One technique some
facilitators have used to diffuse potentially eruptive situations is
to instruct people to respond by saying "Ouch" when they hear
something offensive during a workshop, telling why it is offensive *to them.* The facilitator should help participants process the
event, then continue the workshop with a minimum of disrup-
tion. Other facilitators welcome the emergence of strong feelings during the course of the workshop and use these occasions
as educational opportunities by allowing participants to say anything they need to say in as forceful a way as they need to say it.
No matter which course the facilitator takes in resolving conflicts, participants need to adhere to the guideline of respecting
others' opinions and not engage in any sort of attack (verbal or,
of course, physical).

Personalize Knowledge. To get the most out of the workshop, people should be encouraged to speak from their own experience and not to speak for others.

Value Risk Taking/Expressing Emotion. If you have created
a safe environment, after a short while people will take some

risks in sharing personal information or showing emotions, and this should be encouraged to maximize personal growth.

Take Care of Personal Needs. Depending on the situation, people should be encouraged to get up and stretch, go to the rest rooms, or even separate from the group for a short time if they need to.

Heterosexual Nondisclosure While Gays, Lesbians, and Bisexuals May Disclose If They So Choose (from Cooper Thompson). Although often controversial, this guideline provides gays, lesbians, and bisexuals the opportunity to share their sexual identity while asking heterosexual participants not to disclose. This creates a greater degree of safety for gays, lesbians, and bisexuals and sensitizes heterosexuals to the conditions many people within these groups are forced to face every day of their lives. For the heterosexual members who are being asked not to self-disclose or for others who choose not to, the neutral term *partner* can be used when referring to a husband, wife, or significant other in their lives.

4. Working Assumptions (Climate Setting Component)

Each facilitator walks into a workshop with her or his own assumptions, and these can be listed at the beginning (from Equity Institute):

Homophobia is a devastating and insidious form of oppression.

Homophobia, as well as all the many forms of oppression, is pervasive throughout the society.

It is not our fault, we are not to blame, but we must accept responsibility for it within ourselves.

Individuals and organizations can and do grow and change.

Working to end homophobia is a lifelong process.

Homophobia hurts *all* people.

A true sense of commuity, where *all* people are valued and supported, is a goal worth working toward.

5. Working Definitions (Informational Component)

Many of the terms that are used at antiheterosexism workshops are either not completely understood or have varying definitions. Therefore, for the purpose of clarity, you might wish to display your use of some of the terms you will be using. These might include the following.

Homophobia. The fear and hatred of those who love and sexually desire those of the same sex. Homophobia, which has its roots in sexism, includes prejudice, discrimination, harassment, and acts of violence brought on by that fear and hatred.

Heterosexism. The system of advantages bestowed on heterosexuals. It is the institutional response to homophobia that assumes that all people are or should be heterosexual and therefore excludes the needs, concerns, and life experiences of lesbians, gays, and bisexuals. (Some people choose not to use the word *homophobia*, preferring *heterosexism* but expanding its traditional definition to include that of *homophobia*.)

Coming Out. The process, often lifelong, in which a person acknowledges, accepts, and in many cases appreciates his or her lesbian, gay, bisexual, or transgender identity. This often involves the sharing of this information with others.

Heterosexual Ally. A heterosexual person who supports and honors sexual diversity, acts accordingly to interrupt and challenge homophobic and heterosexist remarks and actions of others, and is willing to explore these forms of bias within himself or herself.

Community. Since this term has a number of possible definitions, have participants come up with their own working definition. Throughout the workshop, use this definition as a reference point to judge whether they are working toward it within the workshop and how heterosexism, and indeed all forms of oppression, limits our ability to achieve that goal of community.

Oppression. The systematic subjugation of a disempowered social group by a group with access to social power, or prejudice and power (Equity Institute).

Prejudice. A set of negative beliefs, generalized to apply to a whole group of people (Equity Institute).

Social Power. Access to and availability of resources needed to get what you want and influence others (Equity Institute).

Oppression = Prejudice + Power (the "ism") (Equity Institute).

Opening "Icebreaker" Exercise (Climate Setting Component)

At the beginning of most workshops, participants, while feeling expectant, walk in with a certain amount of anxiety, or even fear, and need to be put at ease. An "icebreaker" exercise, right up front, can help reduce this anxiety and set a comfortable and accepting tone.

The most effective icebreakers involve movement of some type: standing in a circle, walking around the room, passing around an object (seated or standing), etc. You can design an activity considering the needs and composition of your group. The purpose of the activity is to loosen people up and can, but need not, connect directly to the topic of the workshop.

An activity that has proved successful for me is one I call "Diversity Balloons":

Materials. Balloons, Magic Marker.

Physical Layout. Preferably, participants are in one large circle or a few smaller circles around the room. If in fixed seating, participants can remain seated.

Instructions. Set the scenario (examples below): toss balloons one at a time into the center of the circle.

Process Activity. Possible questions: "What did it feel like having to keep all these balloons in the air?" "What strategies did you use?" "Which balloons did you choose to go after and which did you allow to drop to the floor?" "How did you feel when a balloon fell to the floor?" etc.

Example. Staff of a school or college. Announce to the group, "As concerned educators, you attempt to support all your students and keep them afloat both academically and psychologically, thereby hoping to prevent them from dropping out. I am going to toss out a number of balloons of varying colors and shapes representing the diversity of your students, and it is your job to keep them afloat by any means possible." As you toss each balloon into the center of the circle, shout out the groups (e.g., African-Americans, lesbians, etc.) that that balloon represents. You may also write the categories on the balloons.

Possible Groups to Include on the Balloons. "Gays," "lesbians," "bisexuals," "transgender people," "heterosexuals," "African-Americans," "Latino/as," "people with disabilities," "Asians," "Native Americans," "Jewish people," "Christians," "Muslims," "Hindus," "Buddhists," "atheists," "women," "men," "Euro-Americans," "working class," "owning class," "middle class," "old people," "young people," "middle-aged people," "large people," "small people," etc.

Introductions (Climate Setting Component)

Introducing participants individually aids in the networking process and also helps involve them more fully in the workshop. A variety of introductions can be used.

Introducing Your Neighbor. Have people pair up into groups of two. Allow people two minutes to introduce themselves to their partner by telling their name, where they live, and one particularly delightful or funny thing about themselves: what they like to do, a hidden talent, a surprising trait, etc. After all the introductions are completed, the group maintains its original configuration.

Each person, then, in order, introduces her or his partner, giving the person's name, place of residency, and one delightful or funny trait.

Wants and Fears Cards. Hand out 3- by 5-inch cards and give the following directions: "On these cards I would like you to answer two questions. On one side, write down want you would like to get out of this workshop. This is the 'wants' side of the card. On the other side, write down the anxieties or fears you may have walked into the workshop with. This is the 'fears' side. Do not put your name on these cards. After you finish, I will collect the cards, shuffle them up, and pass them back so that each person gets to read another's card."

When all participants have completed the task and have been given a different card to read, post instructions for these introductions on the board in order to keep the process moving as smoothly as possible: (1) give your name, (2) tell where you live, (3) read the wants on your cards, (4) read the fears on your cards.

In those groups where participants might be reluctant to engage in the activities, or in situations where attendance is mandatory and participants might resent being there, I add a third question for them to respond to on the card: "Where else would you rather be right now instead of attending this workshop?"

Read-Arounds (Informational Component)

Read-arounds are short paragraphs handed out to some of the participants and read intermittently throughout the workshop to highlight additional information on the topic, to serve as a transition between activities, and to serve as a change of pace.

Workshop facilitators can produce their own read-arounds tailored to the group. A convenient way to formulate read-arounds is to extract the main paragraph from a news or feature story in the gay and lesbian or the mainstream press or to use personal anecdotes; either should be condensed to one paragraph. Randomly distribute read-arounds to participants. Throughout the workshop provide the opportunity for people to read their read-arounds.

Examples of read-arounds I have used in workshops on heterosexism include the following:

- "Winston Brathwaite, a freshman at the University of Vermont, was rejected by the Acadia fraternity after he told fraternity members he was gay."
- "Some of the colleges where gay and lesbian student organizations have been denied official recognition include San José and Sacramento State universities, the University of Southern California, the University of South Carolina, the University of Florida, the University of Oklahoma at Norman, Colorado College at Colorado Springs, West Virginia University at Morgantown, the University of Tennessee at Knoxville, the University of Missouri at Columbia, the University of Alabama, Georgetown University in Washington, D.C., California State College at Fullerton, Cal Poly at San Luis Obispo, the College of the Sequoias in Visalia, California, the University of Texas at Austin, the University of Kansas at Lawrence, Penn State, and Natal University in Durban, South Africa."
- "The American Council on Education and UCLA Joint Study

concluded: 'The college class of 1990 is more antigay than previous classes have been. A fall 1986 survey of incoming freshmen at 560 colleges and universities indicated that 52.2 percent of students feel "it is important to have laws prohibiting homosexual relationships." For the previous ten years, the percentage of freshmen expressing such a sentiment remained fairly stable at about 47. Survey sponsors attributed the increase to growing publicity about AIDS. The survey results showed differences in attitudes depending on biological sex. Almost 43 percent of the women polled opposed gay relationships; the figure for men was 62.5 percent.'"

- "After living with her lover, Karen Thompson, for over four years, Sharon Kowalski was severely injured in a November 1983 collision with a drunk driver; injury to her brain left her partially paralyzed. Her parents, on hearing of the nature of her relationship with Thompson, forbade Thompson from visiting her lover in the hospital and filed a court suit for guardianship of their daughter. In April 1984, a Minnesota court appointed Sharon's father, Donald Kowalski, guardianship; following a lengthy court battle with Thompson, the Kowalskis gained the right to move their daughter to a nursing facility and completely bar Thompson from seeing her. Thompson fought for many years, incurring well over one-hundred-thousand dollars in legal expenses. In 1989, she finally won the legal right to be with Sharon."

- "Sexual minorities are, in many instances, excluded from protections regulating fair employment practices, housing discrimination, rights of child custody, immigration, inheritance, security clearances, public accommodations, and police protection."

- "In employment, a person can be denied or fired from a position solely on the basis of sexual orientation. In these locales where equal protection is in effect, other reasons for termination have been given to get around the law when no just cause exists. In most instances, it is difficult to prove discrimination on the basis of sexual orientation."

- "In housing, gays, lesbians, and bisexuals can be evicted from rented or leased spaces. Some landlords and realtors refuse to show one-bedroom apartments to same-sex couples."

- "In accordance with a widespread societal attitude that lesbians and gays should not have contact with children, many state and private child welfare agencies have stated or implied policies denying same-sex couples or individuals the right to adopt or serve as foster parents. In addition, gay fathers and lesbian mothers have repeatedly lost custody of their children primarily because of their sexual orientation."
- "Direct violence against lesbians and gays is a nationwide phenomenon. The National Gay and Lesbian Task Force published a study involving over two thousand lesbians and gay males in eight major U.S. cities. Over 90 percent of the respondents reported some form of victimization on account of their sexual orientation—greater than one out of three had been threatened directly with violence."

Guided Visualization (Climate Setting and Experimental Components)

A guided visualization is a story read to participants for the purpose of having them emphathize with the person described in the scenario.

At this point in the workshop, I inform participants that "they have absolutely no responsibilities." All they need do is relax for a few minutes and listen to a story I am about to read to them.

I ask participants to clear their laps and hands of all materials and to get into a comfortable position. I then ask them to clear their minds and imagine themselves as the protagonist of the following story:

"Close your eyes and think of the person you've most been in love with. Imagine that you've gone out for several months, but for some reason you can't talk about this person or be open about your relationship.

"It's Friday afternoon in the residence hall. People are talking about dates for the weekend and getting ready. You are in your room listening to the stereo and thumbing through a magazine. Your roommate comes in with several friends. Your roommate says, 'I'm going out with ―― again tonight. We're going out to dinner and then to the dance at school.' The others mention their weekend plans and talk about who they're seeing. One asks you, 'What

are you doing tonight? You're not going to study again, are you?'
You reply you don't have any big plans, that you're just going to
mess around.

"They try to fix you up with someone. You reply, 'Maybe some
other time.'

"They continue talking about their dates and plans. Whenever
you can, you smile, nod your head, and joke with them about love
and sex so they won't be suspicious.

"You think about your friend who you've been seeing for three
months. You wish you could tell your roommate and friends about
the good times you've had and how it feels to be in love. But you
know you can't say anything.

"Finally, they all leave for their dates. You take a shower, dress,
and meet in front of the residence hall.

"Although you're really glad to see each other, you can't hug or
kiss each other. You just smile and say hello.

"You go to a restaurant for dinner. You sit across from each
other rather than on the same side. You can't look too long in each
other's eyes. You can't touch each other.

"After dinner, you decide to see a movie. You both wanted to
go to the dance at school, but since you can't dance together in
public, you opt for a movie. At least in the movie theater, you get
to sit beside each other. But you can't touch. When you come out
of the theater, you'd like to put your arm around each other or hold
hands, but you can't. Instead, you clamp your hands behind your
back.

"You wish there were some place you could go together. You
wish you could go to your room, but people might wonder why
you always go there, plus your roommate could walk in. You can't
even go where other young couples go to neck. You wish that you
could go tell the world about your love, but you're afraid that you'll
get disowned, that you'll get kicked out of school, that your friends
won't talk with you, or that you won't get the job you want—just
because of whom you love."

Process activity by asking participants what were the thoughts,
feelings, and emotions that surfaced as you read the story. Also,
you can ask the following question: "Have any of you ever been in
a situation where you were seeing someone of whom your friends

or family would not approve?" Because of the intimate nature of this activity, you might want to have people divide up into pairs, or dyads, to discuss this scenario to provide a greater degree of safety for people to share their feelings. (The Guided Visualization can be modified to suit the needs of your particular group: high school, work setting, family setting, etc.)

Concentric Circles: Epithets and Stereotypes (Experiential Component)

Concentric Circles are used to provide an opportunity for participants to engage others in the group in dialogue, and this, along with the dyads, can be used to ventilate emotions, which is often a necessary step in the process for change to occur.

I use the Concentric Circles technique to bring to the surface the many names, myths, and stereotypes commonly associated with lesbian, gay, and bisexual people.

Directions. Either have people count off by twos, or place numbers in ascending order on people's name tags. Form two concentric circles. In the inner circle are all the number ones in the count (or odd numbers on name tags); these people face outward. In the outer circle are all the number twos in the count (or even numbers on name tags); these people face a partner from the inner circle.

Give the following direction: "People in inner and outer circles face one another. Each person should have a partner. Each person will have two minutes to answer a question I will give to you. We will begin with those in the inner circle, and then after two minutes I will announce 'switch,' and you will change to give people in the outer circle a chance to answer the question. Those doing the listening, please give undivided attention to your partner."

Question 1. Growing up, what were all the names (positive, negative, neutral) that you heard related to gays, lesbians, and bisexuals?

When both circles have had a turn, ask members of the outer circle to rotate two people to the left so that everyone has a new partner. Repeat the process with Question 2.

Question 2. Growing up, what did you hear about lesbians, gays, and bisexuals—the stereotypes?

At the conclusion of this process, the outer circle moves two more people to the left.

Question 3. What were some of the things you heard about these groups growing up that you have come to find out were not true?

When both circles have had a turn, people return to their seats.

(Facilitators can ask participants a number of different questions using the concentric circles model, depending on the workshop focus.)

Processing Activity. The purpose of this activity is not only to expose the myths that we have been taught about homosexuality and bisexuality but also to provide a space where feelings can be ventilated and processed. For some of the more reluctant workshop participants, it helps to reassure them that they are not here to be judged or blamed for their thoughts and feelings. I have found that this activity taps deep emotions, especially for the lesbians, gay males, and bisexuals in the group. Therefore, processing this activity is crucial.

Ask participants what were some of the names and stereotypes that surfaced in the circles. Some of these can be listed on the board or on newsprint.

Facilitator's Mini Lecture. "In our early learning, three primary situations revolved around our learning about the topic of homosexuality and bisexuality" (Cooper Thompson).

1. We heard nothing. Gays, lesbians, and bisexuals were invisible; therefore, they did not exist for us.

2. We heard something, but we were given misinformation loaded with negative stereotypes and epithets.

3. We were given correct information.

"Especially in our society, chances are higher that most people fall into one of the first two categories. I would invite you to consider the possibility you too might have either heard nothing about these groups or been given false information. I am going to give a chance for us to clear up some of these myths."

A *Final Note on Name-Calling.* Emphasize that what we did during this exercise was to bring the epithets, myths, and stereotypes to the surface. Although it was appropriate for this exercise, it is not appropriate to use these names or to perpetuate these stereotypes outside this room. These names and myths come from a place of distress and hatred and can be very hurtful to those they are directed against. They have no place in a society that prides itself on freedom and justice. Therefore, it is in each person's best interests to interrupt negative comments about lesbians, gays, and bisexuals when they are heard.

Kevin Berrill, director of the Anti-Violence Project of the National Gay and Lesbian Task Force, and Daryl Cummings-Wilson devised a three-phase model to empower people in the face of homophobic remarks. Their method can be used in stopping the whole range of name-calling in schools and other public settings.

The three phases can be summarized as follows: "Name It," "Claim It," and "Stop It." In Phase 1, you name the behavior ("That is harassment"). In Phase 2, state how it makes you and others feel ("I don't like that. The other members of this class [other people on this bus, in this restaurant, on this street] don't like that"). In Phase 3, tell what you want to happen ("So stop it").

Participants can divide into dyads to practice the model with a partner, or the facilitator can set up a role-play scenario during the workshop.

Myths/Facts (Informational Component)

Purpose. To dispel myths about lesbians, gay males, and bisexuals by giving factual information.

Direction. Prepare myths on separate sheets of newsprint before the workshop (or write myths that emanate from previous group discussion). Turn over the first sheet of newsprint with a myth. Ask participants to comment giving information that contradicts the myth. Facilitator will include additional information. Following discussion, ask for a volunteer to come up and rip the sheet from the tablet and tear it to shreds. Then say, "Let's give this person an energetic round of applause." Continue the process until all myth sheets have been destroyed.

Possible myths to include:

1. *Myth:* I don't know any gay, lesbian, or bisexual people. *Fact:* You probably don't know any who are *out* to you, although a significant percentage of the population is gay, lesbian, or bisexual.
2. *Myth:* Homosexuality is abnormal and sick. *Fact:* According to the American Psychological Association, "It is no more abnormal or sick to be homosexual than to be left handed." Homophobia should be cured.
3. *Myth:* Loving people of the same sex is immoral (sinful). *Fact:* Many religious denominations do not believe this. What is universally understood is that intolerance and hatred is wrong.
4. *Myth:* Gay men are child molesters and recruit children into their life-style. *Fact:* By far, the majority of child molesters are heterosexual men. There are no laws keeping heterosexual men away from children.
5. *Myth:* Lesbians are failed females, haven't found the right man, or want to be male. *Fact:* Most lesbians enjoy being women and are attracted to women rather than men.
6. *Myth:* Gay males are feminized, failed males and want to be female. *Fact:* Most gay males enjoy being males and are attracted to men rather than women.
7. *Myth:* Bisexuals just can't make up their minds. *Fact:* Bisexuals *can* make up their minds; they are attracted to both sexes in varying degrees. Some may be attracted more to males, some more to females, and some equally to both sexes.
8. *Myth:* Gay men, lesbians, and bisexuals are promiscuous and cannot maintain long-term relationships. *Fact:* As do heterosexuals, gays, lesbians, and bisexuals form a variety of relationships, lasting from one night to many years. Besides, some define the term *promiscuous* as "anyone who gets more than me." Also, heterosexuals had a 49 percent divorce rate in 1989, which suggests that there is nothing inherent in heterosexuality that maintains strong, long-term relationships.
9. *Myth:* Lesbians, gay males, and bisexuals could change if they really wanted to. *Fact:* Most studies indicate that those who

are highly motivated to change their sexual orientation may change their behavior, but not their underlying desire. In fact, it is often societal homophobia that forces people to attempt change. Therefore, energy should go into dismantling homophobia so that people will feel comfortable with their sexuality, whatever that may be.

10. *Myth:* Lesbians, bisexuals, and gay men do not make good parents. *Fact:* One out of four families has a lesbian or gay man in the immediate family; heterosexual parents are consistently not found to be more loving or caring than their lesbian, gay, or bisexual counterparts.

11. *Myth:* Bisexuals, gay men, and lesbians are protected by civil rights laws. *Fact:* By 1992, in Wisconsin, Massachusetts, Connecticut, New Jersey, and Hawaii and some municipalities around the country, they were protected in the areas of housing, employment, public accommodations, and credit, but in most places they are not accorded equal rights under the law.

12. *Myth:* AIDS is a gay disease. *Fact:* Although the majority of people infected with HIV in the United States are gay males, AIDS affects everyone. In other countries, it effects equal numbers of males and females, most presumably heterosexual, and their children. The highest increase in recent years in this country has been among injecting drug users, many of whom are heterosexual.

Coming-Out Role Play (Experiential Component)

The purpose of the "Family Psychosocial Drama for Increasing Gay Awareness" is to get people to experience—in an emotional way—what it is like to be gay, lesbian, or bisexual. It is hoped that this will create a higher level of empathy. Facilitators might want to modify this exercise slightly for different groups.

The exercise can be done in a large group with an audience or in a small group without one.

This "Family Psychosocial Drama for Increasing Gay Awareness" was developed by Leah Fygetakis for a workshop presented to counseling psychology graduate students, Ohio State University, 1982.

Set Up. Ask for six volunteer actors. The characters are Mother, Grandmother/Grandfather, Daughter/Son, Daughter's/Son's Lover/Roommate, Father, Sister/Brother. Each character is to play the role as given on the assignment sheet.

Begin by giving the characters their instructions and roles, describe the setting to observers, and then begin the drama.

Setting. The actors are gathered around the dinner table for a holiday dinner. (Give actors their roles on cards or sheets of paper. Allow them a few minutes to read them and think about how they would act out their roles.)

Instructions to Audience. "As you watch this role play, try to put yourself in the roles. Stay in touch with the feelings this role play brings up for you. Are you uncomfortable, energized, relaxed, etc.? Also, try to remember any instances of homophobia that are acted out. How do they make you feel? How does each instance of homophobia in the role play effect the lesbians/gay men? How does it effect the heterosexuals?"

Instructions to Actors. "You each have your roles. Try to become the person described on your card/sheet as best you can." (For those groups inexperienced with role playing, you might want to provide the "structured exchange" included below to help the actors get started.) "When we begin, you play out your role by initiating or by reacting to whatever is said. Remember, *become the person on your card.*"

Structured Exchanges:

GRANDPARENT: So [to grandchild—calls by name], have you met any nice young woman/man [the other sex to the grandchild] at school?

GRANDCHILD: No, Grandma/Grandpa.

MOTHER: Oh, honey, come on. A beautiful girl/handsome boy like you? You can tell us—I want to know. . . . I'm your mother. I wish you'd tell me more about school than just what you and [name of roommate] do together.

DAUGHTER/SON: All right—All right, I have something I want to say. But before you say anything—I want you to know that I love you very much . . . but I just can't stand the distance between us any longer. [breathe.] [Name of roommate] and I are much more than roommates. We are lovers. I love her/him very much, and she/he loves me. We are very happy together. . . .

Actors' Roles (Placed on Cards or Sheets of Paper)

The Person Coming Out

You have a *positive* lesbian/gay identity. You want to help your parents understand you. You want them to know that you love them and that they are not to blame for anything. Yet you are who you are, and you are happy with yourself. You cannot be "changed" and wouldn't want to be anyone but who you are anyway. You invited your girlfriend/boyfriend to be present when you tell your family, but they think she/he is only an acquaintance from school.

The Girlfriend/Boyfriend

You had discussed your lover's desire to come out to her/his family, and you were willing to be present whenever she/he chose to come out to them. As her/his lover, your role is to be as supportive as possible. You may demonstrate this in any way you wish.

The Mother

You can't understand how your child could be lesbian/gay. After all, you tried to provide a nice home for your family. You feel hurt and guilty, and you make this known in any way you wish.

The Father

As a military officer for twenty-five years, you are also the authority around your home. When you find out about your child's sexual orientation, you are extremely angry. You won't believe that any child of yours could be lesbian or gay. Even though there may be lesbians/gay men in the army, you won't have any child of yours being a bull dyke/faggot.

The Grandmother/Grandfather

Her/his main opinion is that homosexuality is a sin. She/he is afraid that her/his grandchild will land in hell. Nevertheless, she/he tries to act as a mediator between parents and children.

The Brother/Sister

He/she loves and is supportive of his/her sister/brother. He/she tries to get his/her parents to see it from the sibling's point of view.

Processing the Role Play. Give the role players a break by asking the audience members some questions:

"What were you feeling as you were watching this?"

"What did you feel toward the mother, father, daughter/son, lover/roommate, sister/brother, grandparent?"

"What made you feel this way?"

"Which stereotypes emerged?"

"What instances of homophobia did you observe, and how did it effect both the lesbian/gay people and the heterosexuals?"

Now ask role players how each of them felt in their roles.

Next, ask everyone who they most identified with. It is not necessary to share out loud, but think about whom you are most like (in terms of values and feelings that were expressed). "Ask yourself what this means about you as a friend/counselor/helper of someone who is lesbian, gay, or bisexual?"

"Does anyone have any additional comments?"

Panel: Speak Out

A panel is a semistructured activity that allows people to learn about the experiences of others firsthand. There are a number of ways a panel can be organized. Listed below are two versions.

1. Utilize the services of speakers from outside your group to tell their stories. These speakers can help audiences see them as real people and not merely as an abstraction. In many cities and on many college campuses, gay, lesbian, and bisexual speakers bureaus provide individuals who are trained to speak to audiences about their experiences. Nothing is more effective in chipping away at homophobia than real people presenting true stories. It is much harder to cling to the stereotypes we have all learned when we are faced with facts that counter those stereotypes.

Things to consider before inviting outside speakers:

- Allow at least two weeks notice prior to the speakers' presentation.
- Request at least one man and one woman.
- Try to allow at least one hour to maximize participation.
- Introduce and discuss the topic with the group prior to the speaking engagement.
- Have workshop participants write out anonymous questions beforehand if you think there might be some resistance to asking questions in front of others. You may also want to have participants write down their expectations of the speakers.
- Obtain approval, if necessary, from appropriate school authorities.
- Urge participants to ask questions but to be aware that speakers may choose not to answer some that they are not comfortable responding to or that seem overly personal.
- Emphasize that the speakers do not represent *all* gay, lesbian, and bisexual people; rather, they are speaking from their own personal experience, which may differ from others'.
- Do as much follow-up as possible after the presentation, exploring participants' reactions to the speakers.

The typical speaking engagement consists of short introductory comments by the speakers reflecting their experiences as gay, lesbian, or bisexual people. This gives workshop participants a chance to formulate questions. Following the introductory period, the speakers can open the floor to questions.

2. *"Diversity Panel."* Another type of panel is composed of workshop participants themselves. It can be used to emphasize the clear links between heterosexism and other forms of oppression. Since it draws from the experiences of people within the workshop, it is more highly structured and therefore ensures the emotional safety of panel members.

This is an opportunity for people to speak about their own experiences, using the questions listed below as a framework. For the listeners, it provides a rare opportunity to hear stories not often told. No questioning of participants' experiences is allowed.

Set up. Ask for individual volunteers from one or a few of the following target groups: Jews, lesbian-gay-bisexual-transgender people, women, people of color, people with disabilities, people with HIV, old people, young people, working class, etc.

The panelists will be seated in front of participants. Panelists will each have four minutes to answer the following questions, which you, as facilitator, will guide them through. Place the questions in front of panelists on newsprint on the floor.

1. What do you love about being a ——?
2. What is difficult about being a ——?
3. What do you never want people to do or say to ——?
4. What do you want your allies to do to support you?

Following the panel, workshop participants will break into dyads and discuss among themselves what they got out of the speak out and what it brought up for them. (Panel members remain seated in front of the group and dyad with other panelists.) Following the dyads, participants will give appreciations to the panelists (thirty seconds for each) without the panelists responding. Participants will not discuss with the panel members the information and feelings that were brought up following this exercise, although they may continue to give panelists appreciations afterwards (developed by Equity Institute).

Small Group Activity (Action Component)

The purpose of this activity is to provide the opportunity for participants to solve problems presented by a number of different scenarios that may come up in their lives. It gives them something concrete to take away from the workshop.

Set up. Break down into small groups of five to seven. Brainstorm how you would deal with the following situations. Have someone record the suggestions. Come back to the larger group and read those suggestions.

Possible Scenarios. These can be tailored to meet the needs of workshop participants.

1. A student in your class is the target of homophobic harassment in the form of name-calling and occasional physical altercations. You believe that this student may be gay, lesbian, or bisexual. Because of the harassment, the student is isolated from peers. What would you do (1) to eliminate the harassment, (2) to support the student in coming to terms with her or his emerging sexual identity?

2. A lesbian/gay/bisexual teacher in your school is being harassed by a small group of staff members. Homophobic graffiti appears in the rest room, and one teacher advises students not to take classes next semester from this lesbian/gay/bisexual teacher unless these students are willing to "put out sexually" for a good grade. What can you do as an ally of the lesbian/gay/bisexual teacher?

3. Your state legislature has just passed a bill that states, "The Department of Social Services shall not place a child in the home of a person or persons whose sexual orientation would create a physical or psychological obstacle to the well-being of the child. Homosexuality and bisexuality shall be deemed to be such an obstacle to the physical or psychological well-being of the child." What position should a union/school/business that represents lesbian, gay, and bisexual people take on such a law? (Before considering this scenario, try substituting the words *African-American* or *Jewish* for sexual orientation and *gay, lesbian,* and *bisexual.*)

Contract (Action Component)

A "Contract" is used to help participants commit to taking action following the workshop.

On a sheet of paper write one new action you plan to take as an ally (to a targeted person or targeted group different from your own.) You may ask participants to share this in the larger group. Examples of actions members might take include interrupting heterosexist comments when they hear them, initiating antiheterosexism workshops in other groups in their lives, renaming their gay and/or lesbian group to include the word *bisexual*, etc.

"Homowork" Assignment: On Newsprint (Closure Component)

To continue the sensitization and learning process, suggest "homo-work" for participants to try following the workshop. Activities that you might recommend include:

1. Purchase a gay, lesbian, or bisexual periodical or book and read it in public. Write the details of the experience down in a jour-nal describing what you were feeling. (This exercise can also be assigned prior to the workshop and processed as one of the first experiental activities.)
2. Keep your heterosexuality in the closet for one week by not disclosing it to anyone.
3. Be aware of the generalizations you make.
4. Assume there are lesbian, gay, and bisexual people where you work, where you go to school, etc.
5. Wear prolesbian, -gay, or -bisexual t-shirts and buttons.
6. Hold hands with someone of the same sex in public.
7. Challenge heterosexist jokes and epithets.
8. Initiate serious discussion or coordinate workshops on the topic of heterosexism.

Handouts (Closure Component)

Distribute additional informational handouts for participants to re-fer to following the workshop. Handouts can include community resource lists, fact sheets, articles, bibliographies, etc.

Closing Activity (Closure Component)

As is true at the opening of the workshop, it is important to end with a "light and lively" activity to add a sense of closure. You can read a joyous poem or play a game. I include here one that has been well received in my workshops.

Directions. Group participants form a large circle. Facilitator gives the following directions: "I would like you all to think of one word that you would like the other participants to leave with today. I have a ball of yarn [or string]. I will hold one end of the yarn and toss the rest to one other person in the circle, letting out my word simultaneously. That person will then hold a part of the yarn with one hand while tossing the rest of it to another person, saying his or her word while doing so. We will end when everyone has a chance to toss the yarn and complete our 'web of life.'"

Evaluation

For your benefit and the benefit of workshop participants, take a few minute at the conclusion of the workshop for participants to fill out a one-page workshop evaluation form. You can invent your own questions or use some that I have used.

1. What were the high points of the workshop for you?
2. What would you recommend we change when we run this program again?
3. Some things I learned about myself are:
4. Some things I learned about others in the group are:
5. Additional comments:

NOTE

1. U.S. Department of Health and Human Services, *Report of the Secretary's Task Force on Youth Suicide,* ed. Marcia R. Feinleib (Washington, D.C., January 1989).

FURTHER READINGS

Cooper Thompson and Campaign to End Homophobia. *A Guide to Leading Introductory Workshops on Homophobia,* P.O. Box 819, Cambridge, Mass. 02139.

Gay, Lesbian, and Bisexual Speakers Bureau of Boston. *Speaking Out: Manual of the Gay, Lesbian, and Bisexual Speakers Bureau of Boston.* P.O. Box 2232, Boston, Mass. 02107. (617) 354-0133.

Equity Institute. *Training of Trainers: Intensive Program Manual.* 6400 Hollis St., Suite 15, Emeryville, Calif. 94608.

The Human Advantage. *Opening Doors to Understanding and Acceptance: A Facilitator's Guide to Presenting Workshops on Lesbian and Gay Issues.* By Kathy Obear, Suite 125, 6 University Dr., Amherst, Mass. 01002.

CONTRIBUTORS

MICHELLE M. BENECKE, B.A. University of Virginia, 1983, J.D. candidate, Harvard Law School, 1992. She was a military officer from 1983 to 1989. She has written an article (with Kirstin S. Dodge) that appeared in the *Harvard Women's Law Journal* discussing how the U.S. military is using its antigay/lesbian policy to root women from nontraditional jobs. She is cochair of the Women's Law Association at Harvard Law School.

WARREN J. BLUMENFELD is coauthor (with Diane Raymond) of *Looking at Gay and Lesbian Life;* author of *AIDS and Your Religious Community: A Hands-on Guide for Local Programs;* coproducer of the documentary film *Pink Triangles: A Film Study of Prejudice against Lesbians and Gay Males* (Cambridge Documentary Films); associate editor of *Empathy,* a biannual journal for people working to end oppression on the basis of sexual identity; instructor and lecturer on gay, lesbian, and bisexual studies; and antioppression workshop facilitator. He serves on the Executive Board of the Gay, Lesbian and Bisexual Speakers Bureau of Boston and is a member of the AIDS Coalition to Unleash Power (ACT UP/Boston) and the Gay and Lesbian Studies Seminar at the Massachusetts Institute of Technology. He served as features editor of the *Gay Community News* (Boston) and outreach educator for the Public Broadcasting Service series "The AIDS Quarterly." In 1971, he founded the National Gay Student Center of the National Student Association, Washington, D.C.

MARCIA DEIHL, M.A. in feminism and folk music at Cambridge-Goddard. She was one of the creating forces behind the feminist New Harmony Sisterhood Band (1973–80), the book *All Our Lives: A Women's Songbook* (1976), the record *Ain't I a Woman* (1979), and the tape "New Harmony Sisterhood Band Reunion." She was music editor of *Sojourner* (a feminist monthly) and has written songs and articles on women's music, sexual and bisexual politics, feminism, and recovery. Today, she works at Harvard's anthropology library, sings with the Oxymorons (a four-person "odd-cappella" music group), and is active with Boston Bisexual Women's Network, a group she cofounded in 1983.

KIRSTIN S. DODGE, J.D. candidate, Harvard Law School, 1992; Rotary International graduate fellow, University of Fribourg, Switzerland, 1988–89; B.A., Yale University, 1988. She has written an article (with Michelle M. Benecke) that appeared in the *Harvard Women's Law Journal* discussing how the United States military is using its antigay/lesbian policy to root women from nontraditional jobs. She is cochair of the Committee on Gay and Lesbian Legal Issues at Harvard Law School.

GARY E. DOUPE studied theology at the Wesley Theological Seminary of the United Methodist Church in Washington, D.C., receiving a Master of Divinity degree in 1969. While serving pastorates in Pennsylvania and New York and, since 1975, as United Methodist campus minister at Hartwick College and SUNY Oneonta in upstate New York, he completed (1982) a Doctor of Ministry program at San Francisco Theological Seminary. His doctoral thesis was a study of the Christian Institute of Southern Africa, an interracial organization that struggled against apartheid. Since 1983, he has served part time as pastor to two rural congregations in addition to his college chaplaincy. He, his wife, Elaine, their three sons, and three cats live in Bainbridge, New York.

DAVID EBERLY is a poet, critic, and gay activist whose work has been published nationally for over twenty years. He is the author of *What Has Been Lost*, a collection of poems published in 1982 by the Good Gay Poets collective. His book reviews appear regularly in *Bay Windows*.

DIANE ELZE, a longtime lesbian activist in Maine, is cofounder of and adviser to OUTRIGHT, the Portland Alliance of Gay and Lesbian Youth, a support group for gay, lesbian, and bisexual youths twenty-two years of age and under. She is a caseworker at the AIDS Project in Portland and the president of the Maine Lesbian/Gay Political Alliance.

JEAN S. GOCHROS, Ph.D., is a board certified diplomate in clinical social work. With over thirty years' experience as a therapist, she has taught on marriage, sexuality, sex education, and women's issues across the country and overseas and has written on these topics for both the lay and the professional press. She resides in Honolulu, where she maintains a private practice. In the past few years, she has also worked extensively in the area of AIDS, both in an HIV-testing site and on the AIDS Team of Tripler Army Medical Center. Her most recent book, *When Husbands Come Out of the Closet*, was published in 1989.

PHILLIP BRIAN HARPER received his masters and Ph.D. degrees in English from Cornell University. He served as assistant professor of English in American literature at Brandeis University, where he taught twentieth-century English and American literature, African-American literature, and contemporary cultural studies. He is currently an assistant professor in the Departments of English and African-American Studies at Harvard University. He has contributed articles and book reviews since 1981, coedited the Black History Month issue in 1989, and is a member of the Board of Directors of the *Gay Community News*. He is currently working on a collection of essays on the representation of African-Americans in contemporary popular culture.

MARGARET HOLUB is the rabbi of the Mendocino Coast Jewish Community in rural northern California, where she also rides circuit to other small, rural Jewish communities in the nearby mountains. A graduate of Hebrew Union College–Jewish Institute of Religion and the University of California, Santa Cruz, she worked for many years as an organizer on Skid Row in Los Angeles with the Catholic Worker Community and other agencies before moving to the country. As a rabbinical student, she served as rabbinic intern at Congregation Beth Chayim Chadashim, the first synagogue with a specific outreach to gay and lesbian Jews to be recognized by the Jewish Reform movement.

JEFFREY LEVI is an AIDS and health policy consultant based in Washington, D.C. From 1983 to 1989, he worked for the National Gay and Lesbian Task Force as Washington representative, director of governmental and political affairs, and executive director. He also served in various offices, including president of the D.C. Gay and Lesbian Activists Alliance. He holds degrees in government from Oberlin College and Cornell University.

B. JAYE MILLER earned his B.A. from Stanford University and his M.A. and Ph.D. from Yale University. His training was in history and humanities with strongest interests in the areas of religious thought and social action. He taught gay and lesbian history at San Francisco City College and was part of the core course faculty at Kresge College, University of California, Santa Cruz. His mate, Robert Filomeno, died of AIDS in 1986. He lived for several years with his former wife, Donna Haraway, and her companion, Rusten Hogness, in the country outside Healdsburg, California. Jaye died of an AIDS-related illness in August 1991.

ROBYN OCHS, Ed.M., is an escapee from New York City who now lives in Cambridge, Massachusetts. During the day, Robyn is a not-so-mild-mannered university administrator. In her "free time," she helped to found the Boston Bisexual Women's Network (BBWN) in 1983 and the East Coast Bisexual Network in 1985 and continues to be hyperactive in both organizations. She is a member of both the BBWN Speakers Bureau and Boston's Gay, Lesbian, and Bisexual Speakers Bureau. She loves to write, speak, and do workshops on topics including bisexuality and coalition building.

ANN PELLEGRINI holds degrees in classics from Harvard and Oxford universities. She is currently completing a Ph.D. in the study of religion at Harvard University, where she has the unfashionable idea that theory can and must be held accountable to political practice. She has been active in abortion rights organizing with the Boston and Massachusetts chapters of National Organization for Women (NOW).

DIANE RAYMOND is coauthor (with Warren J. Blumenfeld) of *Looking at Gay and Lesbian Life* and editor of *Existentialism and Philosophical Tradition*. She is chair of the Philosophy Department at Simmons College. She has published a number of articles on medical ethics and feminist theory and is active in the reproductive rights and feminist movements. Diane is also a lesbian mother.

COOPER THOMPSON was the coordinator of the Campaign to End Homophobia until 1991, an independent trainer and consultant on issues of oppression, a cook in a community hot meals program, and a mediocre trombone player in Cheek to Cheek, a (mostly) lesbian and gay swing band. He is the author of curricula on sex roles, sexuality, and homophobia.

AMANDA UDIS-KESSLER is a writer and musician in the greater Boston area. Her writings on sexuality and social justice have been published in a number of books, journals, and newsletters; she also composes, writes songs, and plays in an area folk-rock band. Current and near-future writing projects include such topics as the sociology of eating disorders, a new take on heterosexual privilege, the rise of the American bisexual movement, a feminist analysis of *The Rocky Horror Picture Show*, and a fresh look at the "P.C." debates.

CARMEN VÁZQUEZ was born in Bayamon, Puerto Rico, and grew
up in Harlem, New York. For the past fifteen years, she has
been involved in the lesbian/gay movement. She was a conve-
ner of the Lesbian of Color Conferences held in San Francisco
in 1986 and 1987 and of the Dynamics of Color Conference on
Racism in 1989. Currently, she is cochair of the Lesbian
Agenda for Action (LAFA) and works for the San Francisco Department of Public Health as Coordinator of Lesbian/Gay
Health Services. She is a free-lance reviewer for the *San Francisco Chronicle Book Review* and has had her essays published
by *Bay Times*, the *San Francisco Sentinel*, and *Nicaraguan
Perspectives*.

WALTER L. WILLIAMS is professor of anthropology and the study
of women and men in society at the University of Southern
California. He received his Ph. D. from the University of North
Carolina and has taught at the University of Cincinnati and at
UCLA. He has published several books on interethnic relations and gender variance, most notably his award-winning *The
Spirit and the Flesh: Sexual Diversity in American Indian Culture*. In 1987–88, he was Fulbright visiting scholar to Gadjah
Mada University, in Yogyakarta, Indonesia, where he did research leading to his most recent book, *Javanese Lives: Women
and Men in Modern Indonesian Society*. Williams is also the
director of postgraduate research for the Institute for the Study
of Human Resources.